John Dewey

Modernity and Modern Public Education

J. D. Stewart

Acknowledgments

Many thanks to Richard Dagger for his insights and conversations concerning Dewey, and the Alan Ryan book he gave me that Ryan had signed in which he wished me luck on my" journey" in writing this book. Also the reading of this book material by Jerry Haughton was very important as was the conversation and encouragement of James McSwain and William Marty. Many thanks to Cosimo Classics for allowing me to cite their 2008 edition of Sidney Hook's book, *John Dewey: An Intellectual Portrait* which was originally published in 1939. And finally for my wife, Barbara, thanks for all her hard work and without whose patience, advice and diligence this book could not have been written.

ISBN-13: 978-1494236458
ISBN-10: 1494236451

Preface

Have you ever had a conversation in which you discovered that someone has a belief that is in conflict with your belief system? The differences are unmistakable, and yet your friend does not seem to be bothered that they could not both be true. On the face of the disparity is a clear understanding for most that the two positions are diametrically opposed to each other, mutually exclusive of one another. This encounter may have left you unsettled, wondering where such an seemingly unreasoned understanding could have arisen. The answer could be found in this book. Such tolerance in issues of epistemology and morality, by this view, are meant to be inclusive and to be held without fear that they might be corrected or the holder coerced.

Modern values are far from the traditional understandings by which people lived just a few decades ago. A growing number of Americans believe that each person is responsible for determining what is true and what is acceptable behavior. The dogmas of the past have been replaced by what one thinks is good for him or her. Why is there such a drastic change in so short a period of time? It could be that society has finally seen to push back the margins of propriety and do just as they will. Authority has shifted from the good of societal directives to whatever please them. Children and adult citizens find legal issues serving as only for others, while morality has become an issue to protest and truth has been labeled intolerant.

Individualism once meant that each person was to assert self in responsibility for others, to make a good name for oneself and ultimately serve as a role model for those who need a guiding light. Egoists were seen as unacceptable for mimicry. Those that looked out for others, were charitable to their neighbors and those in need, were lauded for their self-sacrificial habits.

We are to look at what has replaced recent tradition, thinking that has changed American society and personal authority that has left us unconcerned for others, while taking all that is given us and still wanting more. These are the issues of our times. These are the marks of unbounded self often cloaked in group purpose.

We must also ask what has happened to the institutions that once were an authoritative guide in codifying for the dispensation of group and individual action. The government finds truth where it wants, education dispenses programs based on theoretical truths and the national unity once seen in America as a melting pot has been divided by cultural, provincial and parochial interests.

J. D. Stewart
September 26,
2013

Table of Contents

Introduction

What are the roots of change that took America from a country of traditional values to a modern or postmodern understanding of its individuals and institutions? Those influences which have brought westerners from lives following a philosophy of simple realism to one of individualistic pragmatism leads inextricably to one man, John Dewey. Although my initial quest and inquiry was not the genesis of twentieth century social philosophy but the agencies of influences that brought about changes in traditional public education, Dewey seemed to have been a linchpin of both. Although schools seemed to have felt the revolutionary influence of Dewey's pedagogy very quickly and deeply, the concomitant changes in the larger culture were immediate but only marginal, arising to prominence over a longer period of societal soul searching to find an often unquestioned home in our time. Both in society and the school Dewey would prophesy of a social meaning to American life that it had never imagined. Dewey would proffer an optimism and singularity that would draw a nation to what is now a modern society and a diffident and struggling public school.

The key to understanding his influence on the Culture is to understand the school. Dewey saw educative practice as more than school instruction but instrumental in the process of acting intelligently in every area of daily life. His understanding of American culture was in ways only secondary to his brief practiced efforts to experimentally reconstruct the school. At the (Dewey) Laboratory School at the University of Chicago from late in the nineteenth century and for only 7 years, Dewey was to assert pedagogical influences that linger to this day. He would also father a sociological understanding which would put authority into the hands of the individual which would come to maturity in more recent times.

Horace Mann and John Dewey seemed vaguely familiar as ghostly cast members from teacher certification training many years earlier, but now I was to see a clearer path to their ideas which had been given quarters in modern public school practice including my own classroom. Furthermore John Dewey's name arose as a successor to America's Horace Mann and the Common School and proximal to those who studied under Dewey for whom he was mentor and teacher. Notable among them were William Heard Kilpatrick and Margaret Naumberg. Kilpatrick and Naumberg each brought non-traditional educational ideas to myriad public school teachers, school administrators and parents thus changing forever the standard praxis of traditional public education. Dewey's ideas were to resonate with our people, and, empowered by his philosophy of the present, he selectively and prominently borrowed from Plato, Kant, Rousseau, Charles Sanders Peirce, William James, Hegel and Emerson in molding a purely American view of man, society and public education. And despite the passage of over a half century since Dewey's death, no one has stepped up to take his place. John Dewey was to become a prophet of modern American educational understanding, America's philosopher and the prophet of American society in modern times informing personal practice and socialization.

Over and over again his name found mention in both praise and derision. The name John Dewey, the preeminent America philosopher and pedagogue of modern ideas, is reflective of an almost Delphic transfer of philosophical understanding divined by moderns, often closely suggestive of his thinking. I would come to believe that he was a key to understanding the philosophical moorings of the modern public school and the world outside its doors.

John Dewey looked hard at our nation of pilgrims poised to wrest world prominence from The Continent and spoke to a determined American entrepreneurial spirit bred in vast numbers of determined citizens beyond the school house door. A prophet of American modernity, of shadowy truth, moral particularity, societal inclusiveness, unlikely unity and dubious authoritative behavioralism better describes contemporary cultural leanings than that adoptive of Dewey's time. Dewey sketched a social gospel that gravitates to earth inviting all to attend yet denying authority of the gods or their place at the communal table.

My judgment against Dewey became ameliorated as my attitude toward his pedagogy grew ambivalent, absolute disapproval in issues of authority and complicit in practice. My valuation of his contribution was to prove split: on the one hand the philosophy as a whole seemed disastrously influential while his practice proved quite intellectually challenging at its apogee. When I reflected on my own classroom and instructional methodologies, many proved identical to Dewey's own ensconced classroom practices at the Dewey School. Relating to the student's experience, cooperative learning and the mandate for an interesting lesson are all traceable to Dewey's school practice and to my own classroom. But his understanding of the child and negotiating lessons did not seem to fit with my understanding from classroom experience. Still many of the standard practices which I saw as practical and broadly educational were his. If Dewey were to bear responsibility for the state of modern public education, and, if the technical practice were at fault in any way, then I was guilty for my lack of understanding of his influence in my teaching practice and possibly complicitous in promoting ideas that I could not consciously support. Still I believed that group learning, appropriate learning methodologies and reduced emphasis on testing were worth pursuing in the classroom.

Colonial and early American education's prominent theorists, reformers and political mavens were a resource for absorption and choosing. Dewey merely brought to educational theory what he found instrumental to teaching and learning. The term instrumentalism came to refer to Dewey's understanding of pragmatism. Only later did I realize after reading his books that, despite the fact that he has left public education in the lurch for over a century, he, at the same time, was responsible for bits of an illustrious pedagogy, which has in hard practice been ignored or misrepresented. It is in society that his ideas have taken root and grown beyond all propriety and reason and continue to influence the schools. Dewey's understanding of the individual and community was to eventually emerge as the key to understanding why America's public school purpose is in perpetual flux. The destroyer of public education, as Dewey has been so often labelled, is not a totally justified epithet; he is not the lone Frankenstein monster by which to judge a patch-worn public school pedagogy. Society absorbed many of his ideas or at least found such ideas useful in the practice of daily life as a general belief in modern, pluralistic and democratic America. America more and more was choosing to see daily life as both communal and egalitarian. The individual would find freedom within a community context. Within the community of school, the student-individual would find, as adults in the larger society, the same freedom to begin to grow beyond permissible margins. School's inability to educate American children has come to be seen by some as failed and exclusively attributable to the school in locus or effect. The modern student-individual taught by a broader school of cultural influences is incompatible with a community of learners, and public schools struggle for authority to teach amid our present cultural and academic malaise.

Sidney Hook's book *John Dewey: An Intellectual Portrait* has really been relied on heavily to make sense of the cultural and societal implication of Dewey's impact. Often accused of inadequate communication of ideas, Dewey is given great care by Hook in relating his mentors ideas and goals. Much of what Dewey had to say on myriad issues has been cited, when helpful, in his own expressive writings in *Human Nature and Conduct, Democracy and Education* and *Reconstruction of Philosophy*. An attempt was made to capture the definitive measure of his ideas which were given more or less in permanent form, if not in detail, in his early writings.

I have also depended heavily on William James writings to fill out his and Dewey's understanding of pragmatism for which their were differences but also strong agreement.

Expect to see here the implications of Dewey's philosophy: its dangers in society and in the public school, an area for which he had no reservations in applying his pragmatism, a philosophy permissible to be equated to all areas of daily practice due to Dewey's unified philosophical understanding. The West has become Dewey's living ideal in many ways. Prophesying if not affecting, the uncertainty where certainty once held sway, the drift of morality, questionable authority, an American optimistic meliorist view of life, the myth of unity, the necessity of experimentation in knowing have all come into our societal psyche inspired by Dewey, and these issues which play into man's wont to control his life and gives us a new way to see ourselves, others and the world.

There have been so many books written about John Dewey, most concerned with a broader perspective of his ideals and ideas, in support or disparagement, but with the exception of the intellectual biographer, Sidney Hook, the man who knew his ideas best, the best chronicler of Dewey was Dewey himself. It is from these two sources that I have tried capturing the feeling of the ideas that have changed us all. The chapter topics were chosen based on the topics that tend to summarize Dewey's basic understandings. Quotations from the books previously mentioned are presented in order to give expression in his use of language and, at times, to demonstrate in his own words avoidance of decisive meaning employed so as to, as he claimed, render his ideas more inclusive of that of others. My disagreements with his views are likewise given where considered necessary and may have embolden my expression. That is the way that Dewey affects analysis.

This book is a topical analysis of a philosophy that resists subdivision and takes a simplified view of the world - objects as objects and environment as environment, as well as other earthly elements - which aids Dewey's purposeful reduction of areas for conflict while ostensibly unifying his species of pragmatism. This book also presents his views which can resonate or abrade with those perimetric philosophical views which draw distinctions to the work of Kant, Hegel, Locke, Aristotle, Plato, Socrates, Rousseau, Berkeley, Hume, Nietzsche and others. More than a topical guide and appraisal of Dewey's philosophy this book has an extensive reference-topical index which permits a more systematic approach to discovering the derivation and often the implications of Dewey's ideas.

Chapter 1
Soil and Seeds

> Contemporary American culture has for so many years been under the influence of John Dewey that it is hard to realize that his philosophy has had a history... But it is important to know that he developed out of a philosophical tradition which he helped to undermine...
>
> - Sidney Hook, *John Dewey* [1]

John Dewey's ideas were prophetic of contemporary America's uncertainty and particular morality. And even as modern individualism began to trump a cultural understanding of self, it asserted itself through group preference: justification for action would arise from narrow group purpose. The appeal of the cultural melting pot, over decades, was slowly replaced as individualism was to find a home often behind the authority of self-seeking groups. This basic change in the way that America saw itself was to change dramatically under the philosophical and pedagogical weight of dubious authority asserted by John Dewey.

But Dewey's influence was not characteristically direct nor always accurately transmitted. It was his students, however, who would carry his instrumentalism into schools and churches, to an institutional understanding of action. He was merely the conduit for what was seen as a new free reckoning. His alloyed ideas were to come at a critical time in the early history of the American school. Under an imperative to educate for an informed democracy - considering the vast immigration to America in the mid-nineteenth and the early twentieth centuries and the meteoric rise of industrialization - Dewey's optimistic values, as seeds in the growth of a young ebullient country, would hold hope for work and social opportunity for a rapidly expanding citizenry. At inclusiveness Dewey was unparalleled and this was one goal that must be acknowledged despite other fragmenting effects to be discussed later. John Dewey figures prominently among those providing distributive influences in determining the character of our nation.

Dewey did not generate a social philosophy in an historical vacuum. Everyone is tied to the seed roots of their beginnings, and so Dewey could never have been capable of completely emancipating himself from colonial and earlier American influences, those bundled in seedling root and stem. The distinctively American character of this fecund land was to give itself an indeterminate understanding of what it would become. The American individual, through Dewey, would ultimately adopt pragmatic ideas which would prove important to his developing a uniquely American cloak of confidence, while harboring confusion concerning a social understanding of authority under the cowl of Dewey's ideas which rendered a persistent uncertainty.

In a country of optimistic frontiers Dewey came to adulthood, with unlimited prospects and new individual opportunities, he found experience in the community of his youth not unlike, in many respects, that of early colonial settlements. Citizens took from a largely traditional practice of their work and their belief system, and grew into a well-established and integrated people. Dewey was to draw from this communal experience conjoined with academic pioneering to create a distinctively American and one-off integrated philosophical variant.

Pragmatism, an individual philosophy of useful action in daily life, was adopted by Dewey, and was to find its genesis, in part, in the experiences of his youth. Sidney Hook traces the earliest influences on Dewey to his life in the community practice of "Scotch realism." This was a common sense understanding of an intuitive, active, timely life style, "safeguarded from skepticism, doubt and challenge," harboring a transcendent inner faith in God and a common sense understanding of an external teleology. "Scotch realism" recognized in intuitionism, emerged from each person as truths that are innate and not learned. Despite a belief that there was a God, there was no attempt to create an extensive hold on the mind through "intuitions to the details of Biblical history." "[C]ausality was one of necessity, that

God exists," but theology was infused by a nurturing "liberal" "religious atmosphere" which required no Biblical understanding of the world. This religious-community commitment, would belie his later rejection of theology as superstitious metaphysics on the basis that transcendence was unable to provide necessary solutions to daily problems (Hook, 11, 12). [2]

Dewey proposed to have forged a unified philosophy which has inhered consistently in his understanding of epistemology, morality, individualism, society, unity and pedagogy. The faithful practice of his ideas and at times misapplication of those ideas by others has resulted in an ill-defined, or better, undefined seemingly irreformable American society which has left the American individual to be swayed by ideas without certainty of a philosophical telos and to slide from one experience to another with doubts about ever finalizing meaning. Influences from his youth as well as cherry-picked philosophy from the ancients on, culled and reassembled, embellished and unified, are a key to his ideational genesis and serve in understanding his mark on modernity, society and American public education. Tracing the twisted threads that weave Dewey and his progenitors into a common fabric of current pedagogical practices will point up the systemic obstacles which have prevented the realization of the long-held promise of Dewey's true democratic society and subsequent true democratic public school.

Grown in the soil of pioneering optimism Dewey was to find his philosophically based ideas in Charles Sanders Peirce, the author of American pragmatism. William James gave pragmatism its name and it was James who gave Dewey the early link to the assumptions of pragmatism. Through experimentation and instrumentalism, two descriptors of the Dewey's philosophical methodology, truth, facts and theories were only useful, meaningful as instruments, as they provided solutions to everyday problems. These "instrumental values" were merely "means" to problem solving through experience, as studies and not as a firm "hierarchy of values" (Dewey, DAE, 279- 281).[3]

As Sidney Hook, perhaps Dewey's most devoted student and supporter, tells us, "John Dewey was born in Vermont, developed his philosophy in Michigan, Minnesota, and Chicago, and brought his thought to a rounded completion in New York, the cultural metropolis of American." Dewey was to ultimately merge a communitarianism with an academic understanding of philosophy (Hook, 5,8).[4]

At the University of Vermont where he did his undergraduate studies, Dewey was exposed to Hegel. The soil in which Dewey was to farm for true democracy and individual freedom had been furrowed decades before his sowing. America at that time was romantically poetic, lingering in a transcendental inwardness emblematic of Ralph Waldo Emerson's idealism. Dewey, who would be referred to as a Vermont Transcendentalist due to the influential professor and president of the University of Vermont, James Marsh, who had predated Dewey but had left his mark on the University, aligned with both transcendentalism and Hegelian philosophy. Dewey, although exposed to Hegel, would never become an "orthodox Hegelian" but found Hegel's idealistic universalism of interest and would glean and parse Hegel's dialectic as a method of resolving practical understanding of the real world.

Dewey, we are told by Hook, was attracted to Hegel because of his aversion to dualism which he felt denied the interdependencies within the world. With dualism comes "disjunctions" and "alternatives." (Hook, JD, 13).[5]

From societal separations to oppositional ideas, like mind and body, in all examples of opposition, Dewey was to see unification where other philosophers had seen disparity, as in education, as "the unity of method." Dewey would find in Hegel a way to see opposites as integral as the mind must have the body to act on and the body without the mind has no direction (Dewey, DAE, 376, 377).[6] It is in this opposition for others that Dewey finds unity; these are propositional dependents. In nature there is but unity and the forces of "instinct," "impulse" and "action" moving to remedial purpose (Hook, JD, 13-15).[7]

As surprising as his draw to Hegel was Dewey's interest in Kant on whom his doctoral dissertation was written at Johns Hopkins University. It is interesting that the one who would become the quintessential American pragmatist of the twentieth century would find more than passing curiosity in Kant's idealism. Yet, over the decades in his consistently propounded philosophical framework, in Kant he found an optimism of man's ultimate good will in action which seemed to fit with Dewey's central faith in the individual's ultimate purpose through society. Man would become through positivity of action the basic element of a democratic and productive society. Kant's categorical imperative was seen in modification through Dewey's optimistic view of man: to ultimately find good activity with others yet not to prescribe or proscribe particularly for him through individual thought and action. Duty was to be individually found but not by any Kantian rigor of duty, a duty that was subjective in thought and impersonal in action. Dewey would make the practical purpose of community the unifying action of all in membership (Dewey, DAE, 405-418).[8]

The individual will and the collective would find no practical delineation for action as duty. Dewey's philosophy would have to answer to a charge of conflicted interests as well as a future expectation for the unification of the One and the Many. Idealism, which he consistently eschewed, will be seen in his hopeful prospects for salutary individualism to adopt collective goals while entering into a constructive membership at one with the willed purpose of the group. This coalescing of wills must "be voluntary" and clearly understood. Dewey saw coercion, from "superior physical power" or "threats," of "duress," as precluding "choice" or "personal disposition." Thus will, under such circumstances, cannot be willfully actionable. If one is in one's right mind, then to be denied one's will is to lie about "intent" of an action (Dewey, E, 176, 177).[9]

Not that Dewey felt that all activity was acceptable and that the individuals would find immediate purposeful membership among others.

> Individuals are certainly interested, at times, in having their own way, and their own way may go contrary to the ways of others. But they are also interested, and chiefly interested upon the whole, in entering into the activities of others and taking part in conjoint and coöperative doings. Otherwise, no such thing as a community would be possible. And there would not

> even be any one interested in furnishing the policeman to keep a semblance of harmony unless he thought that thereby he could gain some personal advantage. (Dewey, DAE, 28, 29).[10]

There is "interest" on the part of the individual that draws him or her to the group, and, in the conjoining of One to the Many, the individual must be given "direction, control, and guidance" (Dewey, DAE, 28).[11]

Dewey manipulates these terms to his own purpose. Direction, in part, and guidance are not coercive, as intends their use, so he must explain away control which is imposed from without and against resistance.

> Control then denotes the process by which he (the individual) is brought to subordinate his natural impulses to public and common ends. Since, by conception, his own nature is quite alien to the process and opposes it rather than helps it, control has in this view a flavor of coercion or compulsion about it....Control, in truth, covers the regulation gained by an individual through his own efforts quite as much as that brought about when others take the lead (Dewey DAE, 28, 29).[12]

If it is not totally coercive then "control" would seem to be a joint effort of the individual and an external authority. The "flavor" however is not distinguished clearly. Dewey seems to bring in the "government" and "theories of the state" to further roil the water, making application impossible, and definition ludicrous. Dewey still standing on his jumbled explanation adds to the defense of a partial 'coercion or compulsion": "But there is no ground for any such view." This is one of several positions that Dewey felt that he had effectively taken that had allowed either inappropriate practice or misunderstanding in principle (Dewey, DAE, 28, 29).[13] Kantian duty was against one's will, one would have to coerce self to do what might or should be done but would not want to do. Dewey could not support the loss of freedom by forced compliance but did retain free input from the individual as the critical actionable agent.

It was in Michigan and Minnesota that Dewey, Hook tells us, was to lose all his "metaphysical lumber." Hegelian ideals proved presumptive of consequences without expectations of predicability. He came to see the power of experience "in action," rather than an innate understanding of action (Hook, JD, 5, 8, 14,15).[14] Dewey would shed what he felt was the last of Hegelian idealism. He began to see life as a procession of practical problems. But what was to become prominent in his ideas was the indisputable value of the group, interdependency, which was ingrained from his youth. People of Dewey's community took from largely traditional practice their work and their belief system finding group solidarity in established commonalities of "wealth," one's "standard of living" and in judgment of one another according to displayed actions. An overall emphasis on the practical, true to his rearing, would find its ultimate focus on these issues in daily experience (Hook, JD, 5, 7, 12, 15).[15]

Dewey came to see life as a series of practical problems which were new each day. It would be in considering the change associated with day-to-day problems, that in his "early maturity" Dewey came to believe that one could reap a more "flexible" harvest from practical philosophy by tending to experience and its associated problems simply by knowing "their problematic contexts." He eventually realized to his own satisfaction that what counted for knowledge was to become individualized and dependent on the world around and not being informed about the world by the mind by simply making general inquiry. On this point turned knowledge which thus seen would become individual and particular. Furthermore, and here is the foundational mooring of knowing, it "involves doing." But Dewey's insight that philosophy and education were united, as they were both informed by "doing," opened up a unifying understanding of "genuine learning" and was the child of academic intellectual inquiry (Hook, JD, 7, 8, 13).[16]

At the University of Chicago he arrived at philosophical unity, unity as he understood it, through a progressive philosophy concerned with real life as a practice (Hook, 5, 8).[17] At the heart of Dewey's epistemology was the idea of change which he took from

Hegel. Hegel's historical approach to philosophy was ideal, the Absolute end, which would mark the culmination of change. Dewey dropped the historical dialectic for nature, for a change that was not necessarily to an end, but, by the individual mind within community, change was to bring "good" although not any assertion of finality (Hook, 14, 15).[18]

Dewey ultimately carried a complex epistemology into his philosophy thus ridding himself of intuitionalism, that is, that there are things that can be known innately independent of any necessary proof. Although explored in more detail later, but for now:

> Hegel's insight that knowledge is never immediate or self-certifying, that its truth or falsity depends upon something other than its own occurrence, ... [thus freeing] himself [Dewey] from the last vestiges of intuitionalism (Hooks, 13).[19]

Unity, as Dewey understood it, yielded a progressive philosophy of real life. Aspects of his philosophy would predate and span insights into existentialism and postmodernism which were to arise later across the sea. Dewey must be seen as a prophet of modern thought, trends reaching out a century into the future and remaining in the thoughts and actions of society and pedagogy until now. The seeds of his ideas have been so broadly sown that today they are deeply rooted in American society in the way that we understand ourselves and others. But his celebrity and influence was not restricted to being known widely in the United States. Dewey found receptivity in distant lands which "he visited on educational missions." It was, however, in his own country that his ideas have "had institutional effect, and even here, not everywhere, nor in their full bearing." Dewey would become a theoretical harvesting field for acolytes and for ideas often grown in misrepresentation (Hook, JD, 5, 8,9, 10).[20]

For both science and education Dewey would offer methodological critique. In fact Dewey would address "all problems of human existence" by what he would consider "methods" of "inquiry." (Hook, 15-17). [21]

Individual inquiry, he believed, was the work of a lifetime as he would draw from Hegel's view of a progressive methodology. According to Dewey

> History is reason in its progressive unfolding in man. An individual becomes rational only as he absorbs into himself the content of rationality in nature and in social institutions (Dewey, DAE, 350).[22]

Dewey was to find the absolute in the "content" of the social domain, in the orderly organization of "public concern," not in the individual, but the individual was given a place in the public interest and accountable to the public and "less to the workings of private self-interest." A country-wide educational system was necessary to provide for the intelligent who would find acceptable communal behavior. Dewey felt that this understanding although it moved man in the proper direction, to the group or nation, did not account for experimental inquiry or the modification of the society by the progress of man and therefore to the collective. The individual rather than the community would be the agent of actionable experimental inquiry but in the context of group purpose. Authority for the group would be found, it must be imagined, as the collective good intentions of the individuals that comprised it. But when the individual takes control of action without the group as in education, "physical distance" and individuality can result in a lack of learning measured by social activity(Dewey, DAE, 350 - 353).[23]

Constraint on passing judgment by group authority would make hierarchy and culpability virtually impossible to enforce. There would be no definitive bisection into the authority of the individual or that of the group just a loose expectancy by which the One would be imagined to eventually come to the service of the Many. Idealism, as we shall see, was not removed from Dewey's ideas but formed the basis for a failure to clearly delimit authority. This failure (more to come later) would prove to be a critical error in Dewey's sociological and pedagogical understanding.

Still with time his philosophy, though not broadly sold by Dewey himself, was to find support in practice. Despite the temptation of the hedonistic draw of utilitarianism by which pleasure is maximized and pain minimized or some variation on these diametric positions, Dewey' saw experience, in the case of stimulus and response as important even in the consequence of pain. A child being burned by a flame, was pained but so would the teacher of a valuable lesson, a painfully learned lesson. Dewey thought that utilitarian ideas were good to a point, but, when the materialism of ownership, which could not be avoided when this philosophy took its extended measure, then "security" would lead to abuse not in having what was needed but to make having the ultimate goal. The problem with pain was that sensationalism is merely "immediate stimulus and response" rather than an issue of "knowledge." Sensations are not "cognitive and intellectual" but are "emotional and practical." But the individualistic drive to own above concern for others eliminated the utilitarian understanding of promoting the good and the "organic" society where the individual and the group are in "correlative" agreement in mind and action. Utilitarian ideas rely on the fixity of goals and necessarily, in time, the conflict of one's ends with that of another's strived for good. Dewey felt that in society fixed goals must be moderated for the good of the group. (Dewey, RIP, 86-88, 182, 183, 187, 188, 166).[24]

Dewey's pragmatism would come to find a strong allegiance to individual freedom, uncertainty and the flexible use of language and meaning which was also attributed to Emerson, Thoreau and Bronson Alcott, three of the premier transcendentalists of nineteenth-century America. Those three distinctives are to be mined from Emerson's statement, "What have I to do with the sacredness of tradition, if I live wholly from within" (Emerson, E, 17).[25] Thoreau and Alcott had been teachers and left their romantic brand on the practice. The romanticism of German idealists and American transcendentalists were to find an optimism in a young America, an optimism which has never been lost. Pestalozzi and his students Froebel and Herbart were to bring idealism to American education and William Heard Kilpatrick and Margaret Naumberg, although they differed in pedagogic philosophy from their mentor Dewey, they too were steeped in tempered idealism. Dewey' optimism was seen in the form of meliorism. Meliorism was the optimistic view that the actionable world could be made better, and with Dewey that better world would arise not from "within" the individual but through an common group determination and the outcome of purposive group action. This hope was based on the ultimate authority of one's chosen community.

Dewey fashioned a pragmatic philosophy of interaction and unification. In a generalized fashion, Emerson had proposed a oneness with respect to the physical world and its inhering morality. Dewey would propose a holism of the inner thought world, the physical world of objects and morality. Inwardness and outwardness were to find philosophical unity in Dewey as all metaphysics was to be replaced by a physical understanding of the world. Dewey's unified his methodology of instrumentalism by linking action with thought. Unification required action, such that a proposition could find justification in the action realized, and, although action did not have to follow what had been proposed in thought, by his method, thought and action would find proof of unity in the resultant event.

Linguistically, Dewey would state his positions more flexibly for other philosophers and scientists. At the University of Chicago, Dewey's philosophy began to take on a technically challenging "vocabulary" that was by his philosophical contemporaries not broadly understood. They had not "grasped its revolutionary implications in their bearings on the traditional intellectual habits fostered by diverse philosophical schools." Hook contends that pragmatism would ultimately be found to have "penetrated" the culture bringing with it a challenge to the traditionally unquestionable. Having for so long broadly been sown through the academy and his written words, his ideas and their derivatives have found a home deeply embedded in the daily operation of American society and its public educational system. The extent to which his ideas have come to nest in the practice of the nation is debated, but he has had his "influence." He found people who were at odds with one another in philosophical opinion, who found a safe harbor in Dewey, who strived for inclusivity through his ideas and who found agreement outside themselves in practice (Hook, 8-11).[26]

America would forever see itself differently. His ideas were not always understood. For example, Oliver W. Holmes was reported to have commented after reading *Experience and Nature* that he was sure he had read a "great book," although he could not put his finger on a reason for its greatness (Hook, 22).[27]

The "penetration" of which Hook refers is probably more subtle and absorptive than having a driving breach of the Culture's mind set, but the more important question is whether Dewey was consistent in his ideas and whether in practice they meet a consistent standard. On this point consideration of his ideas linger and fester. The question that could be more broadly put; is there any philosophy that proves ultimately consistent? Niezsche found all philosophies more than creating "impasse" but as self-serving and "tyrannical," for

> [i]t always creates the world in its own image; it cannot do otherwise; philosophy is this tyrannical impulse itself, the most spiritual Will to Power, the will to "creation of the world," the will to the causa prima. (Nietzsche, BGAE, trans. Helen Zimmern, vol. 12, T.N. Foulis, Edinburgh, 1911, 9).[28]

Although the tendency is to doubt what Neizsche claims since this is philosophical self-certification itself; this at least raises the necessary question of whether Dewey's philosophy has felt the caress of a less accusatory construction. A bind seems to appear in his practical understanding of the individual's relationship to the group. There is the question of an irresolvable discontinuity among the Ones within the Many, the problem of collective unity. His understanding of the individual is that the One is but a necessary element of the numbered collective, while the Many try to compensate for individuals and their often detrimental effects on the whole. Some are not truly dedicated to the group purpose and its membership. These individuals are first out for themselves. This may be a timeless proposition or it may be more true today than during Dewey's lifetime. Regardless of the ravages of modernity, both idealistic and potentially dangerous to organization are the implications of assuming a functional unity of any societal group such as a school or a government when individuals in membership are not committed to cooperate in carrying out the group function. When individualism runs amuck and society is to wait for the One to self-reform, since Dewey repudiated the use of coercion, we must propose self-remediation, and school and society may become little more than a dysfunctional mockery of commonality. The unfailing dedication to the purpose of the polis or an educational institution should be viewed with extreme skepticism. Individualism today has no bounds; self-interest is indefatigable; and community must and does cede to the pervasive unrelenting needs of the One.

This is the bind of communitarian dedication. Dewey's ideas cannot be laid to rest without satisfactorily addressing dichotomies, conflicts between individuals and group interests. As Dewey left the philosophical door open wide to welcome philosophical travelers, grappling at expectations for allies, unsure, a squinty view of what he may have considered irresolvable philosophical tenets, impossible to alloy with his general ideas, finite inexpressibility, due to what he believed were limits on linguistic expression, these were the difficulties Dewey found in attempting to explain his unified philosophy, but equally impossible was the prospect that a lack of limpidity may have served as a cover for a painful philosophical bind. That bind, linguistic or loose, would ignite a conflict between the One and the Many which would burn into the twenty-first century in both American society and in its public school. Given Dewey's propensity for inclusive language, a flexible approach to procedural action would separate Dewey's ordering of experience from the logical positivists, their laws and those that would tout universals. It is no wonder that Dewey would come to question the Enlightenment project and the authority of certainty.

Bacon, Descartes and Locke found only methods for investigating the physical world and each by a strong reliance on the machinations of the mind. Bacon was a utopian of knowledge, dreaming of *New Atlantis* as a world in which man would find the cure for disease and through technology produce a paradise given by God in provision for mankind to tend. Bacon saw himself as God's own hands for sorting out the puzzles and problems of the physical world (Bacon, NA).[29] Descartes could only believe in what was in front and around him through individuating a necessary proof, only mentally connected to the objective world which thought creates. Unlike Descartes, Dewey felt that without action the inner direction was not authoritatively creative. Dewey saw experience as individuated, but, unlike Locke's understanding there was no ultimate "bias" or conceptual framework by which to assign teleology, causality, to an experience, or a generalized grouping of experiences to some proposed purpose-claim of mind or theory. Dewey's view of "instinctive tendencies" was to draw a fine line no less committed to the possibility of "innate ideas" of Descartes or the dependence on " Sensations" extolled by Locke. (Dewey, RIP, 35, 50, 82, 89; and Dewey, DAE, 312).[30] For all four philosophers, there existed non-empirical expectations which were beyond experience, expansionistic, biased and optimistic.

Yet Dewey's requirement for an acceptable empirical test for knowing was, he claimed, to be holistically natural such that neither by mind or action apart was experience to be certified. Rationalists had argued that to merely be the free expression of individual occurrence required that empiricism stand firmly on "rationalism" as a basis for experience. "Reason" was to negotiate relationships among experiences if they were to be more than spurious occurrences, "without binding and connecting principles" (Dewey, RIP, 81-83). [31]

As long as experience was instrumental in giving "usefulness", Dewey found no need for experience to lead to a "universality or principle," something to bog down experience, which he felt had happened in Kant's understanding. But the test for experience was met with obligatory formal preconception, *a priori*, in which the individual by "laws" and "principles" would be subordinated to reason (Dewey, RIP, 98).[32] Hume, Dewey points out, saw that the "chaotic and isolated particulars" of "sensationalist empiricism" gave no authority to experience but necessarily required reason.(Dewey, RIP, 83).[33]

There were no provisions for empirical purpose from economic considerations to a divine first cause, both self-establishing and absolute. Perhaps epistemology by any strict definition does not capture the pointedly direct dependability of life as a hard science. Dewey would offer an unsure footing, a shore of shifting sand, an uncertain nature of knowing in everyday life rejecting formulaic meaning while attempting to find meaning through sequential occurrences, a consideration from which Hume receded.

The theism to which Bacon, Descartes and Locke would resort for authority was not acceptable as the foundational understanding of the world. Dewey believed that the individual not following the model of "exaggerated self-sufficient Ego which by some magic creates the world," could indeed create a new, intelligent reconstruction of the world, if given direction by an "agent who is responsible, through initiative, inventiveness and intelligently directed labor for re-creating the world, transforming it into an instrument and possession of intelligence"(Dewey, RIP, 51).[34]

Under these orders epistemology becomes suspect, if not arising from experience of individual knowing, or exclusive experience. But even this knowing was subject to replacement, no guarantee of permanent usefulness. Dewey's empiricism was to constitute a soft Enlightenment project of its own. His epistemology was experimental while being practical, empirical, methodological, yet, individual and with the likely prospect of temporal and replaceable usefulness (Dewey, DAE 309-323). [35]

Morality was not fixed in Dewey's understanding. No one should be judged by the same point of law or rule. Common sense without method was unreliable as resultant consequences suffered from antecedent "judgment" and "choice" to "overt action" in a "moral situation" (Dewey, RIP, 100,163,164).[36] Dewey saw the traditional view of "common sense," lingering from his childhood, in "opposition of Sense and Thought, Experience and Reason." Considering "professional philosophers" harmful, he wrote: "Men who are thrown back upon 'common sense' when they appeal to philosophy for some general guidance, are likely to fall back on routine, the force of some personality, strong leadership or on the pressure of monetary circumstance " (Dewey, RIP, 100).[37]

Dewey felt that philosophy which finds useful practice is different from that which has no practice, which he was to describe as "artificial," that is, when a serious consideration does not lead to an actionable outcome. Useful practice may be seen as educative. But Dewey gave more import to the broader view of usefulness. When philosophy leads to "fundamental dispositions, intellectual and emotional, toward nature and fellow men, philosophy may even be defined as the general theory of education." In any philosophic directives that reflect on "experience," a concomitant "program of values" must be borne out in "conduct." Only through Dewey's "general theory of education," given true democratic freedom, could an individual, society, community or an institution, such as public education, be truly and effectively free to carry out its duty. For any philosophy to be useful it must accept divergent competing philosophies, uncertainties and flexibilities of action. "Education is the laboratory in which philosophic distinctions become concrete and are tested" (Dewey, DAE, 382-384).[38]

An understanding of epistemology and relationships with others was to be seen in his pragmatism, an all-inclusive view of experience and its usefulness. Pragmatism, the name given by William James to the parent philosophy of Charles Sanders Peirce, was to become influential in the way that many American's viewed life as doing what works in its representation among the cultivars of an evolving modernity. A radically tolerant, unanalyzed and fragmented understanding of the events and implications of those events in our day-to-day living would take hold.

The consistency with which Dewey presented his ideas were over so many years astoundingly confluent. Dewey' pragmatism was just one of many variations. James was to embrace the term "radical empiricism" to describe his variety of pragmatism (James, RE).[39] Hook does tell us that despite their differences they were nonetheless accepting of one another, and James even "welcomed Dewey as a peer." It is not hard to imagine Dewey's acceptance of James as he was even magnanimous toward those near his own ideas and even moved to inclusion of those merely seeming to gravitate toward the broader pragmatic family. Dewey was to find access to many corners of society through his writings which spanned "psychology, education, law economics, sociology, politics, art, religion, and the philosophy of science." It was his ability to absorb diverse views that increased the value of his stock and thereby allowed accessibility to those who otherwise might not have been able to buy in to agreement with each other (Hook, 8,9).[40] Although the formulary of ideas knit into Dewey's philosophy was deliberately general, or even vague, the purpose was to obtain maximum inclusion which he thought foundational to his general pluralistic philosophy of unity, and, therefore by extension even to the health of his pedagogy (Hook, 9,25-27). [41]

Dewey's writings may be considered tenebrous, awkward and difficult, but never the less more than a half century later his books and articles continue to communicate a message. The details of his ideas have had great influence as people find use in his general philosophy and pedagogy. Hook contended that the effect that Dewey's philosophy has had on America "in qualitative terms" is difficult to pin down, and those that hold to his ideas "are not always aware of their source." From over six decades ago, Hook describes Dewey's influence.

> The daring vision of yesterday is the commonplace of today ... The amazing thing however is that Dewey has made a greater impression upon the younger men of each decade since the turn of the century than he has upon his own strict contemporaries (Hook, JD, 25, 26).[42]

Society has embraced Dewey by absorption and assumption. America was ripe for Dewey's pragmatism; practicality in the schools and in society at large was to become a primary goal in the work of twentieth-century America. Dewey's prescription for the public school system has been sowed broadly and deeply. Many of his pedagogical ideas, remarkably consistent ideas, reside in public school practice today. His appeal to education and American society must be seen as his ideas have knit together philosophical, psychological and pedagogical understanding taken down from the shoulders of philosophical giants and cobbled together to engender a philosophically tempered groundwork for an alternative to a traditional American understanding. The young country which Dewey influenced with his ideas are amazingly consistent in many of the philosophical similarities which had previously emerged to drive national optimism. It is my contention that this impress is more than a coincidence or following in step. He commandeered American education with often nothing more than good intentions, yet it is maintained that in pedagogy and public life, Dewey's philosophy has been a driving force and a scapegoat for failed modern life styles as well as failed educational theory and school practice.

Dewey was grown in a century of Emersonian optimism lacking sufficient order to affect the stabilization of "opportunities of present life." Dewey would not see "thrown to the wind" all "consistency" in an undisciplined exertion "against all organization and all stability," but like Emerson and the other transcendentalists, Dewey, did not pursue "fixity" and rigidity either (Dewey, HNC, 100).[43] Dewey would find for order for the Many and to the their purpose. Emerson would take the mechanism out of man to free him from being "only the tender of a machine," "into spiders and needles" (Dewey, HNC, 144).[44]

Dewey opposed rigidity in the extreme, yet the opposite extreme also was to be feared in its excess. Lives lived "under the guise of a return to nature dream of romantic freedom" nor "a continual source of improvised spontaneities and novel inspirations," "in which all life is plastic to impulse" "which stands in defiance of organization and institutions" would not provide the "steady reorganization of custom and institutions" which Dewey felt was possible through "utilizing released impulse" intelligently for saving the individual from romantic "ideals." Habit replacement Dewey agreed was present in the child for "renewing of habit rendered possible by impulse," but never stops in the adult. "If it did, life would petrify, [and] society stagnate." Dewey favored a controlled response to behavior in which the child's or the adult's "[i]nstinctive reactions" could be "woven into a smooth pattern of habit" and not in "superficial" and "rigid habit" expression (Dewey, HNC, 100,101).[45]

Dewey's fame was to spread around the world in the early twentieth century. Interest in Dewey's theories of education arose in countries including Japan, Mexico, China, Russia, Turkey and South Africa. Yet only in America did his ideas find fertile soil in which to grow and reseed (Hook, JD, 6,10).[46] It was at the University of Chicago where he put his pedagogy to work in the so-called Dewey Laboratory School in which he was given the opportunity to test his idea of the school within a pragmatic community through the application of his experiential learning methodology. He was as head administrator no longer a philosophical rhetorician but the leader of a group of teacher-experimenters. Ironically, Dewey, the pragmatist, never proffered practical guidelines for civility for a broad range of school communities. Today student-individualist freedom in all its excesses is for all practical purposes protected, sacrosanct, preventing proactive measures to forestall disruptions. If the schools do not turn a blind eye to much of the extreme individualism that shakes the public school to its foundation, then it is touted as self-expression and a student right. Dewey's influence in the school has come to sides, some defend others attack his views linked to modern public school practice. Dewey gave us a pedagogy of order but must be philosophically examined, more closely examined. His, so-called, unified understanding of knowledge and ethics are at the center of many of today's school controversies and are inseparable from the theories and reforms which continue to prove the public school an unworthy vessel of pedagogy. Knowing and behavior, as understood by Dewey, have had deleterious effects in producing unwise choices for daily life. But we must take a closer look at Dewey's empiricism and pragmatism which will be examined in chapters preceding his epistemology and his ideas on morality, pedagogy, individualism and unity.

Chapter 2
Empiricism

> Those whose experience has to do with utilities cut off from the larger end they subserve are practical empiricists; those who enjoy the contemplation of a realm of meaning in whose active production they have had no share are practical rationalists.
>
> - John Dewey, *Democracy and Education* [1]

Advocates of an empirical, physical world have held various understandings from Plato's idealism, to Cartesian rationalism and even to Berkeley's immaterialism. Dewey felt that experience in this world had misplaced practical meaning after Plato, and experience had come to be understood through "universals," "prejudices" or "dogmas imposed by authority." Validation of experience by "reformers" of the 1800s and 1900s was fit to expectation" and "was to find protection under august names." "Appeal to experience marked the breach with authority" and authorities (Dewey DAE, 311,312, HNC, 50). [2]

Dewey's empiricism proclaimed the sole authority of an individual's experience in daily-life, a practically-fitted empiricism not Cartesian ratiocinations, which put distance between an internal and an external life. A Cartesian understanding of the world was that it was possibly illusory; it was only secondarily considered, and therefore inappropriate to Dewey's world of immediate physicality. Dewey had come to deny that remote ideas, those apart from objects, could adequately explain common experience. Descartes' foundational dualism of body and mind was to be replaced by Dewey with united action, action driven by thought. Thus, the mind and body dilemma of Descartes became one of inseparable functions where thought was given importance by demonstrable and deliberate action (Dewey, HNC, 19-22).[3]

Locke and Hume could only explain the world as experience: acquired objective knowledge through the senses. For Locke there was only what could be learned through sensationalism. Dewey would take the empirical and, like Locke, reject all other pretenders to knowledge, yet Locke, from experience had allowed knowledge to lie in state and be buried as fixed (Dewey, DAE, 71-74).[4] Dewey would see sensations as "immediate," as "stimuli and response," the path to knowledge in that sensation is the challenge which may alter behavior and lead to understanding, alive and not fixed in the rigors of meaning, maybe a mere beginning to knowing. The senses may deliver the "experienced shock of change," a "necessary stimulus" to knowing. (Dewey, RIP, 35, 81-90).[5]

Locke's apperception of an objective materiality preceded the consideration of any object by the observer. Representative realism of Locke was still closer to Dewey's pragmatic object-related realism than that of say Bishop Berkeley who denied the very ability to know the nature of materiality of "substance," thus cautioning the draw of inference from the world of objects. For Berkeley, essence and secondary characteristics were merely mental, therefore any object so described was only to be known by thought not substance in a sort of rationalistic empiricism (Dewey, QFC).[6] Locke and Hume were also considered not to be "truly empirical at all but to answer to certain demands of their theory of mind." Dewey would never deny the fact of objects, the fact of real daily life and experience. There was no immaterialism in the real world: objects existed beyond sensationalistic empiricism (Dewey, RIP, 87-91).[7] Kant's noumena and phenomenological knowing were separated in knowing - the noumenal, the thing in itself, and the phenomenal, or the sensation of the thing. The former was in the purview of philosophy, and the phenomena the haunt of everyday life and the empiricism of science. The latter was a way of knowing reality, quotidian empiricism, "the practical affairs and utilities of men." (Dewey, RIP, 23).[8] Dewey would unite both noumenal and phenomenal issues in individualized experience, in recognizable relationships and in a possible sequence of related events. Hume could not find a necessary need for the coherence of separate but possibly related experiences. Kant's imperative to prescribe for others, Dewey would see as failing to adequately understand the uniqueness of individual experience. Hume would look to reason to turn the world into "a heap of chaotic and isolated particulars," and only through "the logic of sensationalistic-empiricism," experience reasoned, could experience "be furnished with any binding and connecting principles." Dewey could not see life as "chaotic" with meaning lost in "particulars," finding meaning only in the mind's reasoned faculties (Dewey, RIP, 83).[9] Dewey world is not lived as isolated events. There is no imperative to see the world in a particular way but rather to find order in the world among real objects and events and interactions.

But empiricism and experience-directed understanding were not merely " to answer to certain demands of a theory of mind " as with Locke and Hume.

> The true "stuff" of experience would be adaptive courses of action, habits, active functions, connection of doing and undergoing; sensori-motor co-ordinations. Experience carries principles of connection and organization within itself. These principles are none the worse because they are vital and practical rather than epistemological. Some degree of organization is indispensable to even the lowest grade of life. (Dewey, RIP, 89-91).[10]

Hume's fragmentation of experiential sequence was seen by Dewey as avoiding connection. Dewey would propose the idea of "habit" (details of which are to be found in Chapter 11).

> The word habit may seem twisted somewhat from its customary use when employed as we have been using it. But we need a word to express that kind of human activity which is influenced by prior activity and in that sense acquired; which contains within itself a certain ordering or systematization of minor elements of action; which is projective, dynamic in quality, ready for overt manifestation; and which is operative in some subdued subordinate form even when not obviously dominating activity (Dewey, HNC, 40,41).[11]

Habituation could become an intelligent understanding of change in and among objects and events in the world. Change was the force of that "stuff" which was linked to experience. Dewey found a resolution for that change in Hegel. Dewey felt that Hegel's solution upheld a philosophical and physical reality among objects within the environment. No more duality's; the mind and the body, for example, would become one in Dewey's philosophy: the mind would be seen as "biological" and social practice as "institutional" (Hook, JD, 13-15).[12]

Hegel's commitment was to an idealistic world in which rationality of events was not to be prioritized but given unique experience for any real-world happening. Rather than sorting "concrete situations" for appropriateness of response, Hegel chose the "power of sheer survival" as a better procedural approach than ideal sorting. Hegel's understanding of the world which was "already ideal," was incapable of responding reasonably to "specific problems," which called for responses that were procedural, "self-corrective," and made no claims to "absoluteness or finality," nor gave consideration to what might be considered appropriate action. Dewey would come to address "all problems of human existence" by "methods" of "scientific inquiry" as an empirical process rather than by the historical-philosophical traditions. Dewey would also reject Hegelian absolutism as an irrelevant reckoning of remote properties and would replace remoteness with actuality, materially addressed in real time on earth and not by any "metaphysical" understanding. Questions regarding tradition, reason and ideals were to push Dewey farther from metaphysics and raise objections to a fixed world. Inquiry would now be enlisted by Dewey to ask questions of "all problems of human experience." He was to become the philosopher of the "plain man" whose life was ordinary with remediable circumstance (Hook, JD, 13-17).[13]

For Dewey acts would eventually become only useful experimentally, as tools. Old practical tools would be replaced by those found more appropriately useful and without sentimental or transcendent attachments. Theory would only be given place among the real considerations in the acts of life though ideas that would bear fruit. Education would tend to be more practical, applicable and instruction less theoretical. Experience would teach by the manipulation of materials or objects in the environment. In the classroom, experimental referred to hands-on learning activities.

Dewey carried away an uncertainty of knowing from Hegel, a temporality of knowing, and the Hegelian engine of methodology by which uncertainty might be given privilege in a more inclusive understanding. Yet any claim that Dewey was non-idealistic would have to be scrutinized in light of a nagging idealism, meliorism, a metaphysical hold-over which apart from tracking back toward idealism, may need to be rejected as not true to a real-world empiricism imagined by Dewey. The inconsistency is found in imagining a world as free of coercion and democratic yet struggling against the physical reality of entropy. Sidney Hook has suggested that Dewey was to lose his Kantian dualism by seeing the world as unified through Hegel. (Hook, JD, 13,14).[14]

Hegel's history of knowing would suggest for Dewey knowledge was available through individual experience. An Empiricism, without *a priori* beginnings or fixed ends, would produce meaningful experiential and individual knowledge. Truth would come to mean that something can be known which has a meaningful effect on the life of the individual. Dewey points out that historically truth came from deity and it was the responsibility of the individual to reason its authority. Later truth was seen as learned and even later as a right and duty in learning of prescribed truth for oneself. The individual was to sit in the seat of knowledge and become the harbinger of truth as he or she supplanted the lessons of truth. Authority would yield to the mind and subjectivity. According to Dewey the real indication of truth is not the result of individual testing since meaning would not be given in isolation, in "disconnection," but in a "social medium" which avoids the "rupture of continuity" (Dewey, DAE, 341 - 344).[15]

Perhaps Dewey's empiricism is tainted with presupposition and expectancy. Not that he shirks in his condescending appraisal of scientific knowledge, fact and law. Dewey ideas, in part, must be viewed by his empiricism. An inconsistent binding, true of all philosophies, must be considered in Dewey's philosophy and extended to its intrinsic pedagogy. Teaching does not presuppose theory but through general practice is dependent on dogma for exposition. One could not begin to teach a broad sweeping unit on the American colonies without detailed preparation and factual mooring of subject material, no matter how loose the contextual constraints. But conflicts in Dewey's ideas are difficult to assess when informed guidelines for application are so loose, possibly if absent in detail, then awkwardly inclusive. Dewey's empiricism is a creature unto itself, unlike that of any of those of his philosophical progenitors. Dewey's understanding of empiricism would propose ideas concerning experimentalism, a look to experience for life's meaning, and would radically influence modern practice in society generally and to the uncertainty of modern pedagogical practice. Experimentalism, proposed by Dewey, is a doomed marriage of daily experience and agency while giving less than definitive methodology for the expressed claims of authoritative negotiations necessary to prevent the trespass of the individual or the group. His empiricism is compromised not only on the basis of fuzzy guidelines of application, but an inclination to idealistic hopefulness, meliorism, that the One will very likely and voluntarily in time join the presence and purpose of the group.

Dewey's empiricism, on the basis of authority, proposes a fallacy. Individualistic fallacy or a collectivist fallacy, by either name the conflict is the same. Any experience must ultimately be given authoritative agency; it is either by the authority of the One, or an opposing position, the group, which may internalize the experience or the effect of the experience. Any resultant conflict must resolve itself in deference to one of the sides, or author-ship, to be established. Who truly and ultimately should own and find meaning in the experience seems to be methodologically unclear. For only from authority, whether it is acknowledged or not, flows meaning, sanctioned purpose, and, at least in most practices, the right to fit consequences. Empirical conflict almost always has consequences. To let a conflict within the group pass without notice is to subject authority in the matter to trivialization, and even if avoided, there may still be consequences, even if not directly confronted and judged it may run amok among the members and

the group purpose. Universal prescription or proscription according to Dewey does not account for the "irregularity of special cases" which leads to "complete confusion." Dewey suggests that we judge the "idea" by the "consequences"
(Dewey, RIP, 163).[16]

Dewey's ideas would come together as a generalized philosophy of usefulness, uncertainty, and immediacy. At least on these three points, the modern Western world has had its understanding of itself compromised while the school has suffered at the hands of authority in the face of empirical doubt while in the grips of uncooperative student-individualism. This ongoing conflict has been exacerbated by the Dewey philosophy of a replaceable, useful understanding of individual authoritative experience. Dewey's view of empiricism and experience was to be given form through his own version of pragmatism which would compromise epistemology and morality both in the general society and in the school.

Chapter 3
Pragmatism

Establishing Philosophical Distance

> A philosophy should meet your needs... A personal philosophy allows people to experience "Reality"...Rationalism closes the door on the universe. Rationalism and Empiricism come together in pragmatism.
>
> - William James, *Pragmatism* [1]

John Dewey and William James, following the lead of Charles Sanders Peirce, were to bring deductive rationalism to inductive empiricism and united them in fruitful action beyond thought or action alone. Pragmatism, doing what works, however, would never resolve the practical aspects of the uncertainty of not knowing. Knowledge, in Dewey's consideration, was to become questionable and authority could amount to little more than opinion. Both Dewey and James would only give veracity to individual immediate experience. Dewey offered that despite the "all too human love of certainty" there is in life, as James had put it, "alternation of flights and perchings." "Life is interruptions and recoveries" (Dewey, HNC, 242, 179).[2] Ideas that lead to individual action could be instrumental in pragmatic issues.

Experience in pragmatism would in the mind of John Dewey find questionable chronology and modest "perching" due to the rational expectation of change. Experience could and probably would support an expectation of change. Rationalism is the only way to yield to such idealistic expectation. If all is subject to shifts and turns, then even the process of education becomes not only problematic but carrion on which the skeptics may feed. The very assumption of change or likely change does carry with them flights of imagination and temporal usefulness.

Aristotle represented philosophy as a "self-closed" and "contemplative" knowledge; Dewey saw this without evidence.

"Pure Mind," the ultimate knowledge, is unchanging, but Dewey felt that experience is deserted when rules become "fixed, " unyielding to time and situation. An attempt to find certainty where there may be none is Dewey's idea of "a hankering for certainty." Dewey would see this as attempting to resolve problems with right-at-hand answers in issues of judgment. Each experiential rule should be custom fit to every particular situation. To rely on principles and unbending authority is to not see that even standards of measure are comparative in nature and in science, for example, we compare one size with another by use of "the foot rule," an arbitrary standard. Dewey cites James definition of philosophy, and then continues with its purpose. " '[P]hilosophy is vision' and that its chief function is to free men's minds from bias and prejudice and to enlarge their perceptions of the world about them" (Dewey, RIP, 21,110, 111; HNC, 238, 240, 241).[3]

The origins of ideas contributing to his world view and their implications for America and our system of public education may be extracted from Dewey's evolution of pragmatic ideas. Pragmatism knows the world through its immediate action; Dewey was to give cognitive distance to rationalism and idealism. To divide an understanding of the real world into a physically experiential domain and into another of ideals was unacceptable to Dewey; this was the world of Platonic and Kantian philosophy. Dewey rejected Plato's physical world which was directed by universal values external to the physical world. Since this required a rationalism dependent on transcendence and on "modes of knowledge [therefore] inaccessible to the common man, involving not continuous reconstruction of ordinary experience, but its wholesale reversal," Dewey could not accept Plato's authority which was unknowable exclusively through experience of the individual for whom such values were to be accepted as universal (Dewey HNC, 290,291).[4]

Dewey would come to see the world as united through communal practice which would stand as authority among all its members. Agreeing with Plato then the "society is the human soul writ large," the stability of society, Dewey would contend that education, in a broad sense, was a social glue. But Plato saw the elements of social construction as classes, groups of fixed contributors and lackeys ordered for the common good. Dewey saw the individual as the basis of civilization. The enlightenment of the eighteenth century saw "society as broad as humanity" with each individual an "organ." Since there could not be found an appropriate way of carrying out such individual empowerment, the resort was Nature. The idealism of the nineteenth century gave authority to the state in the form of the ruling politicos while assigning the subjection of the individual to the state. Dewey would hold that to define the state to which the individual would submit, it was necessary to know the type of social education it could provide (Dewey, DAE, 112, 115,116).[5]

The pragmatics of education were to hang by the string of democracy. The thread of unity between the One and the Many was to be perennially frayed. It was with Dewey's idealistic knitting of the Ones into the Many that he would attempt to unify groups without a guarantee, merely wishfulness, of ultimate authority to the group.

So society needs to wait around for the loose cannons to join in the war for communal commonality. In a public school system, which has vacillated in uncertainty of purpose in an ill-preposed jumble of programs that have repeatedly failed to meet high academic standards, the social and academic needs of most students in public schools have been compromised if not disregarded by remote control, from outside the immediate learning community. Dewey offered a philosophical framework for democratizing a nation and educating its young through a group-based ceding to individual pragmatism. The individual was the active element but the group was the primary benefactor. Giving what was deemed needed by individual students was to insure the effectiveness of educational practice and would result in student civility as well. This is a reversal of communalism: the Ones being given the freedom to act as they will even at the risk of the larger group, who will ultimately, and hopefully, arrive at consensus with the Ones.

James addresses the valuelessness of understanding one another in dealing with ideas alone in the following.

> We can never be sure we understand each other till we are able to bring the matter to the test. This is why metaphysical discussions are so much like fighting with the air; they have no practical issue of a sensational kind (James, P, 358).[6]

James and Dewey would agree with a focus on the "test" of everyday philosophy but found at its margins an irresolvable epistemology. Peirce's pragmatic understanding was that of a belief in the promise of science to find hard answers through rigorous scientific investigation. Not so with Peirce's two notable acolytes, for both James and Dewey, uncertainty was lurking in the deepest reaches of scientific discovery. James, though he recognized that the flourishes of science could "dazzle" the mind, stated:

> as the sciences have developed farther the notion has gained ground that most, perhaps all, of our laws are only approximations...a man-made language, a conceptual short-hand...and languages, as is well known, tolerate much choice of expression and many dialects (James, P, 56, 57).[7]

James claimed that the value of science is in its usefulness, no usefulness no value. On this point it seemed that James was a bit chagrined at the loss of religion's prestige in its roll of metaphysical usefulness (James, P, 56, 57).[8]

Dewey would not share James disappointment in the loss of religious metaphysical authority no matter its use but would see all experience as non-transcendent, but only earthly with earthly outcomes. For Dewey pragmatism was instrumental. It must be confirmed in actionable decisions among real issues not in the abstract necessity of any particular issue. As Dewey points out, anything which is "invaluable" has intrinsic value. If something is instrumental, that is has instrumental value, then it may be an option in a choice of options. To eat and to listen to music may be of value, but, if sated, then music may be chosen, if hungry, then food. What has meaning, is instrumental, is the option that will be chosen at that time. This is a real decision involving one choice over another, and that shows instrumental value of the preference and is not intrinsic in its value. "In the abstract or at large, apart from the needs of a particular situation in which choice has to be made, there is no such thing as degrees or order of value (Dewey, DAE, 279, 281).[9]

Dewey's pragmatic approach held that thought, instrumental to its attendant action, may give rise to usefulness and, therefore, meaning. Dewey claims that this is the only way a student will find value in, say, arithmetic. One must show application and not speculate on the possible future uses in the life of the student (Dewey, DAE, 280, 281).[10] Dewey would eventually come to see epistemology and morality as one, a useful holism for daily life. Dewey felt that in his and others' manipulation of the two realms that the physical and mental worlds could be unified as knowing and doing through experience. Empiricism made useful and amendable is pragmatic, instrumentalism gives pragmatism a direction or purpose recognized in its outcome.

There can be no universal law or fixed rules, that do not respond to experimental imperatives. Kant was rejected and in doing so, so was the willing and prescribing of civil action among individuals (Dewey, HNC, 245-247).[11] For Dewey rationalism failed the test of an objective, changing world of objects. Willing universally for others would be presuming that the time, events and situations were the same which they could never be for two or more individuals. Dewey could not accept the fixity of such an imperative of experience to group action. The individual must decide what the behavioral limits should be to individual action and how to instrument its application.

Scientific theorizing and physical laws were to be held to the scrutiny of daily life with experimental knowledge questioned as to any sampling of event, environment and time. To apply to practical life any data-based insight is to hold fact above inquiry, above the process of life and ongoing scientific discovery. Dewey would deny the rush to ends and view scientific progress as merely means to potentially further means. Science was about data, facts; experimentalism was about real life. In underscoring this idea, Dewey made reference to Dickens', Hard Times, in which the character Gradgrind commented, " facts, facts," but for Dewey factual knowledge was of dubious importance when weighed against the immediate experience of life (Dewey, DAE, 221).[12]

Since experiences change facts and data from experience, experimentation could not be expected to be dependably enduring. The implication for school practice is profound in light of a floating epistemology. Dewey claimed, despite his academic and scholarly background, that experience should be the bedrock of instruction "in school" and "out of school" (Dewey, DAE, 416).[13] All school texts must be held in lower regard as well as disciplinary judgments as daily practice within the school or outside the school is equally acceptable as educational, instructional. If facts are to be doubted, then grading class assignments and judging behavioral infractions in the classroom bring question to correctional authority which in consideration would amount to little more than opinion, strong feeling or peer or teacher disapprobation.

Pragmatic conception of pervasive and progressive uncertainty had eroded Dewey's confidence in the Enlightenment project. Bacon, Locke, Descartes had found only a method of investigation where each rendering of the physical world was assumed to some degree accessible through machinations of the mind. Descartes could only believe in what was in front and around him through individuating his proof in thought. He thus projected an insulated individualism among remote objects.

Francis Bacon was a utopian, dreaming of New Atlantis and a paradise in which man would find the cure for disease and the establishing of a technological excellence for mankind (Bacon, NA, especially 575-584).[14] Bacon's pursuit of knowledge was an inquiry into the ways of nature for the benefit of the larger community of man. Bacon saw himself as at least one pair of God's own hands trusted in the sorting out of the puzzles and problems of the physical world for all humanity. Dewey could not accept this utopianism only positivity in community cooperation and the hope that science and technology would be used for the betterment of all. Francis Bacon felt that God had given man the opportunity to fulfill the hopes of mankind through a collective rule over nature. In Bacon, nature and collective man would find a utopian future, and, although he was a man of letters, he was not just a solid proponent of positivism. He felt that the power of empiricism was poised to make science and its discoveries the servant of man, still he was a dedicated student of literature and letters in all respects. And for Dewey also this was the educational goal - to make education expansive to these two poles of learning. Dewey saw Bacon as "the real founder of modern thought" in using science and its empirical methods for the "control of natural forces" and saw that "fantastic learning aped the form of true knowledge" "in scanty and distorted measure" "from antiquity through scholasticism (Dewey, RIP, 28-30).[15]

Dewey could applaud Bacon's sense of communal good and his methodology, all be it flawed, as he would see science as not "already known" but becoming and hence not fixed or possessed. Dewey would use methodology in his pedagogy while holding the Baconian application to science, which Bacon saw as "perfect," Dewey saw as "absurdity.'" Human differences in "ability" could be "discounted" by Bacon's utopian view, while Dewey would always believe in leveling. " Bacon's view of such an interdependence of science and society, as an organized pursuit, was a grand gesture. "Power over nature was not to the individual but collective; the Empire, as he says, of Man over Nature, substituted for the Empire of Man over Man." The individual would on his own find little but "his own self-spun web of misconceptions." (Dewey, RIP, 31, 36, 37).[16]

The scientific method would become the soldiers of Dewey's instrumentalist, pragmatic, campaign of knowing the world. Dewey, after great praise of Bacon, falls out with him for his sharing the glory of man's ultimate conquering of nature with "the creator."

> Bacon may be taken as the prophet of a pragmatic conception of knowledge. Many misconceptions of its spirit would be avoided if his emphasis upon the social factor in both the pursuit and the end of knowledge were carefully observed (Dewey, RIP, 38).[17]

Never would Dewey view reputable science or acquisition of knowledge as other than an earthly and collective responsibility in which "operative and practical character of knowing, of intelligence, is objective" capable of uniting "daily experience" and "rational contemplation" (Dewey, RIP, 116, 117).[18]

Dewey saw Bacon as the modern progenitor of the scientific method.

> ...Bacon eloquently proclaimed the superiority of discovery of new facts and truths to demonstration of the old...Active experimentation must force the apparent facts of nature into forms different to those in which they familiarly present themselves;...Bacon felt, and with justice, that any logic which identified the technique of knowing with demonstration of truths already possessed by the mind, blunts the spirit of investigation and confines the mind within the circle of traditional learning (Dewey, RIP, 31-33).[19]

Dewey extracted from Bacon the idea of methodology, which was not original with Bacon but which he would apply to all of life's experiences. Education would become under Dewey's influence methodical and organized. Science was valuable, instrumental, to Dewey in that through science, using it as a model, he saw daily life and educational methodology as orderly practices. Dewey would question that there could ever be an end to human understanding thus removing any possible sanctions on practice, experimentalism, pragmatism. Pragmatism would become by his definition a what-will-work-now philosophy which was open to the knowledge that issues and understandings could be subject to remediation or remain irresolvable for all time. It would be unavoidable, following the logic of knowledge replacement, that neither scientism nor logical positivism would escape scrutiny.

Ultimate experiential authority was seen differently by James. He took pragmatism in the direction of individuality, while Dewey's held a collectivist position while denying the efficacy of projected collectivism: transcendence or universalism which favored the unearthly for transcendence or absolutism. Supernaturalism, which Dewey attached to the Middle Ages, was not capable of transferring its fixity to the evolving experimental concrete world (Dewey, RIP, 47).[20]

Dewey's influences on education have been in his understanding of community and of truth, knowing and meaning, for which he shared commonalities with co-pragmatist William James. Antecedents to Dewey's brand of pragmatism, Socrates, Aristotle, Locke, Berkeley and Hume had posited pragmatic ideas, but they were only "preluders," their ideas were "forerunners of pragmatism used... in fragments" (James, P, 50).[21] For both William James and Dewey, pragmatism embraced an "empirical attitude" and "concrete action" against dogma. It was of " cash-value" and not "magic," an "enigma" wielded for power. James conferred the distinction on pragmatism contending that it "unstiffens all our theories," always considers "particulars" and always leaves room for "[n]ew truth" to suit individual "needs." "[I]individuals will emphasize their points of satisfaction differently. To a certain degree, therefore, everything here is plastic." But pragmatism has come to be applied in a broader sense as "a certain [particular] theory of truth," "New truth is always a go-between, a smoother over of transitions." Satisfaction, rather than fixity of knowing, shows truth to be but an "approximation," "instrumental" for usefulness (James, P, 51-61).[22] Knowing is only a temporary, stop-gap immediacy, useful as its purpose, but only close to truth.

Dewey with James would carry pragmatism beyond Charles Sanders Peirce's original conception: "that our beliefs are really rules for action." "[D]ispute is idle." Yet the hypothetical only finds meaning in support of action, James added (James, P, 45, 46).[23]

In the words of Emerson: "[G]ood thoughts are no better than good dreams, unless they be executed!" (Emerson, Essays, 348).[24] Rationalism only attends to truth as a proposition. A requirement for action removes the solitary mental aspect of truth and constrains thought to the demonstrable. Only then can thought hope to find axiological veracity. Universality, on the other hand, is also a dream, as thought without action. Since universals have no specific referent action they are no more than that of Emerson's dreams. Dewey's spin on pragmatism would require the action of event and experience, a doing of truth, an experience of truth. Universal, a term that would give authority, Dewey would reckon coercive. Dewey, so Hook claims, came to view individual experience, that is individual thought with individual action, as uniquely authoritative and not of universal importance or rationalistic. No higher mandated rule was given authority over individual, intelligent experience. Knowing was "self-corrective precisely because" no presumption " to absoluteness or finality" could be claimed. Dewey had adopted Hegel as he became convinced that knowledge was "neither immediate or self-certifying" and judgment was based on factors beyond the occurrence of "metaphysical" judgment of "truth or falsity" and therefore could not claim universal authority (Hook, JD,13-15).[25] Through Dewey's pragmatism, absolute knowledge would be supplanted by the value of experiential knowing. Meaning was to come to be seen in doing, while truth, defined by meaning, could be altered by new experience which could in turn reveal new meaning, and so on.

The useful, the pragmatic, is an extension of Dewey's empiricism. Action takes its value, its truth, from being useful and, it would seem for an inability to control what is useful, without regard to the acceptability of the action. Dewey proposed a methodology for societal and school practice that was pragmatic: collectivistic and experiential. Since there is no guarantee of certainty, experimentation is its own goal. Collectivity would endure perturbation by those in membership who would stand for self. Not even membership was certain of purpose as some were out for themselves and were only nominal members. To claim answers in a changing world, without certainty, must be seen as naive and fruitless. Knowing that one knows from what is pragmatic is narrow and unrealistic in such a changing world. Science would have no credible authority since the basis for understanding, facts and data, may be replaced. Science like the pursuits of the daily routine of any individual proceeds through a pragmatic usefulness called instrumentalism. What is useful, instrumental, is good and worthy. Life like science is experimental with understanding changing with time, situation, event and agency as experience and experimentation are individualized and not transferrable. Schooling and knowing would seem to be arrived at in transcendental fashion, without known thought value nor expectation of meaningful outcome. This calls into doubt the usefulness of Dewey's variety of epistemological arguments.

Dewey being doubtful of causality, however, does not answer the usefulness of uncertain knowledge. It limits the way that we may understand the world and those around us. Dewey's understanding of causality in knowing is no better than Hume's. Either way knowledge loses its authenticity; there is on either ground no way that such skepticism can certify knowing.

Empiricism which embraces rationalism is in direct conflict with Dewey's pragmatic ideas: what to do with the why to do it. Lock's impenetrable resistance to knowledge having its origin in interiority was not shared by Dewey. As will be detailed later, Dewey maintained that development of the individual occurred through instinctive and impulsive eruptions from within the individual which may be challenged by the environment, but these are valid. Ideation for Dewey was thought, useless unless it was joined to action. But that action could never be linked causally to personal propositions or motives. We cannot be sure that we may know why human thoughts are brought to action. Seeing the empirical evidence does not give us assurance of causality only mere speculation. Dewey would consider "consequences broadly" since it is not possible to flawlessly "judge dispositions" (Dewey, HNC, 44, 45).[26]

Pragmatism would come to impose itself broadly on the Western world. From postmen to presidents, the fallout of such a forced empirical order has exacted dramatic effects on society, its communities and cultures. Individual perception would bring chaos to group understanding and purpose. Whether in the greater society or in the school culture, the rule of the One would reign in knowledge and human relationship as rationalism ran amok among the leitmotif of modernity. The schools are adrift in the often fantastical whim of student authority, while the theorist understand their ideas by conjecture and the schools have little authority to teach and struggle to hold up civility. Both theorizing school practice and the ultimate consideration of the individual are resurrected as guiding theories from historic and more modern rationalism. If pragmatism is given to the One before the Many, then the One will always think of self first and secondarily of Others, if at all.

For Dewey practical experience was the great teacher; it was individual and gave authority. Rationalism, pure thought, as well as any protected definitive experience, as in scientism, could be discarded. Empiricism and its hard Enlightenment principles had to give way to the unique experience, changeable experience, of the One which would permit authority of exclusive experience. The value of any experience was in its usefulness, its practical advantage not in its elitist pedigree.

Empiricism based on active individual experience was to find meaningful authority in Dewey's philosophy. Locke who would accept nothing but the evidence of experience, found no method of linking experience to idea except by trial and error and without guaranteeing causality. Thus Locke brought another obstacle to educationally useful knowing of the world and the living of each day. To experience the world without the surety of understanding is an idle prospect. Setting aside school authority creates social riskiness, like crossing a street while blindfolded during rush-hour traffic. The ultimate absurdity of an experimental approach to everyday problems is a dubious pragmatism.

As kings were replaced so the length of royal feet. Dewey would hold that such is the temporality of much, if not most, which is considered knowledgeable and known. The very implication that knowledge is subject to change as a principle of knowing damages the credibility of not only the knowing but the very methodology by which one is to know. To replace facts is not the core problem since knowledge must give way to correction, but to cast aspersions on the very process by which knowledge is corrected, if called into doubt, can only mark the death of any dependable knowing. Judgments in the courts are all suspect and deny evidentiary ruling. The impact on education of such procedural uncertainty is immeasurable as that of society. Not only is any knowledge to be questioned, in effect, but the serious pursuit of knowledge is found unreasonable. Pragmatism compenetrates under unique aegis, the justification for doing what One wants.

But like truth Dewey will show acceptance of individual actionable thought, if it has positive social impact in its action.

Chapter 4
Epistemology

> The only literally true thing is reality...Truth...is a property of certain of our ideas. It means their "agreement," as falsity means their disagreement, with 'reality'... Truth lies, in fact, for the most part on a credit system. Our thoughts and beliefs "pass" so long as nothing challenges them, just as bank-notes pass so long as nobody refuses them.
>
> - William James, *Pragmatism* [1]

> I never can catch myself at any time without a perception, and never can observe anything but the perception.
>
> -David Hume, *A Treatise of Human Nature* [2]

Dewey gives truth collective meaning pragmatically in requiring it to serve the greater good. This may seem on the surface a minor wrinkle, but Dewey would only have social or group understanding of truth. If individual truths were asserted, say, from two or more people, even if they conflicted in their assertions, each could claim veracity, if each had positive social significance. If the issue were of little consequence, this may be laid down to interpretation, but whether to walk in the street during rush hour is of far greater concern.

Even as Dewey eschewed rationalism and idealistic thinking, his philosophy could not rid itself of these influences. Pragmatism, the philosophy which Dewey would perennially defend, was measured by a fixed and certified standard, individual action. Authority was not based on the judgment of experience and usefulness of One among Many but given to the individual through unchallenged freedom in all experience. The choice of action might not be fixed but the authority of judgment rests with the individual. The standard is the individual will which cannot be refuted or coerced.

Suffice it to say, to question causality is to question the basic workings of society and the school and indeed that of the whole of the physical world. Certainty would be undependable, unable to settle practical questions. Ends become suspect and seen as primarily new means by which pragmatism works to find new means with no guarantee of ever finding resolution, an end. A looming future could bring new understanding leaving former beliefs no more than means through which still newer means would surface. Dewey's optimism was permitted under these circumstances, since the authority for meaning and truth was individualistic. Individualism or particularity, whether an issue of the individual or of the scientific laboratory, could harbor extrapolative meaning yet be doubtful as authoritative in any transfer of particularity to another individual experience or another experiment. Time, event, situation, all aspects of agency interfere with dependable transmission of what to do, how and when and ultimately what it all means.

The individual not only may not be clear on considerations leading to judgment but may fail in the reasoning of intended action. The civility of society and the school have been compromised by implementing this pernicious practice under the weight of societal pressure which has empowered extreme individual authority. Doing what is pragmatic has come to mean do what you want. Object and agent interaction, predicated on thought, which may be antecedent to action, may join with action as activity.

Epistemology for Dewey was pragmatic: does what one knows have use and therefore meaning for life and learning. Any context of study, Dewey concludes, must have "connections" to real people and situations, and it is within experience that one is to find knowledge. He denied that teaching facts retains the necessary humanity needed for educative learning (Dewey, DAE, 246).[3] The ongoing pragmatic, useful understanding of truth and knowing offers little initiative for values and must be relegated to an itch and whimsy. Do what you want, and feel good about it. If others find value in what you did then they may acknowledge your social contribution or the change induced by you. Action will contribute to a non-defendable and an unquestionable evolution within society.

The knower is granted the parochial margins of experiential authority in the present. The One has the vantage point to meaning and truth within the event-horizon. What then is immediate and useful may be viewed as meaningful but only as present events prepare the way to future understanding. Recalling lines from Tennyson's "Ulysses" we look to a bright future but live in experience which is lost as we walk in the present toward the future. "Yet all experience is an arch wherethrough Gleams that untravelled world, whose margin fades For ever and for ever when I move (Tennyson, Ulysses).[4]

Knowing, truth, is lost in the past and dims in expectation of the future. If it would seem Dewey's concept of truth is puzzling; James would not claim a complete understanding of Dewey's view of truth, claiming Dewey's pragmatic ideas might diverge in "postulates" or in "implications," but not necessarily in substance. James distinguished Dewey's view of pragmatism as a much broader species. Dewey held that objects not in consideration of experiential judgment would transcend activity and would, therefore, be outside the realm in which such entities could be necessarily considered extant. However, this was not necessarily a denial of their existence, only a reluctance to give a host to reality outside of immediate experience (James, TMOT, xli-xliii).[5]

So Dewey could not see ideas apart from objects and actions. Knowledge, was for Dewey, eventful practicality for the One. The individual, unique experience among "objects," "things," in ongoing activity, as things are part of a "continuously developing situation, instead of taking them in isolation" (Dewey, DAE, 161). [6] James tells us that a terminal experience on which everyone could agree, would not be a matter of truth but rather the experience would be seen as "real" (James, TMOT, 134).[7] Dewey granted knowledge to the ordering of any practical experience as "real." "Genuine knowledge has all the practical value attaching to efficient habits in any case" (Dewey, DAE, 397).[8]

But order requires a reasonable alignment of occurrences, even some that would appear to be dependent on one another especially in problem solving. In Hume's epistemology the sequence of issues accrue but find no resolution in combination to permanently solve problems. Each issue becomes an individual, non-transferrable knowledge event lacking the ability to serve in finding a practical solution. This sort of empirical reductionism isolates activities and precludes the possibility of prediction. For Hume there was no requirement of teleology among particular events but merely a random grouping of events and nothing more. Knowing in its ultimate form is indefensible: "Truth is disputable." Each person finds subjective truth in Hume's view (Hume, ECHUTPOM, 3).[9] Dewey at least saw a possible sequence of particulars making sense together for directing subsequent action, but within the context of a collective resolution.

Objects become useful according to our preconceptions. Appropriate to conception is that a pen knows only to write. That is what pens do, write on paper; what we do is to pen paper by our own power to our own purpose. But Dewey held that all "things" are intrinsic to the experience, whereas the rationalistic mind stays outside the experience determining "truth-relations," categorizing among "parts" and concluding by merely "uttering the name truth." The "anti-pragmatist" then has only a perspective of One who must "stand outside of all possible temporal experience" "obdurate" to the end. A "known" and a "knower" are separated into their own categories of objects.(James, TMOT, xxxvii). [10]

The habits of use are integral to knowledge, as knowing to the known. Dewey perhaps has carried the agency of knowing a bit farther a field. The individual forms understandings of the world through first hand experience. The individual mind is "the Agent of Reorganization." "Men must observe [the world] for themselves, and form their own theories and personally test them." Knowing was to result from an inductive, individual experience and not the deductive process of drawing from any "dogma of truth" (Dewey, DAE, 343).[11]

There seems to be value, as Dewey would see it, in considering the inclusiveness of an appeal to knowing. Instead of harming the pragmatic line of truth, Dewey would loosen the reins on truth-controlling so as to allow more flexibility in the on-going process of knowing. Still even with the best intentions in mind, Dewey has created by redefinition, or devaluation by openness, a loss of dependable and specific knowledge while at the same time trying to bring knowing to pragmatic utility. Though of doubtful terminus, Dewey's words make our prospects to know no more assured then couches knowledge in a lagging process: "[L]earning takes place in connection with the intelligent carrying forward of purposeful activities [which] is a slow work" (Dewey, DAE, 161).[12]

As the "margin fades," to revisit Tennyson, so our exclusive claim to experiential knowledge fades, so fades the present and the future. Dewey's empiricism may have reluctantly depended on immediacy in valuing and revaluing knowledge. Immediacy in awarding trust in knowing was not necessarily less valid than knowing accrued over extended time. The former, if arrived at through direct experience, would be even preferable to accrual. Time frame and personal agency issues of knowing must raise doubt concerning the retentive usefulness of any knowledge in learning, of even traditional education itself. Yet as Dewey considered the storing up of knowledge, whether accumulated or amassed as a totality of learning, he saw a control of acquired information, facts, and not the result of a experiential action.

> Deliberation is not calculation of indeterminate future results. The present, not the future, is ours. No shrewdness, no store of information will make it ours. (Dewey, HNC, 207).[13]

Knowledge is slowly acquired at best, and storing information only contributes to dogmatic traditionalism and standing in the path to interfere with new understanding. "[T]he entire scientific history of humanity demonstrates that the conditions for complete mental activity will not be obtained till adequate provision is made for the carrying on of activities that actually modify physical conditions, and that books, pictures, and even objects that are passively observed but not manipulated do not furnish the provision required" (Dewey, HWT, 100).[14] "Pupils are taught to live in two separate worlds, one the world of out-of-school experience, the other the world of books and lessons" (Dewey, HWT, 200).[15] This appears to be an admixture of experience and remnants of Dewey's romanticism.

When words and ideas are given apart from activities of "personal inquiry and testing," then "meaning" becomes semiotic and "[l]azy inertness" results in the acceptance of "ideas that have currency about them" (Dewey, HWT, 176, 177).[16] Understanding is absorbed from the environment without the activation by initiating experience. Dewey believed that "words" and "things" should not be taught but rather their "meaning" certified by experience. After which "[w]ords can detach and preserve a meaning (Dewey, HWT, 176).[17] Meaning derived from knowing and knowing itself, however, is not patently transferable but the result of "personal inquiry and testing." Heidegger and Dewey both felt that each individual being was to find limits to understanding. As we shall see, Dewey has placed a wall between the individual and the hope of the individual securing any specific claim to knowledge. It will be hard to hold on to knowledge as time, event and circumstance conspire to alter the thing known by the knower and, thereby strengthening the improbability that a viable claim to whole knowledge could not be sustained. From Dewey's discussion of "natural resources" we are confronted with the limitations of "natural resources" which may amount to, we are told, "he (the teacher) has sold when no one has bought, as to say, he has taught when no one has learned." It is difficult not to see that the acquisition of knowledge due to failed methodology or limitations of the teacher or disruptive students additively constrain to incongruity in the classroom (Dewey, HWT, 29-44). [18]

Dewey's views on truth and knowledge might conflict but could share common ground if broadly assumed among other prominent theories. Over a century ago, Harold Joachim sorted through asserted theories or perspectives of truth-claims. One such theory, correspondence-notion, was found to depend on "two factors determinately related to one another" as factors in each of two comparable wholes. In "accordance with" or "in conformity to the facts," correspondence is "faithfully" abiding in "real things" (Joachim, TNOT, 7-12).[19] Since the "mind" and "interpretation" weigh on this method of getting at truth, the knower may miss "significance," fail to give completeness to its meaning or "convey a thoroughly false impression." All judgment hangs on the correspondence which must stem from the perception of the individual. Truth may not effectively arise from "correspondence." Truth may be created in the process of the mind's own activity." The narrative "portrays" the facts; and the narrative is a whole of simple and abstract elements in comparison with the fullness and concreteness of the "occurrences" (Joachim, TNOT, 16, 17).[20]

So as one individual "portrays" through narrative, so does another describe the same event. Each individual's description of the same event is different; neither has duplicated the other's tale. Each has his own vision which neither may exactly capture, and yet each may judge a faithful likeness. Correspondence by this example may seem only to represent a limited contribution to the potential of recording an event. Skewed by each One experiencing and recording the likeness, each may be true to the event and correspond on multiple features rendered by each individual. "Thus, the image in the mirror 'reflects' the face; and the image is a less concrete expression of the idea, an expression in a simpler material" (Joachim, TNOT, 17-24).[21] There are "a plurality of meanings by correspondence"..."the judging mind constitutes as it judges" (Joachim, TNOT, 16-22).[22]

Dewey would allow the replacement of truth as needs require. He would find it difficult to avow replacement based on personal "utility." He felt that this was a utilitarian disposition in the legacy of Jeremy Bentham which was "so abnoxious" and amounted to "a mere tool of private ambition and aggrandizement, that the wonder is that critics have attributed such a notion to sane men" (Dewey, RIP, 157).[23] As a pragmatist, Dewey saw the event as action. Each individual experience must have meaning, each individual ostensibly told an intelligent tale, each of which could be acceptable in correspondence, yet various unique experiences may share the truth of an event without the truth serving as a convenient tool to private purpose and selfishness.

Thought is what is "in our heads" or "goes through our minds." "Thoughts grow up... without reference to the attainment of correct belief...Such thoughts are prejudices." (Dewey, HWT, 1, 5).[24]

Mental separation from situations represents the mind/body duality of Descartes and denies that the mind and appropriate objects are conjoined in action to express the physical world. Unity of mind and matter, for Dewey, denotes, objects, situations and experiences, relationships involving these elements in an ongoing reconstruction.

This understanding of knowledge does give more flex to knowledge but makes it possibly unrecognizable or undependable when communicated to others. If truth is found in the correspondence between subject and object in the world then to change the subject reveals a changed understanding of the object in an inseparable subject-object relationship within the world. When the subject changes, the subject-object relationship becomes a new relationship, and, when the object changes, the relationship is likewise changed. Two subjects may relate the same story with each far from the details given by each narrative yet both be correct in their correspondence to the actual world event. Each bestows the authority on each experience of truth. No one holds exclusivity to completeness of truth but merely some general agreements possibly concerning another's truth.

In some sense of progress, correspondence seems to get close to another truth theory. Joachim's analysis of epistemological theory, the coherence-notion, which in considering truth and fact is judged by "conceivability." Truth and knowing must maintain a "systematic coherence" which can be reasoned from the "significant whole." Elemental portions of the whole must find cohesion free of "discursive thinking." (Joachim, TNOT, 64-68).[25] One story may emphasize the event, while yet another the situation under which the event took place. Serious "coherent" models create a fuller rendition of the narrative but must so render a mutually reinforcing alikeness. Coherence theory allows for an acceptance of narratives without judging the stress on details as evasive. Coherence is maintained if details or stresses are not singled out or ignored to skew points of inquiry in constructing narrative. Furthermore, what is considered in each experience-narrative must not be in conflict with One another for the construction of any bona fide meta-narrative. Internal agreement of cohesive parts must be in the "whole" of "single concrete meaning" (Joachim,

TNOT, 66).[26] Narratives must be in agreement to support and strengthen coherence.

For Dewey there is "conceivability" in meaningful truth as it must be derived from experience. Truth and knowing must find a "significant whole" within the world of objects. The correspondence of seemingly conflicting truths was not a problem for Dewey. Dewey's epistemology is by comparison still looser on this point than represented by the theory of coherence. Knowing is considerate of the differences among meanings and knowledge held by different individuals. Time and new experience stoke the fires of change and persistently threaten as perennial knowledge burns behind and on all sides. Dewey's truth is foremost collectivist. Holding tenaciously to conflicting ideas does not build agreement and community. But the plurality of meanings for Dewey was to be viewed as a communal understanding in progress, evolution and equilibrium which through "discord" could potentiate progress in "discovery" over time (Dewey, RIP, 108,109).[27]

In keeping with Dewey's inclusiveness, conflicts may only serve to drive the collective understanding to new commonalities of acceptable truth. Conceivable conflicting views may be coherent and even correspondent to a progress toward this commonality of truth. For Dewey who holds the knower responsible for the known, as long as the known is represented in the world of objects, any knower has authoritative control over the truth of knowing, for its time. Joachim suggests that a position like Dewey's does not hold truth to the coherence requirement of "a single concrete meaning." This approach to truth is characteristic of a more scientific or philosophical understanding of truth (Joachim, TNOT, 66-68).[28]

Convergent theory of truth, loosely held, could also prove acceptable to Dewey with openness to an evolution of veracity, to hope that the future will allow a consensus among conflicting or multiple perspectives resolved or even conjoined. This form of truth theory would give Dewey's inclusiveness a possible option as an ongoing procession to establish truth that would give distance to the epistemological demands of any or any combinations of time, place and agency. As Dewey felt that truth was an unfolding and not an end in itself, so in a convergent theory of truth, Dewey would have found an open-ended acceptance. All individually held truths place evolutionary pressure on the resolution of social needs and may ultimately find themselves the synthesis of antithetical influences.

Dewey saw a tendency in depending on common sense to direct ones actions as a "fall back on routine, the force of some personality, strong leadership or on the pressure of momentary circumstances." Common sense has "confused and hampered" and the liberal and progressive movement of the eighteenth and earlier nineteenth centuries had no method of intellectual articulation commensurate with its practical aspirations (Dewey, RIP, 100).[29]

James saw common sense as a way of rationalization by which "categories of thought" in systematic order register impressions (James, P, 171).[30] "The common-sense categories one and all cease to represent anything in the way of being; they are but sublime tricks of human thought, our ways of escaping bewilderment in the midst of sensation's irremediable flow" (James, P, 186).[31] He understood the turning to categorizing smart judgment as a method of dealing with our not knowing under the bombardment of "sensation's irremediable flow." James claimed that "it is only the highly sophisticated specimens, the minds debauched by learning, as Berkeley called them, who have ever even suspected common sense of not being absolutely true" (James, P 182).[32] James emphasizes his lack of faith in common sense: "Retain, I pray you, this suspicion about common sense" (James, P, 193).[33] Dewey claimed that the reason that common sense has failed is because it has

> fallen back on faith, intuition or the exigencies of practical compromise. But common sense too often has been confused and hampered instead of enlightened and directed by the philosophies proffered it by professional intellectuals (Dewey, RIP, 100).[34]

They rely on "fixed principles transcending experience, to dogmas incapable of experimental verification" rather than depending "on fruits and consequences in experience" (Dewey, RIP, 100, 101).[35] The fixity that Dewey eschewed was reactionary in the sense that it precluded any new understanding. Dewey forestalls admission to hard knowledge issues by claiming that such fixity would appear to be ends - final understanding - but were no more that merely means to additional means.

> Means and ends are the names for the same reality... To bear the end in mind signifies that we should not stop thinking about our next act until we form some reasonably clear ideas of the course of action to which it commits us. To attain a remote end means on the other hand to treat the end as a series of means. To say that an end is remote or distant, to say in fact that it is an end at all, is equivalent to saying that obstacles intervene between us and it. If, however, it remains a distant end, it becomes a mere end, that is a dream (Dewey, HNC, 36).[36]

Dewey saw an "end" as "vague, cloudy, impressionistic" (Dewey, RIP, 36).[37]

Such teaching of ends is confusing to most students. Doubt concerning "knowledge" shows tolerance to other understandings of truth without offering much more than a method for establishing such doubt. Any experiential theories of truth, although not necessarily inharmonious with pragmatism, may in some respects find a degree of comfort within pragmatic claims. Pragmatism would necessarily decline rigidity in justifying truth. Dewey showed a reluctance to define truth stating that:

> it is nominally agreed upon as a commonplace that definitions to spring out from concrete and specific cases rather than be invented in the empty air and imposed upon particulars, [that] there is a strange unwillingness to act upon the maxim in defining truth. To generalize the recognition that the true means the verified and means nothing else places upon men the responsibility for surrendering political and moral dogmas,

> and subjecting to the test of consequences their most cherished prejudices. Such a change involves a great change in the seat of authority and the methods of decision in society (Dewey, RIP, 159,160).[38]

The fallout from defining, itself a process of fixing knowing, would bring about a tremendous change in the way we view our world. Authority would be given to the thought of being hypostatic, and authority would at best be shared with the individual. Certainly any pragmatic theory of truth, unlike a constructivist theory of truth, must allow both meaning and truth to emerge from ['a]ctive experimentation" "as torture may compel." Although Dewey's understanding of truth was far less stringent, although not necessarily in conflict with loose understandings of coherent, correspondence or convergence ideas of truth, he did draw sharp departure by eschewing a constructivist approach to knowing and truth. The constructivist employs " [p]ure reasoning as a means of arriving at truth...like the spider who spins a web out of himself. The web is orderly and elaborate, but it is only a trap." Dewey cites Bacon's view on inquiry to truth contending that the "spirit of investigation," pragmatically empirical in nature, must address truth without preconceptions and must be sentineled with "critical scrutiny" (Dewey, RIP, 36, 32, 33).[39]

He did not want truth to bind, and, yet the risk is more to loose the point of truth to whatever is abroad. With any instrumentalism, the One, the individual, is the experiential authority to knowing. If defined, then it must be by the experiential authority of the One. The implications of Dewey's ideas on truth and knowing must necessarily be drawn to education, for which his ideas are still circulating, often without antecedent thoughtfulness. In fact, relying on Dewey's idea of truth, events could not be related through time, as the present is all that is extant. Dewey's narrow historical representation of the chronological seems by his own statement to be, while imagined abstractly referent to the adult, mute to the young. "Subjectmatter" reels and the curriculum suffers in this confusing context of truth and time. The past is a product of "accidents," "systemized mistakes and prejudices of our ancestors," their "ready made knowledge upon which learned men rested." (Dewey, RIP, 35).[40]

Knowing becomes, for Dewey, an active, new understanding replacing the bias of yesterday on which for immediate usefulness we must depend and in effect are given to useful "imagination." History becomes little more than winking at narratives of past episodes. Dewey, for all practical purposes, takes up Hume's discontinuity, a skeptical history of events. What most teachers would consider history would be at odds in the strictest sense with a subject matter for the "imagination." To grow with knowledge is to deny "prejudices" of history which have fallen chronologically into disfavor as "innate knowledge" did for Locke (Dewey, RIP, 35).[41]

> If we verify a judgment about a past event by its effects or consequences in the present and future, and if we verify a judgment about a present event in the same way, what is the difference between past and present events? The difference would lie in the fact that past and present events have different kinds of present and future effects (Hook, JD, 85).[42]

The implication for science is crushing. We will see that Dewey liked the methodology of science, but did not trust science in an ongoing unfolding of the constructivist world. "Science does not trade in certainties, nor does it derive trustworthy values from the structure of the physical world, not to speak of guaranteeing them" (Hook, JD, 84).[43]

Since Dewey felt that the laws of the physical world were naturally subject to change, those laws of the physical world were only given from outside of the real world. Once again he spurned the supernatural for the earthly. "Law is assimilated to a command or order. If the factor of personal will is eliminated...still the idea of law or universal is impregnated with the sense of a guiding and ruling influence exerted from above on what is naturally inferior to it" (Dewey, RIP, 64).[44]

In using modern methodologies of science and experimentation as a basis for much of his educational directionality, Dewey's practice of pedagogy was solidly committed to science as an invaluable educational tool, even given the relatively primitive technological understanding of his time. Paradoxically, science for Dewey was both to be feared in the wrong hands and to be welcomed as a potential tool in the growing of a democratic public educative force. "In general ... science marks the emancipation of mind from devotion to customary purposes and makes possible the systematic pursuit of new ends. It is the agency of progress in action (Dewey, DAE, 261).[45]

On the other hand, to hold a preoccupation with speculative "pure science" over "systematically, intentionally" "applied science is to lose sight of man and the material world" (Dewey, DAE, 264, 266, 268).[46] Dewey still had reservations about science and its uses, since even the usefulness of science could be assigned to the "old ends of human exploitation" (Dewey, DAE, 331).[47] If "human exploitation" is set aside and man set fully in view of purpose, then science is at best a source of the useful. And experience tells us that truth stands "temporarily satisfactory" under the pressure of the "process of change."

> But, owing to the fact that all experience is a process, no point of view can ever be the last one. Every one is insufficient and off its balance, responsible to later points of view than itself (James, TMOT, Chapter III, 89, 90).[48]

We can really only know what we have experienced as we inhere in the experience. Just seeing something happen is not true experiential knowledge of the event. Dewey refers to a man in the path of a carriage and his "participant" denotation as opposed to a "spectator" who may be "indifferent to what is going on;" we never can "call anything knowledge except where our activity has actually produced certain physical changes in things, which agree with and confirm the conception entertained" (Dewey, DAE, 146, 147, 393).[49]

The significance must be brought back to Kant who questioned the idea of *a priori* knowledge, that which can be known apart from experience. Kant felt that their was assumption in the intuition of pure thought. Dewey, as previously stated, dumped his intuitional beliefs, so claimed, for pragmatic, replaceable and suspect knowledge - from what we do to those thing in the environment. Dewey rejected what he saw as a habit from Middle Ages' scholasticism which left science with a faith in thought-knowing or "Pure knowing." Facts could exist impracticably in solitude and isolation, fixed and understood through authority of such purity so as to be found transcendent to worldly meaning (Dewey, RIP, 29, 30, 110, 111).[50]

An understanding of "idea" is based on the "knowledge [which] is a process of getting ideas, ideas are the life of mind." " Yet no idea in science whether as premise or conclusion, postulate or law, rule or description is regarded as self-evident." Dewey was concerned that "some" of what was called knowledge by scientists, generally thought to be a pristine body of reliably understood cases was actually "derivative." So Hook gave a practical reading of the dilemma: Agreement, consensus, seems to be the measure of recognized knowledge (Hook, JD, 53-58).[51] Since science as fact was to experience the constraints of time, then observation tends to become "fixed and inflexible." (Dewey, RIP, 32, 33).[52] Such absolutism could not be "objective" nor knowing "operative and practical" (Dewey, RIP, 32, 33, 117).[53]

Dewey's process or methodology of educating the student is reduced to "absorb and learn from the environment." (Dewey, DAE, 51).[54] "[I]t is impossible to procure knowledge without the use of objects which impress the mind" (Dewey, DAE, 313).[55] Kant was revisited by Dewey for merging the physical world and the metaphysical world. Dewey would seek a synthesis, a hybridization, of these two realms of knowing in thought and action.

Perhaps Dewey held on to at least a portion of Kant's idea of individualist perception of objects. Kant expanded the ideas of knowing to include what he called "*a priori* synthetic judgements." It was his contention that we must have intuition of preconceived knowing in order to propose or understand an experiential event. Our perception determines what we will know as objective. Our resultant understanding of a car, say, is dependent on the perception which we have of a car. In this sense the observation of the car is both synthetic for it is experiential and *a priori* because we have rationalistic preconceptions of the car we experience in even knowing it is a car. (Kant, COPR, 7-9).[56]

Dewey combines the thought and the action for experiential outcome. The thought is only the result of experimental suggestion. The intuition and a concept of the event combine as thought with action to perceive the experiential outcome. Dewey combines thought and action in an event, but as we shall see he sees action as a way to direct thought. Where Kant sees a hybrid of *a priori* and *a posteriori* factors in an action, Dewey would claim that the intuitional thought was a product of action, to re-appropriate that thought to further action. This directed and possibly repeated behavior he describes as habit. Kant would claim as Dewey asserted that each event was individual and under the influence of time and space. Dewey would even claim that truth was meaningful until it was replaced by more meaningful information by even the same agency differing in time and space (Kant, 21,23).[57]

If knowledge of science or any knowing raises skepticism, then, paradoxically, even not knowing must be questioned as a possible source of knowing and in step with the ancient philosophical skeptics one must refuse a final judgment. Although Hook, Dewey and certainly Peirce would distance themselves from such an interpretation, at least Dewey and Hook would always look to means upon means and not be comfortable with other than a skepticism toward ends, a different way to see meliorism, no doubt. Dewey would in his inclusive philosophy see greater numbers of possibilities by not giving exclusive veracity to one understanding but remaining open to new means, as what is designated ends may prove to only be new means in time, thus keeping with a form of idealism and perhaps optimism, a tenderness for the future.

Science must venture to admit it is a process which is marked by unpredictable change. History is a process of change by its very nature and therefore was only good for general study. Dewey, in "My Pedagogic Creed," has said of history: "When taken simply as history it is thrown into the distant past and becomes dead and inert." He would have the student accept history rather as a "record of man's social life and progress" for it is in this way that history "becomes full of meaning" (Dewey, MPC, Article Three).[58]

Shades of Derrida are seen in this postmodern understanding of context and meaning. The value of knowing specific information out of time, based on Dewey's view of history, must cause questioning of the value of history in the school - a liberal view of learning having found support in balancing social perspectives on education and denigrating academic knowledge. If the question was to be put hard to Dewey's understanding, then it would seem difficult if not impossible to justify a solid academic education based on fact and concept or even defend academics to students at all. The past, in any definitive way, is off the table and the student could only feel the experimental reconstruction of history while facts and concepts could not be collectively investigated, since each student's opinion would be guarded and the transfer of ideas and fact based understandings could not be informatively productive.

The educational implication, considering Dewey's rejection of fixity in any form and his dependence on individual experience to direct action, is to loosen the hold of language, its meaning and its application, giving the individual an experimental invention or derivation of word usage thus threatening to leave pedagogy, if not meaningless, in its strictest sense, stripped of conforming direction and substance while allowing philosophically skeptical inquiry to hold the only authority not delimiting language. "Because of our education we use words, thinking they are ideas, to dispose of questions, the disposal being in reality simply such as obscuring of perception as prevents us from seeing any longer the difficulty" (Dewey, DAE, 169).[59]

When words are used in "triviality and meagerness" in a child's books, they tend to "shut down the area of mental vision." But Dewey concedes that words are a necessary part of life despite the "liability to infection" (Dewey, HWT, 181,174).[60]

The value of literature is as a follow-up to experience, since it is "the reflex expression and interpretation of social experience" (Dewey, MPC, Article Three).[61] All be it the experience of another, it is not given authority since its influence is merely individual.

Math becomes, in the extreme of this view, a collage of numbers and symbols. If certainty cannot be claimed in at least basic calculations based on mathematical laws, then the idea of gaining mathematical understanding is no more than whimsy. Dewey's views on mathematics are, if not a denial of authority of numbers, are little more than undervaluing by declaring its remoteness. By drawing such a distinction, the math of utilization and theoretical formulation would seem to displace the objective forms. Mathematics becomes a confusion of propositions and processes. Mathematics must be made experiential in real inquiry with measurement units rather than idealized and abstract with out dimension. But it can be argued that all experience, all measurement, is grounded *a priori* or by intuition, and as discussed earlier with regard to the foot rule - it is arbitrary. As it has been suggested the framing of the question has the quality of answer implicit within it. Without a predilection or introit there would be no context in which to understand events or ask questions. Daily life must be met with the flexibility and immediacy. Any fixity of perennial knowing is founded on preconceived ideas and traditions which do not address current needs and understandings. Dewey believed that the gravitation toward fixity of knowing sprang from the "Love of Certainty" and an "acceptance" "as an aspect of man's devotion to an ideal or certainty" (Dewey, HNC, 236, 237).[62]

The need for facts and truth, in a traditional sense would have provided, as Dewey saw it, a familiar and comfortable knowing but only to justify theory. Without action, thought cannot be knowing, but with action thought may be successfully judged or given meter. For in Dewey's world, theory needs to be anchored to action not employed to bolster data propounding theories without definitive verification. Failing falsification of basic contentions and never forming alternate schema, theory has failed to give accountable representation to theoretically difficult data by finding ways to account for inconsistency based on theories already in place and sanctioned. In which case, there is a strong temptation to massage the data and resurrect essentially the same retread ideas for continuing on the same journey. Without a calculus of effectiveness scrutinized against objectives, theories are not justified, nor are they necessarily disposed of for more promising theories. Thought apart from the laboratory of experience is often pre-established or an escape from reality, as "dreams" and "reveries". (Dewey, RIP, 138 -140).[63]

Those theories having gone down in defeat may be salvaged and relaunched with a different name but constitutionally remain the same.

> An ounce of experience is better than a ton of theory simply because it is only in experience that any theory has vital verifiable significance. An experience, a very humble experience, is capable of generating and carrying any amount of theory (or intellectual content), but a theory apart from an experience cannot be definitely grasped even as theory. It tends to become a mere verbal formula, a set of catchwords used to render thinking, or genuine theorizing, unnecessary and impossible (Dewey, DAE, 169).[64]

Like common sense and theory, there is a scripted understanding of rationalistic logic which is self-certifying. To be subjected to external authority, Dewey was to lose individual freedom at the expense of flexibility of knowing.

> Reason, universal principles, *a priori* notions, meant either blank forms which had to be filled in by experience, by sense observations, in order to get significance and validity; or else were mere indurated prejudices, dogmas imposed by authority, which masqueraded and found protection under august names (Dewey, DAE, 311).[65]

True "connections" are sensational and without "dogmas imposed by authority."

Pragmatism for Dewey is the instrumentalism of experience. Truth, fact and knowledge are tenuous and find utility in immediate experience. Absolutism is transcendent to daily life. There are no fixed answers or truths. We only can have utility of knowing in the present. The wisdom of the past is biased and does not represent the needs of the present. We may learn from the past but only in a broad and diffuse understanding. Absolute truth of the past or present are preconceptions and theory without action is a "dream." The agency for knowing is the individual through experience. Other ideas about truth are not necessarily in conflict with Dewey's instrumental understanding. Truths may embrace correspondence, coherence, convergence but common sense, constructivist science and abstract logic are non-individual in their weight of assertion. On truth Dewey offered few specific delimitations for knowing. When truth is viewed as a dependable concept or a necessarily communal holding, Dewey's truth fails to show substantial usefulness unless the purpose of claiming truth is to extend internal group tolerance to as many of the membership as possible. The more inclusive, the less likely that the embraced concept would serve many of the group and so not the whole assemblage. This inclusiveness was thought to be an advantage for building Dewey's collectivist position, but as experienced in pedagogy the lack of definitive treatment of knowing produces significant if not insurmountable obstacles to teaching and discipline.

History, mathematics, literature, logic are reduced to individual opinion. What works is truth without specific commitment, merely a glimpse into immediate experience. All learning is in consideration of individual student interest. All knowing is chosen by the student according to individual interest. Among all the differing programs implemented and theories asserted about public pedagogy, there is little that unites these experimental issues except an uncertainty of outcome and a failure to reconsider the theoretical basis for its perpetual reissue. This is a serious legacy for society and the modern school. When there cannot be consistent agreement on authoritative agency, purpose or the content of law or rules and teaching in the public school, based on an interminable abridgment of dubious practiced and loose epistemology, judgment is lost.

Knowing determined by oneself will not necessarily be extrapolated to another. Dewey's guarantee of individual knowledge may prevent not only the verification of that knowledge, but it may not be transferable to a Group including shared experiences. There is no guarantee that any matter known by One can be transferrable to another. Understanding must be seen as a compromise, which, even in some small way, may result in a change or recertification of the newly modified group purpose. To broach this point of knowing and truth pedagogically is to question the very nature of education, knowing and acting on knowledge while expecting reproducibility. The One not only does not have to will for Others, according to Dewey, the One cannot do so for Others without compromising their freedom. "The slave is the man who executes the wishes of others, one doomed to act along lines predetermined to regularity" (Dewey, HNC, 304).[66]

Freedom comes to the knower by experiencing the known as a free individual accountable only to free thought with reservations toward the group. Knowledge becomes disposable in personal experience. No authority of knowledge may be assumed or imposed on understanding. What knowledge can we keep and what can we release to dreams and well-wishing? The school mandate to teach everyone becomes undoable in practice, unjustifiable by Dewey's standards. For in the extreme, mere interpretation and fleeting observation cannot give rise to thoroughgoing knowledge and therefore judgment. The life experience, giving power to the moment not trapped by the past or losing the present for an impossibility of controllable future prospects, is individual and to others alien. Dewey would see history in large experimental swaths, history would become in essence the experiences of others painted with a broad brush. Dewey was to find dubious meaning, if not implausible fact, in his own pragmatic experimentalism.

But Dewey's understanding of truth, which will here be referred to as an optimistic skepticism - that which may have "meaning," at least on some level, but is still held in doubt - cannot add a commitment to acknowledged veracity, to what we know to the extent that we are willing to commit our trust, yet unreservedly to ultimately find correspondence in a systematic understanding of community. When learning is not given importance beyond the student's own experience, not by necessity to that of any other student in the class, then you have a recipe for ignorance and eliminate the communal aspects of learning. In addition, if the subject matter is to be understood for its "meaning" only as an analogy or self-referent but never committing to the subject matter as each part has a common systemic interdependence with every other part, not as correspondence, coherence or convergence in fact, then learning has no specific engaging value or meaning. When students are called on to use imagination when the factual basis for conjecture is not solidly grounded in fact and concept, the lesson is useless to the process of learning and building on what could be known. Truth thus becomes no more than a personal analogy by which to give ones own questioning of reality and transcendence a place to reside. Dewey's pragmatism at some level lets the imagination or possibly unjustifiable fantasy grow larger than the daily life which pragmatism praises, forfeiting the latter for the former. This is where the individual alone and unencumbered may be found, away from Others to do what is desired without regrets, responsible to no one, creating a singular epistemology without assumptions. This is ironically prescient of existentialism and postmodernism that would follow. For Dewey epistemology must be graded a misnomer.

Chapter 5
Morality

> Man's life is a progress and not a station.
>
> -Ralph Waldo Emerson, *Essays* [1]

> 'The true,' to put it very briefly, is only the expedient in the way of our thinking, just as 'the right' is only the expedient in the way of our behaving.
>
> - William James, *Pragmatism* [2]

In addressing moral theory, as with epistemology, Dewey avoided writing in detail, occasionally by analogy and rarely by example. Everyday concerns such as how society and school could maintain against civil disruptions was not explicitly covered. Since authority was individualized, Dewey posited an individual working-morality which could only guarantee the freedom he felt the individual must have to learn and grow in pursuit of individual interest. To prevent the subjectivity of such an empowerment from producing an autonomous disregard for others, Dewey believed within the group the individual would probably or eventually find communal meaning through an evolution of experiential action to a mutually acceptable outcome. An eventual attitudinal averaging among the general will and purpose of the group would then smooth any rough edges of conflict. With time the natural evolving will of the group would move toward practical moralities, the nature of which would be determined by group acceptability. The ultimate character of the membership would be dependent on the judgment of individual activities, but no reckoning could be coercively rendered, since the nature of temporal identity of group or individual could not be assessed for the purpose of imposing will.

Morality becomes for Dewey an adhesive, a communal glue. Dewey held that our goals give us standards for morality, an "end-in-itself," yet these are not really ends but rather "terminals of deliberation, and so turning points in activity." Not only are these ends "ends beyond action," but they are opinions that "differ in their notions of what the ends are." The effect of suspended or abolished ends was to remove man from the Aristotelean natural world of a "regulated" "moral theory," to a spawn of "science" without being subject to the "intellectual revolution" that occurred in the seventeenth century. As science was not to be assumed but studied and changed as needed, so "human action" should have received like attention. Dewey felt that any form of fixed morality was dependent on pre-selected ends, or "foreseen consequences." Morality becomes "some fixed end beyond activity at which we should aim." Predetermination of moral "forms" could not answer immediate needs especially if these "forms" of strict adherence were dependent on the direction by remote superintendence. (Dewey, HNC, 223 - 225).[3]

When human action is to be judged free of predisposition of ends, responsibility for unacceptable behavior is spread thin. Since the individual is responsible to the group and the group to individual, it is difficult for blame to be assessed on moral grounds. The group bears responsibility through "social partnership in producing crime" (Dewey, HNC, 18,19).[4] To correct the culpability of the community, Dewey tells us, "[w]e must work on the environment not merely on the hearts of men" (Dewey, HNC, 22).[5] In the mean time, destructive behavior in society and in the school finds no basis for correction nor consequences for unacceptable action nor clear culpability, no coercion.

Although Dewey would opposed Mill's belief in elitist authority which would justify Mill's opting out of the authority of social convention; both would seal individual unconstraint. Dewey's view on behavior, as moral activity, seems extreme: "self-control denotes a self which is contracting." The moral concern for the "welfare of others," "altruism" may have some advantage in its reaching out beyond self, but the ego is served by settling for what exists and not looking for "a self which shall be more inclusive than the one that exists " (Dewey, HNC, 138, 139).[6] In keeping with Neizsche's view of charity, Dewey would echo that the "self-sacrificer" was truly the self-server (Niezsche, BGAE, 90).[7] Furthermore, to try to "act for the welfare of others," is to risk limiting or "harming them and to indulge ourselves under cover of exercising a special virtue" (Dewey, HNC, 293).[8]

This negative view of charity seems to come dangerously close to an objectivist perspective. To promote another without "widening the horizon of others and giving them command of their own powers," is a harm. "There is a sense in which to set up social welfare as an end of action only promotes an offensive condescension, a harsh interference, or an oleaginous display of complacent kindliness." Dewey would agree that giving a man a fish is direct and is an end in itself; he would give to potentiate the powers of the one in need. But there can be no mistake that although this view is admirable, the condescension begs a hesitancy to act and avoids the needs of others which Dewey referred to as "a soup-kitchen happiness" in the giver (Dewey, HNC, 292 293).[9] Adam Smith contended that: "The man who desires to do, or who actually does, a praise-worthy action, may likewise desire the praise which is due to it, and sometimes, perhaps, more than is due to it" (Smith, TTOMS, 113).[10]

This, as a lesson to the young, is to make them skeptical of doing good works and considering others for fear that others will be harmed and that conceit will inflame the giver's ego. Furthermore, there seems to be a lingering determinism which finds acceptance in the failed lives of others as a wrong impression to suggest to the young of any community. Or more frightening is that the idea of charity, honestly and empathetically shown might not even strike a cord of kindness in the heart for the blindness of the ego. Community under such reservations takes on hollow meaning when associated with the idea of community.

It is true that character does not exclusively and necessarily follow from good works rightly thought. It is not a given that character can be seen in altruism. The character of an individual is a dicy proposition. Dewey would not give the measure of an individual except in "extensive and minute observation of consequences incurred in action" (Dewey, HNC, 44-57).[11] It would seem a difficult proposition to take measure when we must "place the particular consequences of a single act in a wider context of continuing consequences "but comparable for each individual as a physician's analysis taken from a "complete clinical record" (Dewey,

HNC, 46).[12] This is not a fixed record and obviously any hard knowledge of moral character is a life-long process of action and consequences only to be settled on the demise of the individual. "Virtues," we are told, "are ends because they are such important means" (Dewey, HNC, 47).[13] For Dewey, "In every case a result or 'end' is treated as an actuating cause" (Dewey, HNC, 136).[14] One has the feeling that the uncertainty created by such a view of bottom-line morality has little practical value to the community but only to the One. Causality is reduced to little more than Hume's collection of unrelated ideas or impressions, and morality to what ever one wants to call a moral act.

Not only are there questionable "ends" if they exist at all, but the determination that a "trait of character" is "desirable," may not always produce desirable results " (Dewey. HNC, 47).[15] Dewey has given little hope of finding a moral act and One with the character to perform it. A fixed "moral good" fails when considered apart from its "consequences " (Dewey, HNC, 47).[16]

Since the resolution of pronouncement on any issue is potentially an "end" only upon the death of one whose character is in dispute, this "means" and "ends" relationship may be relegated to at least the realm of antinomy or dispute. Whether irresolvable or indeterminable with respect to the living, the character of an individual can never be adjudged while he or she lives. Living role models are to be with uncertainty honored or vilified in the grave, and everyone is correct to see the one side or the other. This is a dangerous lesson for citizens and students who need to know a dependable way of living and one that considers self and others in a respectful way recognizing exemplars. Students are to not judge an act until comfortably knit into the garment of a whole life.

Issues of morality were handled more directly by Kant as action to be willed by all rational persons. The implication of such individual willing is that reasonable judgments will determine action not just for the One willing but for Many. Kant has it that each individual wills, as Dewey might contend, from a "controlled self" instead of Dewey's "experiment in creating a self." Kant's deontology, in Dewey's view, cannot reliably predict consequences of action or teleology. Despite our best intensions we will at least occasionally give in to self-absorbed inclinations. Every teacher knows that a child, who may understand what to do and why, will not always be an obedient child and do what is asked. And the action willed will not necessarily be appropriate to all Others especially since a child, as may also be true of us all, to some degree, can only with difficulty remove self from consideration in specifying for their group. To depend on voluntary compliance by a rebellious child, or any child for that matter, is a formula for disciplinary disaster on the street, in the home or in the classroom. Dewey's ideas suffer in real-life examples of names and deeds, but, beyond reluctance in modeling good behavior, he would oppose behavioral norms by claiming that prescribing obedience may be to "exaggerate the herd instinct to conformity" (Dewey, HNC, 5).[17] Subtly these ideas, as many of Dewey's ideas, have succeeded in societal penetration and by extension have left much of street acceptability and school disciplinary policy without reliance on convincing authority.

Even if the group could safely, effectively and indirectly control individual behavior by the shear weight of group influence, by winning over through communication the marginal extremist individuals, any suggestion that behavior as knowledge could lead to elegant moral action and perfection of habit, was rejected by Dewey. Behavior as in any other consideration of daily life was changeable. The notion that educating could produce knowledge and knowledge in theory could produce a moral basis for living has been given by Plato and Aristotle, in their "classic philosophy," a traditional understanding of fixed "values." (Dewey, RIP, 17).[18]

The individual is the seat of immediate behavioral authority and the community in evolution is the undirected ultimate authority. Children must not have adult authority imposed on them by "insolent coercions" resulting in their "curiosities [being] dulled" (Dewey, HNC, 64).[19] Dewey believed that life lessons for the individual, in all hope, would produce good behavior by replacement of bad habits, yet such modification, no matter how thorough, would never lead to behavioral perfection. Life, under the influence of community, would shape the interrelationships among individual members thus replacing old habits for new and more appropriate habits. Education was a lifelong pursuit in the broadest context (Dewey, DAE, 411, 412).[20]

The ultimate control over behavior is the community. In his definition of control we see a loss of a basis for enforcement of authority where needed. "Control, in truth, means only an emphatic form of direction of powers, and covers the regulation gained by an individual through his own efforts quite as much as that brought about when others take the lead" (Dewey, DAE, 28, 29).[21]

So, according to Dewey, the school's disciplining of the student-individual is subject to the most immediate perspective of experience, that of the student. Situational truth of any violation of rules is tantamount to a non-eventful judgment of someone else's unique experience such that no one holds ultimate and fixed authority in judgment of others. "The foremost conclusion is that moral has to do with all activity into which alternative possibilities enter." Some activities that are good and others that are better may be determined by the "situation" under which they may be judged (Dewey, HNC, 278).[22]

> "Business" absorbs a large part of the life of most persons and business is conducted upon the basis of ruthless competition for private gain...The convictions that obtain in personal morality are negated on a large scale in the collective conduct, and for this reason are weakened even in their strictly personal applications (Dewey, et. al., E, 286).[23]

Looking to the past, families worked together and yielded acceptingly to the cultural "rules of caste." "Castes of workmen may take the place of mere kinship ties...[becoming] a hindrance to individuality and must be broken down if the individual is to emerge to full self-direction" (Dewey, et. al., E, 37).[24] The individual becomes like all others and prospects will be found only at a " low level." To get ahead in life's work "one must control impulse with reason." Purpose is not allowed to change for those dedicated to success in the work world (Dewey, et. al., E, 36, 37).[25]

Shirking the reality of the blame of individual extremism again, Dewey did not let just the One off the hook, but looked to the individual as the moral good-will agent of community. In the positive and optimistic attitude rampant in young America, however, Dewey found in Kant, the optimism of man's ultimate good will in action to be at the center of his ideas. Dewey was taunted by meliorism, constrained. Not utopianism, but an ongoing belief in the improvement in contributive membership of collectivism in a true democracy. Not by Kant's mechanical duty, did Dewey see good coming to the community. For Kant's idea of duty, in moral action, was to be seen as coercive in that universal imperatives to duty removed complete freedom of authority from personal initiative of immediate and responsible action. Dewey saw absolutism inherent in Kant's philosophical conscription to duty and ultimately rejected Kant's *a priori* reasoning in which a fixed understanding of experience was not given authority over direct individual action. Dewey saw imposed "order" along with egoism and universals stripping away individual freedom (Dewey, RIP, 50-51, 98,99).[26]

As we shall see in a later chapter action was to give authority to thought which when directed consistently to that action would produce habit. Dewey we will see was to put the cart, action, before the horse, thought.

Dewey's optimistic, if not utopian outlook, despite his denial of such an outlook, surrendered authority to the individual with the expectation that the individual who, though extreme and selfish, would be brought into the fold. Yet the One was not coercively prevented from being coercive in the treatment of Others. Coercion of One to prevent the coercion of the Many was still coercion. Coercion, if allowed in less than extreme and dangerous instances, can not be considered an acceptable response. Any individual determined to offend and deny the rights of others, it was believed, could be joined to the group in purpose, in time, without stifling individual freedom in the process of absorption into the group. Dewey understood group solidarity and the absorption of the individual into group harmony, at least when seen as a process, as methodology not to be confused with re-programming by coercive means. In a sort of non-directional, irresolute becoming, Dewey envisioned society as a mutually regulating confluence of individual experiences without imperatives for action by "strong leadership" (Dewey, RIP, 100).[27]

Such a proposal by Dewey would seem little more than Hume's stream of sequential events and would in effect remove any hope of determinative value in morally-actionable considerations. Without a formal procedure of evaluation, writes Bentham as he asked and answered his own question, " Is it possible for a man to move the earth ? Yes, but he must first find another earth to stand upon" (Bentham, POMAL, 6).[28] The specific "earth" on which to stand and the specific "earth" to move must be found and not be in doubt. Any doubt in inquiry destroys inquiry for any practical outcome. Thought does not destroy inquiry but must rise to suggest another specific "earth" on which to stand. Reasonable standards, a thoughtful stand outside inquiry, must be availed to find actionable reason and meaning.

Once again, Dewey proves reluctant to allow the full expression of causality in antisocial behavior according to an assessment of morally good, since the hope of establishing consequences while isolating "a unified deed into two disjoined parts, an inner called motive and an outer called act." He saw motive and action as inseparable (Dewey, HNC, 43).[29]

Authority is not held fast by the community but by the One, perhaps the extremist, the individual which Dewey saw destructive to community. Inquiry rests with the One for whom the more dependable ground is potentially self-imposed. Yet the challenge to the status quo which Dewey could not on principle oppose nor actively discourage, would have been a force for the evolution of society. Classroom and school discipline are, as we have seen, hard to justify on Dewey's pragmatism and appear to under-emphasize the negative effect of extremist behavior and adversely effect the possibility or eventuality of communal unity. Any bright flame of extremism is fed by an inability of Dewey's ideas to give a methodology for finding a "solution" to disturbances. It is clear that Dewey does not value "thinking" divorced from action in the pursuit of solutions. He rejects solution as a loss of freedom for the individual since most thinking is carried out by "external authority," for the "urgent way out" which is absorbed from standards or authoritarianism (Dewey, RIP, 139).[30]

Thinking of solutions is often left to "external authority" or from "higher up." Problems may not be solved but only the thought of them. Dewey did not see solutions as a viable product of pure thought, as from those who are remote leaders and not involved in the activities for which they are not immediately involved. "Wherever external authority reigns, thinking is suspected and obnoxious." The impetus for finding the solution is in finding "freedom from troublesome conflicting factors." The "conflict and problems" are not given "solution," " they only get rid of the feeling of it." For thought is secondary to action and does not precede action. Any decision, made based on thought rather than the fullness of activity is not only incomplete but can not offer any meaningful solution to a problem. Though both are integral to one another, action precedes the thought and without action thought amounts to "that type of Idealism which has well been termed intellectual somnambulism." Even calling an individual down for unacceptable behavior could in itself be damaging. Dewey's was concerned that correcting student error could also induce pathologies (Dewey, RIP, 139-141).[31] Even observation of events cannot be considered by Dewey as "an end in itself but a search for evidence and signs show that along with observation goes inference, anticipatory forecast - in short an idea, thought or conception" (Dewey, RIP, 143).[32] Thought and observation are fraught with uncertainty and resultant dubious action. "The material of thinking is not thoughts, but actions, facts, events, and the relations of things." (Dewey, DAE, 184).[33] For Dewey this would seem to be entirely too cerebral without immediate and individual experiential involvement. Second-person experience claims could not be seriously entertained on the grounds of individual authority and freedom. "Men must observe for themselves, and form their own theories and personally test them" and eschew "dogma as truth," as "philosophic subjectivism" in consideration of truth. "The self, achieves mind in the degree in which knowledge of things is incarnate in the life about him; the self is not a separable mind building up knowledge anew on its own account." Platonic oneness comes very near but not as spiritual unity but that of individual thought and mind "[t]hrough social intercourse" (Dewey, DAE, 343, 344).[34]

Behavior must be allowed without coercion, since ethics and morality are unknowable apart from the group and individual blame and praise are communally held. Values are likewise not individualistic, contrary to a utilitarian view which would claim the central values of one's own good and one's own avoidance of pain. Furthermore, values, Dewey asserts, are either "intrinsic" or "instrumental" and cannot be weighed on a sliding scale.

> Intrinsic values are not objects of judgment, they cannot (as intrinsic) be compared, or regarded as greater and less, better or worse. They are invaluable; and if a thing is invaluable, it is neither more or less so than any other invaluable" (Dewey, DAE, 279).[35]

For Dewey a measureless value, which he defends in a mere word analysis, starts to take on a solitariness or absoluteness in contradiction, it would seem, to his rejection of fixity and the ideal. There is a sense in which the term "invaluable" has become vague in its use, omnipotent in connotation, both of which raise a problem of the agency for valuing. There appears to be a preferential order of values as any number of intrinsic values must be judged by a third, collectivist instrumental value.(Dewey, DAE, 279, 280).[36] Values are instrumental and situational, as means become means for more means, and so on as beliefs are replaced, for

> no standard of belief can issue because it is the very nature of experience to instigate all kinds of contrary beliefs, as varieties of local custom proved. Its logical outcome is that anything is good and true to the particular individual which his experience leads him to believe true and good at a particular time and place (Dewey, DAE, 309).[37]

Dewey contended that when the social aspect of "learning " is absent by a hand-me-down process of schooling, the information is passed to "individual consciousness, and there is no inherent reason why it should give a more socialized direction to mental and emotional disposition." There is then no "socialized direction" and no opportunity for the individual to join in group activities."But the essence of the demand for freedom is the need of conditions which will enable an individual to make his own special contribution to a group interest, and to partake of its activities in such ways that social guidance shall be a matter of his own mental attitude, and not a mere authoritative dictation of his acts" (Dewey, DAE, 351-353).[38]

Dewey meets this modeling of positive communal direction with meliorism, the belief that although utopia will never be attained, experience will show progress, an apparent fixity. It is on the point of meliorism that Dewey brings together both intellect and morality to attend to the earthly work of bringing man into a progressively better world. Man's welfare is found in hoped for melioration, which has more importance to man and his aspirations for a better life than law. It is interesting that Dewey turns this philosophical principle, as might be expected, into a prognosis for education and a hopeful expectation for its future. But Dewey then claims that education has a moral context, in that there is a dependence on one another that ostensibly works to better man in his environment. To see man as independent is to view him out of moral context. The rugged individualist for which Dewey had much concern as an anti-socializing influence was by standards of meliorism immoral. Education was the process of learning not facts but ways to work toward a better community and world. Morality was a group value, since the morality of the individual could not be shown disavowable. Blame falls on the institutions and commerce which should be responding in a democratic manner to societal needs of group members. Dewey's optimism surfaces again. "Democracy has many meanings, but if it has a moral meaning, it is found in resolving that the supreme test of all political institutions and industrial arrangements shall be the contribution they make to the all-around growth of every member of society" (Dewey, RIP, 186).[39]

"[M]oral meaning" in its pluralistic framework tests the individualist cultural groups of politics and industry. Education was the process throughout life by which the individual could expect a hopeful future within community and the world. "Thus the process of education as the main business of life ends when the young have arrived at emancipation from social dependence" (Dewey, RIP, 183-186).[40]

Individual character and behavior over a lifetime of activities and a variety of individual assessments of character among group members could be conjectured of the deceased. Mill's utilitarian subjectivism has been avoided as authority has been ultimately brought back to the group, although posthumously, measuring the extremes of life's moral variance among the membership. Self-advancement would seem more likely for the late communitarian, without immediate judgment, with no set moral standards and few exclusions to potential member action except those to which no one could justify such as murder. This may seem on the surface a self-regulating procedure for group beliefs, but, on the street and in the classroom, authority is not necessarily immediate where immediacy could be necessary to avoid danger to citizens nearby. Not that Dewey felt that no policy of discipline should be in place for those that would feloniously overstep the communal bounds of acceptable morality and safety, but that extremes must be dealt with when observed. Without hard fixed rules but within the changing environment of Dewey's morality and behavioral standards, it would seem that only for the most flagrant behaviors, individual action must be addressed.

Arriving at individual behavioral consequences and assuming that unacceptable behavior could be clearly judged as such, another problem must necessarily arise in the moral and consequential mix. Student action must be competently evaluated in deciding the consequences of unacceptable behavior. Indeed, there is no dependable method for deciding what is unacceptable behavior. And even if judgment were offered up after the fact in an ever changing environment, the immediacy of the event would be a fading history and evidence mere allegations which would have lost any determinative value. Moral issues would not be resolvable. The best and only approach short of judgment of felonious acts, subject to civil litigation, is to appeal to the will of the group. But behavioral management by committee is not only a formula for chaos in any group, but in the extreme is potentially threatening to order and democracy.

Waiting for individual responsibility, waiting for a pattern of voluntary, rational decision making on the part of an individual does not seem to address the need for immediate intervention in the event of threatening actions on the street or in the classroom. Communication under the most controlled environmental conditions, using mutually agreeable language, is idealistically discharged under the most favorable of circumstances. Such expectations are dangerously unreasonable when emotions are running high and reason may become suspended or even foregone and the management, at the very best, in the most comfortable fit, is only effectively maintained under disciplinary constraints. Immediacy must be tossed aside in consideration as morally-valued individual experience, when the group is at risk of suffering at the hands of its own membership, where society or the school cannot risk the evolution to disciplinary chaos or even group morality while the individual finds his or her comfortable behavioral fit within the group.

Dewey's view of laws and rules make it difficult not to see Dewey's attitude at best of questionable authority with law's fixity being legislated in "bias and prejudice." Declaring immorality a violation of rules could raise most assuredly a challenge to tradition. Impetus for such a challenge is the hypocrisy with which laws are met in practice.

Briefly, method in waiting for individual responsibility and acquisition of good habits would be replaced with new behavior and conduct. New understanding would replace old less usable habits. Free application of this optimistic and idealistic understanding has prickly implications. Behavioral expectations must be understood by students along with consequences for violating those standards. The mandate for swift and unbiased action in violations of disciplinary rules turns on the right of all students having an opportunity to obtain an education without being subject to a disruptive environment or even danger.

How can misbehavior be judged? Opposed understandings of behavior may not be easily determined based on the "situation" as held by the student-individual and the school official in a matter of "alternative possibilities." A justification for such "alternative possibilities" was supported by a school psychologist once claiming that to fully understand the "situation" one must consider that the student-individual may actually believe that the infraction was either justified, by it only happening innocuously or contending it never happened at all, but the misbehavior was a mere figment of the teacher's biased imagination. It is not far to go to imagine an alternate understanding of the event in which the disciplinary violation in question was in fact not a rule infringement but rather a student-individuals unique experience for which no other authoritative critique, let alone judgment, may be correctively entertained. The psychologist claim that the student-individual may actually believe the primary story of events seen from his or her own perspective dashes any counseling guidance to a reasonable resolution of the event or future events. In cases of murder in the courts, the methodology would be much the same with potentially more damaging outcomes, in judgment and future behavior.

The fall out from this sort of miry jurisdictional authority of the school staffer, may result in negotiation of the secondary experience, the experience of the staffer, to a lesser infraction by placing the behavioral issue before an administratively higher tribunal. And if, apart from some physical damage to others or their property, the upshot may result in nothing firmly or even appropriately being done, the extent of the infraction may amount to no more than a conference noted and papers relegated to a school administrator's office file. It is, however, almost impossible for teachers and local administrators to be willing to alter details of events such that the student-individual can gain confidence and esteem in disciplinary issues. It becomes difficult to hold back the flood of frustration that teachers and local administrators experience in such situations not to mention the effect on enforcing an ongoing discipline policy which appears to reside in the will of the student-individual and not the policy of school staff.

Remote administrative pressure, it is suggested, must avoid hard judgment among mere shades of understanding and give benefit of ultimate or even definitive understanding to the student-individual who may be backed by a parent or litigious others. It would be fruitless to argue that secondary support is any more valuable than secondary opposition to blanket pleas of student innocence in behavioral disputes. As primary experience is trustworthy for that individual, if that experience is pragmatically meaningful, in Dewey's terms, no one could have more direct access to immediate knowledge of any event than the accused, the principle in the experience. And although the One in question would have the prime understanding of the alleged disciplinary event, it is not even to be challenged in that the event is based on experience past and subject to misreading, failing a test of knowing by Dewey's standards. Neither the student-individual or anyone else in support or in opposition to the student-individuals alleged behavioral violation can claim in Dewey's terms that there is a disciplinary case that can be successfully pursued to assigning behavioral consequences. The teacher who corrects and the administration who seeks to curtail such activities by imposing consequences without ultimate knowledge and authority must bow to the youth's more authentic experience which may itself be of questionable reliability in the recent past, when the event occurred. Uncertainty leaves all decisions about culpability or innocence in doubt. Whether philosophically willed or not, the remoteness of experience on the part of the school board in such decisions, is often decidedly pragmatic and challenges the very authority of the school staff they are elected or appointed to defend when political importance raises its ugly head. But make no mistake the carnage created by the student-individual in the school can easily have far less dangerous resonation when compared to an extreme adult-individual in the larger society who is encouraged to willful lawbreaking.

The idealist company which Dewey is keeping on this point, the source of reliable knowing, is no less than Descartes, as well as Locke and Kant who have been held over in perpetuity as ghosts of Enlightenment individualism. Descartes, however, would find only a knowledge of the mind, and Locke would find only the perceptions of experience. Kant gave up ultimate authority to the personal-integrity offering of the categorical imperative: self-justified responsibility for individual action is an idealistic hopefulness to grant benefit to the collective. So knowledge, or even the more demanding claim of truth, was held on a sliding scale with each responsible action being seen as morally justifiable. Judgment rests with a rational individual. The idea that the individual would never be found in error only shown to be untimely or ill-informed by the authoritative group, did not fit with Dewey's idealism, that the individual would probably not be interminably extreme and selfish.

Charitable assistance is also made unnecessary, if there is to be no condescension in consideration of individuals, community or society while one lives. The message is that One should take what is wanted now without consideration of what will happen to Others. This is a terrible lesson for students to work out for themselves without philosophical encouragement and certainly not wise and caring judgment. Although Dewey was hesitant, if not often mute, on discipline issues of the school and avoiding coercive action against behavioral unacceptability, it was, as it has been said, not what he said about discipline and violation of the group, as it was more what he left unsaid about violations to the group carried out by the extreme and selfish.

Life was one; both the physical and the mental could not be separated as Kant did. Both the phenomena, the actions in life, and the noumena, what lay behind action such as hypotheses and ideas, would find unity as all of life would be seen through the lens of individual experiential authority within an amicable group context. The One would ideally will a non-binding universal consideration for all. Historically such hope has not been shown in abundant experience to have been manifest by allowing individualism to work out its difficulty with the Many. Such belief has invariably failed and proven a hollow and often dangerous idealism, and although Dewey believed that a workable progression was the only realistic understanding of community, an evolution of understanding and group purpose without imposing the coercion of duty has never been perpetuated. Only rebellion can reasonably be expected. In effect, Dewey's plan for morality in action is defined by the One, the authority, in the primary role as the experiencer whose behavior is not required on autonomous authority to show consideration and concern for the fate of the Many. The group, society, community, culture or school could not become in an ongoing processional of change, if subjected to overt coercion or external universal directives, a haven for individual freedom with the inclusion.

Hedonism is what the individual wants for self, and struggles to obtain without giving in to coercion or concern for the effect on

Others. To claim that what is good for the group is what I want is essentially unrestricted individual freedom. The student-individual who is told that the authority in experience resides in her or him is not inclined to favor collectivity but will rather give into self-determined and self-serving purpose. To find a way to justify actions, the student-individual, who has the prime authority of actionable experience, by Bentham's utilitarian understanding, is undeniably correct in self-certifying action with the possible exception of extreme violations of the law. Jeremy Bentham gave his utilitarian understanding to the rule of morality and law. Dewey contended Bentham gave authority to the self-interests of individuals when he wrote: " There is no case in which a private man ought not to direct his own conduct to the production of his own happiness;..." Although Bentham gave each man the responsibility of his "fellow creatures," it seems that the One is the first concern (Bentham, POMAL, 313).[41] Dewey considered this to be individual whim and dubbed Bentham's egoism "hedonism." (Dewey, RIP, 349, 405).[42]

With Dewey the individual is the authority in experience, but Dewey holds to communal benefit with change despite selfish intentions. What of the student-individual who has been irresponsible to himself and others and has demanded by word or deed that individuality trumps freedom and democracy of Others? Is the individual responsible for the freedom of Others? Can we expect a young person to be as responsible and rationally inclined to group needs as we might optimistically hope of an adult? What of judgment outside and inside the classroom where legality is concerned? Is there a way to investigate legal infractions when the methodology for inquiry is limited by a philosophical uncertainty, frustrating a doubtful second-hand perspective? On these questions rests school authority and individual authority. Any free-thinking about the morality of school policy leads inexorably to educative chaos and student-individual anarchy. Yet even in cases of crime, both on the street and in the classroom, there is difficulty in assigning guilt or blame. Invoking Dewey's process of inquiry without certainty can hardly be expected to settle issues of blame or innocents. If certainty in law and crime is difficult to access, extrapolated to the school and often more heinous infractions of rule and law, proof of culpability for unacceptable individual behavior, must be cautiously approached. Dewey, in all uncertainty, does, however, provide his own certain standards of inquiry, yet consequences by his standards could not lead reliably to the judging of moral disputation. Dewey's inquiry method must suffer a substantial bind, since action is not "trans-experiential" and individual accountability is nearly incorruptible.

Morality became for Dewey a referent of community action. Without motivational consideration or levying consequences for violations against community, all of society and school community must wait for non-community minded, selfish individuals to find their comfortable place in the group. Under the aegis of Dewey's philosophy, a theorizing community must at least suffer until the individualist finds unity with the group at some later date. Community, educational community, must wait for the societal regeneration of the individualist to community purpose. Morality and its salving of the "savage breast" has become the responsibility of the non-coercive community. Judgment of waywardness is seen in violation of the community purpose or attitude, an attack on a member or a potential member in their midst. Individuals bare dubious responsibility, yet could destroy the communal bond. Fault cannot be found for actions except for those blatantly in violation of community standards and only then with reluctant confrontation. Generally individual motivation can not be questioned nor can guilt or aegis be likely assigned. Outcomes of crime cannot measure motive, since behavior cannot be separated from thought.

Despite Dewey's optimism and despite his realistic disbelief in utopian hopes, the meliorism is merely a qualified idealism of limits. Dewey's idealistic hope that things will get better hangs on the work of the group to correct problems. Yet over time this belief has not worked in public schools except in the mind of those who have chosen to see it so. Dewey's claim that the democratic milieu which allows this idealistic expression of near group harmony for society and education finds contradiction in his basic premise that the perfect system or environment is never going to be realized in a real world but is merely a process on a long road to better society and better schools. Community, whether the school or the larger society, cannot be formed or maintained when the membership is not united either in goals or in immediate obedience. Extreme individualism, student-individuals, stand in the way of those collectively moral goals. From fact to truth to morality, certainty is equated with intolerance. And action is often the biased measure of morality as it is exteriorized.

Knowing is critical to civilization, man living communicatively with man, student with student. Loss of knowing brings down epistemology and morality and any way to relate constructively to Others. And paradoxically, Dewey offers up a denial of authority of belief from experience. " The man who trusts experience does not know what he depends upon, since it changes from person to person, from day to day, to say nothing of from country to country." "Standing on experience creates conflicts." Dewey propounds that conflict (Dewey, DAE, 309).[43]

Experience is of dubious value to know or to do. Authority to know and do is temporal, present, non-transferable, situational, eventful, remedial and finally individual. It is under these restrictions that knowledge, truth and morality must find usefulness in Dewey's philosophy. Life is the expedient, knowing or doing, not fixed in purpose, a "progress" not a "destination." Predetermined action for the student-individual is a loss of freedom as is the imposition of character as an external virtue. Charity is not a virtue but a condescension to others and a coercion of individual freedom. Dewey's idealism is melioristic, denies his philosophy of immediacy by expectant hope of community which will generate an unexplained bettering of group solidarity and purpose among the membership. What is good for the group or the individual in membership cannot be determined for the future and as a good cannot be said to be but, at best, immediately desirable.

A lack of authority in daily life, in the general culture, is consistent with Dewey's epistemology of uncertainty which has crept into modern life. The particularity of Dewey's sense that things can be only securely known individually, as potentially temporal and non-transferable, not only offers no certainty, but the thoughts of the One and the Others, leaves anyone unable to venture with certainty into any but the most superficially dependable reflexive or instinctive actions in daily life. Courts and communities have also stood in the doorway against certainty, as if to prevent the entrance of hard knowledge into our legal and educational systems. Every idea and principle is diminished by uncertainty. Laws and traditional mores have been so denigrated to permit argument in the face of reason. Student-individualism has destroyed school authority which shudders in dispute with students, parents and other litigious onlookers. Fact, truth, morality and certainty is equated with intolerance today.

Dewey may not have given America a way of seeing the world that gave the individual immediate independence from tradition but would eventually provide a methodology for justifying individual relativistic morality.

Chapter 6
Individualism and Society

Man is the measure of all things.

- Attributed to Protagoras[1]

John Dewey saw the individual as problematic, plastic and inchoate.

> The individual is subordinate because except in and through communication of experience from and to others, he remains dumb, merely sentient, a brute animal. Only in association with fellows does he become a conscious centre of experience...Freedom for an individual means growth, ready change when modification is required (Dewey, RIP, 207)[2]

Dewey maintained that the term individual, considered in balance with "[o]riginality" and "uniformity," had two meanings: the individual thinking his own mind and the individual "finding variations of point of view" "person to person" (Dewey, DAE, 354).[3] In order to be "free" intellectually, the individual must qualify by possessing "a situation favorable to effective thinking." Under this consideration "freedom will take care of itself" (Dewey, DAE, 355, 356).[4] A contention with Dewey, but accepted with resignation, was the opinion that individualism had been "preserved, by carrying it over," from the "habits of thought and feeling characteristic of earlier individualism," as was "transcendence," individualism had been understood in "universal terms" (Dewey, DAE, 52,53).[5] Dewey considered the individual qua individual incomplete not being more fulfilled categorically as in the Platonic sense.

Perhaps his exposure to Hegel's understanding of individualism had a lasting effect despite Hook's claim that Dewey had divested his Absolutism and idealism. "One man is concerned in a multitude of diverse groups, that is categorically, in which his associates may be quiet different." In the larger sense, society is unified. There is a useless understanding of the differences of all within society. A society must have commonalties among members and a true communication with others in the group. Coercion does not make or maintain a cohesive grouping. To have equal representation in the group there must be equality to develop freely and to develop one's own interests without interference. Gangs may even use isolation which may become a glue preventing the personal development of members by the adherence to the prescribed norm (Dewey, DAE, 94-99).[6]

Such conflicting views, dichotomous and dialectical, are hard to resolve and find emulation in other philosophies to the extent that they may be recognizable in Dewey's pragmatic writings. Tracing his ideas from earlier times offers a striking comparison of Dewey's concepts with those of the past, specifically his view of the social- and student-individual, terms used by this author, the latter of the two terms being embroiled in the confusion of modern culture and education, through irresolvable and solipsistic change, who have altered the nature of contemporary society and education. Plato was seen by Dewey as not understanding the direct relationships among the members of the group but saw only a common transcendence that gave everyone the same orientation to purpose and action. Furthermore, Dewey felt that Plato did not recognize the individuality of man, although it could be said that Dewey's keener insight was the result of his recognizing the threatening nature of the individual in the extreme. Dewey admitted to at least an elemental function of individuality in membership, but highly favored social plurality (Dewey, DAE, 102-105).[7] The loss of existence of the individual to a fixed system was not the fate of Dewey's One. Each individual element would find, ideally, according to an autonomous spirit, the core of group values and purpose.

Rousseau saw an inversion of individuality: society was an addendum to the individual in *Emile*. Society was the individual's stage. Nature was the teacher. "And since the natural world of objects is a scene of harmonious 'truth,' this education would infallibly produce minds filled with the truth." Dewey thought that Plato had given Rousseau nature but now nature would manifest "the diversity of individual talent and for the need of free development of individuality in all its variety." Rousseau had replaced Platonic categories with nature "in extreme cases, as nonsocial or even antisocial" and "a wider and freer society" which opposed "the indefinite perfectibility of man and a social organization having a scope as wide as humanity." then from this "emancipated individual" would "become ... progressive society." Emile was to become a reluctant element of society, given the right and free membership in humanity. Dewey saw Rousseau's optimism ill placed. Nature had substituted for education and the individual was subject to "the accidents of circumstance." "Mankind begins its history submerged in nature - not as Man who is a creature of reason, while nature furnishes only instinct and appetite. Nature offers simply the germs which education is to develop and perfect" (Dewey, DAE, 106-110).[8]

Rousseau "identified God with Nature" so no individual or group should interfere with the individual in which arose the good, the wisdom of the "good creator." Dewey held that this position taken by Rousseau was in response to and against the Calvinist issue of "total depravity" (Dewey, DAE, 134).[9] Dewey found Rousseau's perfectibility of the individual a divisive force within community (Dewey, DAE, 143).[10]

For Dewey a disciplined individual is one who will deliberate on considered actions as a student; the disciplined individual finds interest in study material while learning is the realization of activities in which the student is actively involved and concerned (Dewey, DAE, 151-158).[11] Education requires an orderliness and not the mere act of nature on a "savage" child. Individualism was developed in a process in which social participation from "almost at birth" stimulated a child's "instincts and powers" through educative experience by the child's own initial self-education. Any external and ongoing educational direction must be established as the child is given "complete possession of all his powers," enabling him "to give him [self] command." With socialization the individual child may be educated, "controlled at every point," knowing his or her "capacities, interests, and habits" which must be understood in social "terms" for use in "social service" (Dewey, MPC, Article One).[12] The freedom that Rousseau conceded to Emile was that of a wise savage, the transcendental seer, who by ridding himself of weakness became wise and strong against any assault by others; for Dewey this education in the broadest sense required controls without coercion. Freedom does not mean the student may run "ragged." The individual, the One, was polished into smoother compliance by the interaction of the Many. Not by coercion but by real-world, real-time relationships with others, could this social abrasion show progress in behavioral interaction among individuals. Alternatively coercion could only point to behavioral disturbance within the group, but, in Dewey's estimation it could not change individual conduct. Only habit replacement based on an intelligent understanding of the individual's behavior could bring the most extreme individual into meaningful group membership and acknowledged purpose. Discipline in the student, as Dewey saw it, and as behavioral modification has been practiced in schools since Dewey's time, may be more clearly understood in a detailed explanation, indeed the psychological bearing of the student, in Dewey's description of the process of individuation, he would contend, depended not on a theory of growth but of experience, but more on this later.

Solitary experience did not promote freedom nor the development of the individual.

> On the contrary, certain capacities of an individual are not brought out except under the stimulus of associating with others. That a child must work alone and not engage in group activities in order to be free and let his individuality develop, is a notion which measures individuality by spacial distance and makes a physical thing of it (Dewey, DAE, 353).[13]

The freedom given by Dewey to the individual was to be exercised within the community and not individually with extra-community purpose.

Locke's view of "authority in all spheres of life" gave all authority to the experimenter through "personal observation," which moved experience "to isolate mind" in separation from the objective world. The world became only "impressions made upon the mind." One's understanding of the world was merely the reflection of one's mental state. Such "practical individualism" "was translated into philosophic subjectivism" (Dewey, DAE, 342, 343).[14] Each individual had in Locke's philosophy the right of freedom of doing and knowing. To avoid subjectivism, Dewey would give ultimate authority to the group, thinking that if observations were collectivized, it would be meaningful as it would be directed toward group purpose. Giving authority to the group relieved Dewey of this subjectivism since each one did not assume individual authority while freedom of thought was tolerantly counted as an acceptable variance, as room for growth of the individual, while the education of the One was given by intellect and "diverse gifts and interest in its [progressive democratic society] educational measures" (Dewey, DAE, 357).[15]

Dewey did not place blind trust in nature. He, no doubt, found in Darwin a biological justification for change but offered opposition to categorization which tended to promote the agreeable while leaving out the disagreeable or diverse qualities. Concepts should make "other cases come in line" (Dewey, HWT, 127-129).[16] A fixity of nature did not satisfy his ideas any more than a fixity of morality and knowledge. His melioristic view of the world, Nature and human nature, seemed to be focused specifically on the culpable role of institutions and not individualism that worked against communitarian goals.

Indeed it is difficult to know exactly what Dewey ultimately believed about the personhood of the student. In his later works, offered after he left Chicago for Columbia University, he did not seem to alter what he saw as a potential threat to the group by individuality's excessive reach. He still reproached the "economic man" who found the "[c]alculated pursuit of gain" practiced while "separated from the rest of life" (Dewey, HNC, 220,221).[17]

Concentrating his ire on the institutions which he felt abused democratic values, namely government, business, industry and education, Dewey placed little direct blame on the extremes of individual behavior outside of these institutional associations implicitly retaining the idea of individual as only defined within the group context as member. As a humanist, the threat of disunity of mankind in nominal citizenship for solitary purpose, was seen as a condition which group purpose could largely overcome, despite perennial examples to the contrary. Blame had to be spread thin at best since culpability had to fall to the group with which the individual was complicit.

The question must again be raised for all who have tread the boards of the classroom: How can one grant individuality to man in freedom, free from coercion, without reaping a harvest of extreme and disruptive behavior? This is the dilemma that Dewey's philosophy faced then and in perpetuity is facing now in the modern public school today. Individualism was for Dewey as with Montaigne, seeing the individual as inconstant: clay molded over time and by situation, mercurial unto death, living in perpetual development. Montaigne's thoughts are reminiscent of Heraclitus, who saw nature lost in the passing of time affirming that the same man cannot walk into the same river twice. Man was not alone in the flux of change there was also nature. The water and the man, as only two considered variables, it could be argued were a part of a dodgy creation. Nature was always becoming but never being resolved in its character, so, why should the individual find final character definition in this life?

But Dewey saw the individual, morphing and emergent, organized through interaction with the material world to inevitable change through experience within the environment and without intrinsic and terminal identity given (Dewey, DAE, 2,3).[18] The individual as mind was thus understood as an arena in which knowledge comes to bear on the interaction with sensation (Dewey, DAE, 312, 313).[19] The individual is the creation of daily life (Dewey, RIP, 197,198).[20] Dewey rejected the self-containment view of individualism.

> When the self is regarded as something complete within itself, then it is readily argued that only internal moralistic changes are of importance in general reform. Institutional changes are said to be merely external ... The result is to throw the burden of social improvement upon freewill in its most impossible form. Moreover, social and economic passivity are encouraged...Let us perfect ourselves within, and in due season changes in society will come of themselves in the teaching... But when selfhood is

> perceived to be an active process it is also seen that social modifications are the only means of the creation of changed personalities (Dewey, RIP, 196).[21]

Education, in a broader sense, becomes the link from person to person.

> Personality must be educated, and personality cannot be educated by confining its operations to technical and specialized things, or to the less important relationships of life. Full education comes only when there is responsible share on the part of each person, in proportion to capacity, in shaping the aims and policies of the social group to which he belongs (Dewey, RIP, 209).[22]

Not only was personal identity given by society but the individual was an ongoing project of daily reconstruction with each instant and new environmental interaction. The consensus theory of truth was not considered since the diversity of views brought about communal change.

Dewey agreed in so far as man was a creation in the communal works, he felt man could be elevated above nature, exerting "powers" even against the ultimate inward reach of the outside world. This marked a point of departure from Locke's *tabula rasa* and the individual as a blank slate on which to write a "passive" identity. A duality of mind and matter drove a wedge, Dewey believed, bifurcating the physical world into an outer and an inner world. Individuals embodied innate activity which could be ordered by repeated stimuli to selective definition of individual action and knowledge. Any mechanical approach would not avail the individual of the powers of freedom needed in the experiential interaction of individuals through the world's assignation of identity (Dewey DAE, 71-73).[23]

The " 'individual' is not one thing, but is a blanket term for the immense variety of specific reactions, habits, dispositions and powers of human nature that are evoked, and confirmed under the influence of associated life." "[I]ndividuality is not originally given but is created under the influences of associated life." (Dewey, RIP, 198-200).[24]

Associative life reveals the difference between and among others in regard to "character and quality." Alone each individual is "morally neutral" which "is likely to lead to independence of group and customary standards" acting out of "personal and voluntary" interest. The term individualism for Dewey "ordinarily" denoted "selfishness, exclusiveness and primary regard for Individual rights." "It is every man for himself." He associates this selfishness with a "theory of government and economics" (Dewey, E, 68).[25] Dewey indicates that if "people really work out a higher type of conscious and personal morality, it means not only a more powerful individual, but a reconstructed individual and a reconstructed society" (Dewey, E, 80).[26]

By shifting the individual's transgressions to institutions by synecdochic association of extremists with institutional abuse, Dewey seems to offer absolution and voluntary release to the individual to eventually become a supporter of the group and in so celebrates the individual with raising the group to a higher level in the process. The individual thus becomes compositionally transparent as s/he is added to the group revered for progressing in purpose and communication.

But conflicts between individuals and the group "do exist" even if there is no "wholesale opposition between society and individuals." Yet Dewey admits that there are "important conflicts which exist" among "some individuals and some arrangements in social life." But "only an unreal and impossible being, one completely isolated, disconnected, can be put in opposition to society" (Dewey, E, 357-359).[27] In general the group without fixed standards is assumed to continue in its growth to a more democratic unity but never reaching the end or completeness. Dewey's rejection of perfectibility of the individual was based on progress and process, hence his defense of meliorism.

Dewey's individual could lurk in the shadows and not fulfill an identity by avoiding broader responsibilities to civilization, as a "dumb" and "brute animal." Concerns over extremism, the lone nature of the individual, fixed in habit without "growth" and "modification," would be a denial of the freedom to change. (Dewey, RIP, 207).[28]

Community, the world and its objects and associations were creators and teachers. Not forced to fill the slate with rote and routine but to act experimentally within the environment to the desirably endless developing through interaction with the environment. Unformed, unstructured in responsiveness, Dewey's individual would become flexible in personality by the smoothing friction from the environment, its situations and instances. Dewey saw community not as a potential detractor of the individual, nor a wary necessity for Rousseau, nor the scribe of Locke but the authored individual writ large by others and objects in a world of pragmatic experiences.

Due to Dewey's mistrust of hypothesis, "social judgments," "a permeation of judgments on conduct by the method and materials of a science of human nature" accounted for general identity (Dewey, HNC, 321).[29] When natural science is applied to man "it is the knowledge of the conditions of human action" (Dewey, DE, 267).[30] There would be a "coming to be." Mankind is graced with a "will" and "intellect" to "meet new challenges" with "flexibility." Change is ever present; "coming to be" would, however, preclude idealistic speculation, unteachable, immediate but never the less fixed. For in knowing by remote impenetrability of the empirical, experiential world, is to hold an understanding by dogma and predetermination. The world changes and everything in it (Dewey, HNC, 303).[31]

Man is found in the flux of redefinition along with the changing world. Certainty becomes an illusive commodity, nature becomes, as man is part of nature and interacting with it, "a number of diverse objects in space and time" (Dewey, MPC, Article 3, The Subject Matter of Education).[32] In the extreme, Nietzsche's "will to power" could leave the individual with a rigidity of purpose but without reason to hope for dependable outcomes. But random change, in identity or personality or individuality alone, is not Dewey's understanding of the process referred to as "growth". (Dewey, RIP, 194,185).[33] Dewey's individual would grow in freedom responding to the environment by "reconstruction and reorganization of experience...which increases ability to direct the course of subsequent experience" (Dewey, DE, 89, 90).[34] The individual free of dogma will grow throughout the span of life as an environmental object and would provide the impetuous to change under the free selection, revision and collection of new habits, more of which in the following chapter.

Individuality is created; selfhood is only changed by society (Dewey, RIP, 196-198).[35] The individual is subordinate and dumb (Dewey, RIP, 207).[36] Dewey sees the relationship between man and society as "organic," and if an implication may be drawn from this, the individual is the organ of the society and cannot sustain membership without serving the body of individuals of which each makes contribution to the fully functioning social order, a society of interacting organs and organ systems.

> In sum, I believe that the individual who is to be educated is a social individual and that society is an organic union of individuals. If we eliminate the social factor from the child we are left only with an abstraction; if we eliminate the individual factor from society, we are left only with an inert and lifeless mass (Dewey, MPC, Article One).[37]

Destroy the kidney, the lungs, and all function ceases. Remove members from the membership and society fails itself. The soft underbelly of his philosophy, unavoidable in its provision for self-defined freedom yet dependence on the communal effort to incorporate and ingratiate the membership to a common purpose, is insidious and without action, pragmatically working, by which the One may be brought into common purpose with the group. But to coerce into compliance would violate Dewey's principle of individual freedom.

Total depravity, as Dewey saw it, strengthen the motive concept for individual behavior. Considered innate, depraved motive would emerge driving results explainable beforehand and not needing the benefit of experience. But blindly accepting results in place of a depraved motive was little better, for both understandings would then fail to reasonably address the nature of action. The individual will do what he will do. It may be called motive, but only after experiencing the results and both motive and action are evaluated (Dewey, HNC, 118-120, 213, 231).[38]

> The denial of consequences thus turns out formal, verbal. In reality a consequence is set up at which to aim, only it is a subjective consequence. "Meaning well" is selected as the consequence or end to be cultivated at all hazards and end which is all-justifying and to which everything else is offered up in sacrifice...But the root of both evils is the same. One man selects some external consequence, the other man a state of internal feeling, to serve as the end (Dewey, HNC, 231).[39]

Dewey felt that when the idea of "meaning well" is chosen it is "more contemptible of the two, for it shrinks from accepting any responsibility for actual results" (Dewey, HNC, 118-120, 213, 231).[40] From either perspective, action must be allowed to take place even if the extreme individual is the actor, despite the effect on the group.

Dewey's ideas, although consistent in their generalities, can broach no solution to the loose cannon of individuality potentially threatening members of the larger society and the school society. His inability to adequately resolve the limits of individual authority, an essential foundational construct of Dewey's collectivity, has now become a critical concern to community practice in society and the public school were limits are not definite. His concept of freedom has failed to delineate the behavioral requirements of the student-individual and the public school to which he is accountable. Certainly the limits to authority must be dependent on the educability of the individual. Dewey believed that human nature could be changed and that education would not be possible if it were not so. Although there were commonalities among individuals, man is capable of exercising the capacity of "plasticity" as "essentially the ability to learn from experience." (Dewey, DAE, 52,53).[41]

The American extremist adult-individual and student-individual are a modern individualist products, a divisive individual seeking through self freedom to rule society or the school, respectively. Dewey's philosophy of unity and the reasonable expectation of harmony, depended on the ability to define the individual by the Other and not just the One. Today schools suffer from the authoritative individualism of which Dewey so often wrote and for which he seemed unable or unwilling to propose specific pragmatic guidance (RIP, 207; DAE, 130, 131, 259, 292, 293).[42]

To see Dewey as a prophet of his own philosophically flawed community with extreme and unavoidable selfish individualism, is to grasp the anti-communal nature of modern individuals who are sceptered and sit inthroned in rule over societal institutions. Even without usurpation, society and the school have built much of their practice around the anticipation of extremist attacks. Public education can barely sputter and spin as it is given over to a youthful mastery and must now reassert its meager authoritative identity, predisposed to the student's authoritative wants and wishes, affections and affectations.

Dewey felt that the individual was a "psycho-physical " holism finding meaning in "culture and its institutions," and what the individual is "depends upon what other people are" (Hook, JD,118, 119).[43] The individual is still at the center, not bending to the needs of others but tolerating those needs, if not standing contrary to group-held dogma. Education which promoted knowing through drill and hard fact-based instruction would tend to solidify individual dogma while making group solidarity fractious at best. Yet despite man's contrarian "capacities" even to violence, he may be redirected to more social activities (Hook, JD, 125).[44] In schools Dewey's ideas must work for a true democratic community. Competitive and rote education, however, produces "selfishness" encouraging the student to surpass classmates (Hook, JD, 11).[45] Competition among individuals was seen as a detriment to community. Dewey saw individualism as an on going, lifelong diegesis. The actors in the plot must flex to the roles of Others.

To Dewey the individual is the enigmatic and undeniable experimenter. It would seem reminiscent of Protagoras's claim of the individual's unremitting authority. Sidney Hook contends: "There is no measure of physical existence and conscious experience because the latter is the only measure there is for the former. The significance of being though not its existence, is the emotion it stirs, the thought it sustains" "We cannot compare existence and meaning; they are disparate." "The cosmology is just a backdrop for man; for without man" there is no foreground or background in nature at all." To grow in aesthetics and intellectual curiosity, "social conditions" must be first met (Hook, JD, 49, 50).[46]

The student was not an isolated learning unit unfettered and free as was held in practice in some of the child-centered schools. Dewey did make reference to a double meaning of intelligence that embraced his understanding of interdependence. The individual must act for self and with "the stimulus of associating with others." Education for the individual is more than interaction with the physical world. The individual intellect and "body" find "union" in the process of learning. Dewey does not see the solitary process of learning to be acceptable. "When, however, education takes cognizance of the union of mind and body in acquiring knowledge, we are not obliged to insist upon the need of obvious, or external freedom. The individual needs others. (Dewey, DAE, 351-357).[47]

Individual intellectual freedom will be instigated with "initiative and imaginative vision"…"control...impulses and habits" It is through this process of "impulses and habits" that the individual is freed up so that his "own purposes will direct his actions." When "authority" is placed over "the masses" "to take orders," then such fixed learning "is not adapted to a society which intends to be democratic" (Dewey, DAE, 351-357).[48] The consideration of what is too much authority does not give us metrics of acceptable behavior.

Descartes through apperception, perception of thought, found a justifying authority for the One, a transcendence of the mind ostensibly separate from a questionable empirical world. Dewey was by guaranteeing freedom and hence authority to the One, giving each individual authority in knowing objects in the external world. Empiricism was transcended by authoritative consideration of individual interior meaning, meaning of the mind, yet free from transcendent intervention by uniting individual meaning with useful action. Dewey thought he had removed the rationalism of inwardness and unearthly authority in daily life, while he was no more than transcending object-based experiential empiricism with the human agency of individual thought. In removing fixity from the process of knowing or even broadly held empirical standards, Dewey gave authority to individualism, for wisdom or whim, selfishness, or error. The possibility of self-promotion, insouciance or caprice being blindly given as individual authority for personal knowledge or even scientific truth must be, in correctly representing Dewey's philosophy, judged categorically the same; it was the rationalism of the One to know experientially. But with epistemology being transitory, Dewey had only replaced the authority of tradition with the uncertainty of immediacy. The process rather than the knowing would take the individual from one pragmatic understanding throughout life.

Dewey seemed to confuse the unity of the One with the Many in an idealistic hope of individual redemption, the loss of the brutishness brought on by isolation of the individual, only to offer up a Protean individual who like education, science and society, is given to a procession of change and may only be dependably known, if the meaning of the word known is not too compromised in the understanding, by temporality.

The individual, in Dewey's estimation, was ultimately defined by the group without which the "dumb" and "brutish" nature would not be reined in. There was no imposed, authoritative group that was to give structure and direction, but only the alignment sought with whatever and as many groups as desired by the individual. The development of an authentic individuality for Dewey did not seem to be a concern even as he was to open the individual up to potentially varied and undesirable group influences. This seems a bit too hopeful as any group may justifiably exert influence of authority. Without specifying the nature of the influence of collectivity, he held that democracy was dependent on "collective intelligencies" or "cooperative individualities." Experience was to form the individual in a life time of indeterminacy culminating in a debatable character at death. There are no solid models by which to pattern life. The individual is not heroic or evil for that may only be at best subject to interpretation and that only at the end of one's life, if then. The action of the environment on the individual and the individual on the environment determines the actions of the One. The individual is a mind-body holism and may only be seen in unity.

The unity of life, a pragmatic view held by Dewey, is more difficult to resolve. The individual is given experimental authority above the group that ultimately contributes authority over the individual. Although the individual is indeterminate, in a life-long state of flux, he is responsible and yet at the same time has the freedom to be irresponsible as an extremist who would act against the group or societal purpose which ultimately should have authority, if for no other reason, than the group is educative and imbues with learned purpose. The individual must not be forced to adhere to group purpose, but is eventually, Dewey hopes, to be brought into alignment with the group without using coercion to bring this about.

The individual in the classroom could only be allowed to do what ever he or she might imagine as freedom of experience as permission was unavoidably exercised. In this conflict is amplified his unsatisfactory resolution of the practical aspects of theoretical unity of the One and the Many who must be seen as inseparable. Just exactly what Dewey came to believe about the individual is difficult to workout. Just how permissible was the freedom given to the student-individual was left to conjecture in keeping with Dewey's usual avoidance of specifics.

Dewey believed that the intelligent replacement of habits throughout life would preclude the excessive appeal to self and prevent the limitation of "capacity of growth." Dewey's less than worshipful consideration of Nature saw the individual responding to the flux of objective life. The procession of experience would determine the adaptive capacitance of the individual as he or she replaced habits of action.

Chapter 7
Individuation

> But what will a man raised uniquely for himself become for others ?
>
> - Jean-Jacques Rousseau, *Emile* [1]

> We may legitimately hope that among the impulses which arise in minds ...emptied of all "rational" or "spiritual" motives, some will be benevolent.
>
> - C. S. Lewis, *The Abolition of Man* [2]

It is necessary, in order to appreciate the process by which experience develops and individuates, to examine the process in some detail. Dewey had put aside the "Scotch realism" or intuitionism, where logic and ethics comes by intuition naturally and not by education, where truths were fixed and unquestionable and where a schismatic duality existed between self and body and where teleological understanding fell from the loose hand of God. Early on he exchanged this given understanding for what he saw as a more practical view, as a presupposition to "creeds and rituals," to "personal experience" (Hook, JD, 11). [3]

The concept of individualization was for him a natural function of convention, prescribed in any particular time and society. Human nature was a function of the society and not the individual who was perhaps given a universal set of behaviors but a flexible nature. Individuals interacting in community displayed native relationships whose properties can only correctly be referred to as human nature. As individualism is not an inhering motivation, self-generated, identity must be learned. Dewey credited this process of individual creation to the communal environment (Dewey, RIP, 197-198).[4] The process by which the individual is educated to "personality" is through activities that are communally common, which direct and develop and yet allow the individual to venture "beyond the limits of established and sanctioned custom." Allowing exploration of the "margin of liberty" within the environment through active "experimentation," was the growth process through which the individual finds empowerment (Dewey, RIP, 208, 209).[5]

The exploratory nature of the child is where we may begin looking at the process of individual becoming in Dewey's philosophy. Babies are dependent and good children do what they are told; this being part of a particular child's nature. This conventional wisdom pronounces some children to be better than others (Dewey, HNC, 2, 89).[6] Custom and adult restraint are traditionally used to coerce the young into adult understandings and "customs" (Dewey, HNC, 64).[7] The child is protected and given needed help and responds instinctively. Instinctive behavior in babies is short lived, however, and the adult attends to ongoing needs. The imprint of adult authority and control results in the child acquiring behaviors. Custom is not infused through instinct but rather by "conceptions that are socially current" (Dewey, HNC, 89-93).[8] Instincts are "primitive" and man is better equipped to learn from experience such that for man rather than animals "most serviceable actions must be learned." In a process of selection, man has greater plasticity to effect behavioral "learning." A better term in humans for this driving force to habit selection is "impulse" rather than instinct (Dewey, HNC, 105n).[9] Impulse is "indiscriminate" possessing "vagaries and excesses" but through the action of intelligence which acts as a "clarifier and liberator," impulse "rushes blindly into any opening it chances to find" (Dewey, HNC, 254, 255).[10] Erupting "desires" cannot be sustained - as emotion fails to be prolonged - but, if acted on by intelligence, desire may be turned into "plans, systematic plans based on assembling facts, reporting events as they happen, keeping tabs on them and analyzing them." (Dewey, HNC, 254,255).[11]

Dewey was in a sense rejecting the Enlightenment's thought or hypothesis as an organizer of action, although he would retain the methodology as a model for order and inquiry. Dewey put aside the more Darwinian view of the later Enlightenment order that would support that the individual can harness impulses to give advantage over others, through "low aims," knowing how to carry out "materialistic" goals by "shrewd cold intellect that manipulates them" (Dewey, HNC, 255,256).[12] Emerson, no doubt, saw impulse as without necessarily possessing purposefully consistent content, as possibly even a whim given without enjoined action. Dewey would link the impulse to a consideration of action, which though arising in the individual, would ultimately find its true dedicated purpose in the interest of community. It would seem Darwinian survivalism was to be given the boot while the process of natural change was to be embraced at the root of Dewey's personification process, as a consideration of causation, unreliable, if at all orderly or traceable from cause to effect.

But seeing selfish impulse rise to the service of the group is hard to imagine. Extreme behavior is an indication of a failure to find relational place in community. Acting out, as Dewey contends, is the result of adult inculcation of the young with adult habits (Dewey, HNC, 89, 90).[13] It is through broader exploration of life; beyond the express process of education that the child implicitly gains "social capacity." Training molds the young rather than educating them through an appeal to their "[o]riginal modifiability." (Dewey, HNC, 96, 97).[14]

Individualism rightly committed to others cannot grow from acquired, traditional knowledge but must be "created under the influences of associative life." Personality, seen clearly, is found to be the creative product of selfhood through the modifying effect of society. Individualism is not the enthroning of selfhood but the clustering of interpersonal relationships. "The individual is but "dumb, merely sentient, a brute animal," for only only in association with fellows does a conscious centre of experience" develop (Dewey, RIP, 196 -207; especially 207).[15]

Perpetual becoming, lives and the world in progress, was essential to Dewey's philosophy of individualization. He presented a most extensive description of this in his book, *Human Nature and Conduct*. The explanation of the mechanism by which community moves the individual toward an educated state is one involving the intelligent deliberative evaluation of habits. Impulses push through to challenge established habits often borrowed from group context. The implicit process of individuation is an ongoing active replacement of "arrested and encrusted habits." This mechanism looks to emerging impulses to change habits which are no longer useful (Dewey, HNC, 105).[16]

Impulses "rush us off our feet " (Dewey, HNC, 196, 197).[17] As a "practical equivalent " of instincts, impulses are unresponsive to the environmental needs of the organism, they surface "undirected" (Dewey, HNC, 105n).[18] Instinct has traditionally referred more to animals than humans as animal responses are thought to be fixed in purpose, where as instincts in human individuals appear to confront an ever changing environment and existential complexities far beyond the experience of beasts. Instincts in humans are so numerous that they "cut across one another, this, as mentioned before, favors learning. Dewey would disagree that the force of impulse makes it a "law unto itself." An impulse is "an indispensable source" for giving opportunity, for altering activities of the individual and others in the realization that man must live under "conditions that are continually changing" (Dewey, HNC, 155,156).[19] The "opportunity" is just that, a chance to apply intelligence to experience to alter actions even patterns of action.

Life is change. "There is no such thing as an environment in general; there are specific changing objects and events." Event and conditions change and "activities" interact bringing more change. Such plasticity of "response to different conditions" is the basis for what Dewey considers a changing "moral phenomenon" (Dewey, HNC, 154-156).[20] Impulse, it would appear, is to be allowed its expression and may result in the carrying out of "social injustice," while other expressions may be viewed as "normal or desirable" (Dewey, HNC, 156).[21] Direct intervention into quelling undesirable expression of an impulse is not advocated; "impulsive activity" "suppressed" is not destroyed but is submerged only to arise later in some "intellectual and moral pathology" (Dewey, HNC, 156,157).[22] Correcting student-individuals engaged in unsociable or even dangerous activities, Dewey must maintain, could have adverse consequences on the child's development, while intervention could be considered coercion, which he could not sanction, could also produce pathology in the developing child which could be sustained into adulthood.

The psychological significance of such an understanding points to Freud, although Dewey would have not clung to the understanding of the disunity of mind without action nor the past without allowance for progress and change merely accepting the effect of past experience on present action. The Freudian alternative would be but to look to the past and embrace its significance thus living in and out of realized experience from the past. Dewey would look to each new experience to give direction and process as each new habit would free man of the past(Dewey, HNC, 156, 157).[23]

Behavior by any measure is individual, but, experience Dewey would maintain, is relative to the environment on which it would depend for meaning. Saying no to the undesirable repetitive behavior of a student-individual, for instance, could carry little authority. Whereas instincts are homogeneously distributed, yet the outcome of instinctive behavior shows no homogeneity across cultures. Since instinct, therefore, cannot be a logical choice for culturally divergent behaviors; the next choice is that of human nature, but Dewey would look rather to the influence of environment on behavior acquisition (Dewey, HNC, 91,92).[24] Dewey held that impulses arise undirected from the individual to interact with the environment thus potentially changing behavioral patterns, or habits (Dewey, HNC, 95).[25]

This was not unrelated to the intuitionism of his childhood: "indisputable truths about existence" by "virtue of the immediate compulsion with which they asserted themselves in our deeper intuition." It was in the "immediate compulsion" that Dewey found authority for individual action (Hook, JD, 11).[26] Impulse may be reflected on whereas compulsion is driven not by thought but by an irrational drive which may produce an outcome without study and consideration. In Dewey's mechanism of individuation, compulsion is not authoritative, but actions find value in habit.

> Plasticity or the power to learn from experience means the formation of habits. Habits give control over the environment, power to utilize it for human purposes. Habits take the form of both of habituation, or a general and persistent balance of organic activities with the surrounds, and of active capacities to readjust activity to meet new

> conditions. The former furnishes the background of growth; the latter constitutes growing. Active habits involve thought intervention, and initiative in applying capacities to new aims. They are opposed to routine which marks an arrest of growth (Dewey, DAE, 62).[27]

Habits can be replaced by those found more appropriate to time and situation. The "medium" for change is the environment, and "[b]y operating steadily to call out certain acts, habits are formed..." (Dewey, DAE, 15).[28] "Habits reduce themselves to routine ways of acting, or degenerate into ways of action to which we are enslaved just in the degree to which intelligence is disconnected from them" (Dewey, DAE, 5).[29] Reflection on habits is not effective in changing them, but impulses may modify or remove habits as they drive to repeated alternate activity. Acting repeatedly on impulse drives habit formation at the hand of environmental objects (Dewey, DAE, 22).[30]

Education of the young is accomplished "by controlling the environment in which they act, and hence think and feel." But then Dewey avers: "We never educate directly, but indirectly by means of the environment" (Dewey, DAE, 22).[31] Education for Dewey was to minister to citizens and students of a changing world. School was Dewey's laboratory for changing the minds of the young who would otherwise continue in the outmoded ways of the past. Since the environment was the medium in which objects were changed, then any change in environment could bring about changes in what we may have accepted as unchangeable. Dewey parted company with the "recapitulation" of knowledge proposed by education pioneer Johann Friedrich Herbart. Dewey could not imagine "[e]ach new generation would simply have repeated its predecessors' existence." (Dewey, DAE, 85).[32] Dewey was not merely looking to progress but to change in which One is emancipated from the experience of others. This would justify the label attached to James and Dewey ideas as that of "radical empiricism." One can only know for oneself in the time, place and circumstance in which no other can, by having a different environment, have the same experience. Habits must be then arrived at individually, replaced individually, and can serve only pragmatically, only as long as they produce the desired effects based on intelligent replication of action. The authority of habit rests with the individual alone and the reason for the non-transferable nature of knowing.

Although Dewey listed extreme examples of "bad habits," such as those driven by the need for drugs and alcohol, still he saw the loss of control and determinations in action as the unacceptability of these habits which were "not deliberately formed" (Dewey, HNC, 24).[33] But education, learning from "activities" driven by impulses, allows one to "intend consequences instead of just letting them happen" (Dewey, DAE, 90).[34] Under duress individuals are moved to "capricious habits;" in progressive societies learning as active habit formation and replacement can be seen as "continuous reconstruction of experience" (Dewey, DAE, 92,93).[35] It would be hard to convince addicts that they need to "intend" and learn to not use.

Pathology may result from duress when habits are forced on the individual. How could a student be held responsible for an act committed without the student being consciously and purposefully giving authority to action? With regard to school misbehavior, we find in Dewey not only a reluctance to judge negative habits as less heinous than addiction to alcohol and drugs but where consequences cannot be levied against lesser behavioral infractions, the student appears merely a victim of the environment, and the infractions are not sanctioned but met with a dubious disciplinary environment (Dewey, HNC, 25).[36]

After being "ridiculed" for unacceptable behavior and gaining "approval" for acceptable behavior, the individual is "assimilated to those of his group." And thus the individual comes to share in "associated activities" and will likewise come to share in common "beliefs and ideas" (Dewey, DAE, 16).[37] The environment of the school is to change undesirable "features" of an inappropriate environmental influence on habits of the mind "not only ... [by] simplifying but at weeding out what is undesirable...By selecting the best" environment, this can be accomplished "[a]s society become more enlightened...The school is the chief agency for the accomplishment of this end" (Dewey, DAE, 24).[38]

Habits formed by the individual, which are not "native and original," can be replaced by natural impulses as they arise to challenge traditional habits. Confrontation occurs as impulses conflict with established habits. Since impulses arise not just in childhood, adults are also subject to eruptive impulses and progressive habit replacement throughout their lives (Dewey, HNC, 98,99).[39] Habits may be destroyed by conflicting impulses (Dewey, HNC, 183).[40] So under the influence of impulses, habits may be refreshed and, if through challenging old habits which are judged by adequately addressing them, the individual may replace old habits of less useful behaviors. "Impulse is a source, an indispensable source, or liberation; but only as impulse is employed in giving habits pertinence and freshness does it liberate power" (Dewey, HNC, 105).[41] Intelligence makes sense of impulse by working deeper to create "[t]hought" which "is born as the twin of impulse in every moment of impeded habit." Habits that do not become patterned will not effect behavior change. New impulses will appear to continue an ongoing "civil warfare" between "vital" habits and those in "stagnation" (Dewey, HNC, 170, 171).[42] Thought is the only way to avoid pure "impulse or purely routine action" (Dewey, HWT, 14).[43]

When any habits and "unorganized impulses" work on tradition and custom to repair and renovate, "consciousness" and "conscience" are born. The theory of knowledge and that of behavior should be seen as resulting from the same issues in life. This process is the result of the war between habits and impulses in which habits may be replaced. This is the basis for Dewey's "theory of knowledge," and impulses drive the developmental process which Dewey refers to as the "character of knowledge." A unification of responses by the individual in the environment is the sign of an appropriate conduct. From each response toward a consistency of responses, individualization proceeds toward a "continuity of nature and mind." There is a unity found in nature and mind as impulses and resultant habits are selected within the same environment (Dewey, HNC, 182-187).[44]

Habit then directs attention and thought, but, as Dewey states, "The routineer's road is a ditch out of which he cannot get, whose sides enclose him, directing his course so thoroughly that he no longer thinks of his path or his destination." This he claims gives rise to "thoughtless action" (Dewey, HNC, 172,173).[45] For when universality is given to understanding without regard to possible limitations and conditions - Dewey refers to this as the "philosophical fallacy" - intelligence is thus hindered through "supposition" (Dewey, HNC, 175).[46] Thought well considered displaces easy answers: "[t]he essence of critical thinking is suspended judgment " (Dewey, HWT, 74).[47] Dewey was skeptical of knowing as complete, as "[a]ll judgment, all reflective interference, presupposes some lack of understanding, a partial absence of meaning" (Dewey, HWT, 118).[48]

Although Locke believed that all experience was written on a blank slate, a *tabula rasa,* Dewey's understanding of habit formation was also to be written on a slate as each individual's resultant nature was impressed, yet man was not impressing with a Helvetian "infinite perfectibility," but rather erasing any "external superficial barrier to the operation of existing intellectual tendencies" (Dewey, HNC, 106, 109).[49] "Every act, every deed is individual." To fix the nature of each act for Dewey amounted to casuistry and reverting to the "procrustean beds of fixed rules" for which the individual in each act will not fit with others (Dewey, HNC, 240).[50] When impulses arise resulting in habit replacement, forming new perspectives and understandings of the self and the world, the individual is changed by the new habit. Dewey tells us that habits are dicta for new actions which in combination with the other habits of action, evince the self. Habits we are told "are active means, means that project themselves, energetic and dominating ways of acting" (Dewey, HNC, 25).[51] As "demands" for specified action, these habits become the "will." As actions occur through relationships with objects within the environment, the objects purposefully applied become the media of "means." Dewey's analogy of a man with bad posture telling himself to straighten up may only be useful when he thinks about it. The habit of good posture will only be possible, only as the habit of bad posture is replaced. Likewise, habits of action may be replaced as needed over time and not in the thought of the moment (Dewey, HNC, 25-30).[52]

It is no wonder that bad habits are not changed by consequences, Dewey continues. A person's "bad way" may not be changed by telling of the behavior, by interposing the "idea" of the good way between action and the "mind and will." Since ideas depend on habits, simply telling someone to do an alternate action will not change the habit permanently or become an "end." " The act must come before the thought, and a habit before an ability to evoke the thought at will." "Ideas" are merely "thoughts of ends" (Dewey, HNC, 30).[53] "Means and ends are two names for the same reality." "Ends," by Dewey's analogy are the army, while means are the soldiers seen "distributively" (Dewey, HNC, 34-36).[54] If "ends" are "remote"; if "'end' is the last act thought of, the means are the acts to be performed prior to it in time." "[T]hen related means collect over time, except in regard to "social customs" and "collective habit," and become means for more means and so on. Ends are merely the ideas of ends of sequential means. If applied to character without ends, character is merely the habit replacement of a lifetime.(Dewey, HNC, 34-38).[55] Each act seen as a "distant end" is a dream; each act must be turned from an "end" into a "means." Of the intermediate acts [in a series of acts], the most important is the next one." "Character can be read through the medium of individual acts" (Dewey, HNC, 34-38).[56] But character would seem to be an incomplete formation of describable actions without judgment and the potential benefit of praise failing to find heroes.

The implication of the means, ends, habit are staggering to an understanding of not only discipline but also knowing. The individual in Dewey's mind cannot be permanently dissuaded from undesirable action except that habits be replaced and not by orders or holding consequences as deterrents. The student-individual is in this regard incapable of being rendered behaviorally acceptable by any method other than self (willed) transformation over time, until the completion of character formation (end), the end of life. If ideas are ineffective and means are never really expected to lead to ends, ends which may only suffer disaffection or being forgotten, then causality suffers with the inability to effect direct behavior. The student-individual becomes an authority to self, and change waits on the action of the self, on civilizing and cognitively significant erupting impulses.

But what if bad habits are not replaced by the student-individual? When habit-replacement is quelled, the individual may settle into habits stayed on certain objects. William James maintained that passions may be fortified against change and the developmental progress of the individual (Dewey, HNC, 195).[57]

Presumably passions are unresponsive to the moment growing into idolatry with which comes the fixation of passions evidently patently selfish by its persistence of focus or stagnation (Dewey, HNC, 193-198).[58] Dewey conceives of such stagnation as resorting to having "fixed-ends-in-themselves" which would halt growth. Emphatically he declares only means and not ends - "There are in no sense ends of actions" (Dewey, HNC, 224, 225).[59] With regard to over zealous actions of the student-individual, are we to wait for the passions to subside? Shall we wait for intelligent "deliberation" to allow the "working harmony among diverse desires?" Dewey believes that "passions" should be more frequent despite the inability of idea or "Reason" to give direction. The schools inability to curb passions, whether prurient or hostile, removes all claims to civilize and removes the rule of reason by the sheer developmental power of One's self-interest.

We are indeed far from Plato's view of individuals as representations within categories of service to the state assumed by "expectation" of a practical if not connate principle in each person (Dewey, HNC, 134).[60] How do you categorize those who are in unique respect particular, individuals, each one ultimate in authority with a need to an unquestionable right to the uniqueness of One? One need may be for the Other, but that need may be trumped by yet another need, the need to be One, ultimately, extreme in self-need. How are students ultimately to be considered collectively when being One out weighs the Other and the Many ?

The authority dilemma is potentiated by Dewey's deference to the immediate, the "next" act, the next means in the series of means which cannot be considered as acts collectively as ever coming to rest as any fixed end (Dewey, HNC, 34-38).[61] What One wants now is not often that which the Other needs now and in the future. As with character, actions are immediate as useful meaning can only be assigned. Actions are not in the past or the future but now, therefore there are only present actions. Only actions in the present can give rise to means and "[N]ot just singular means but a concatenation of means with no "end in itself" (Dewey, HNC, 228-231).[62] Only actions in the present define "reality." "Fixed rules and habits remove flexibility" and "response from action."

Universals do nothing to address individual situations and actions. "Casuistry" lends understanding to actions and in doing so robs "individual cases" of their unique character while substituting "infallible certainty" (Dewey, HNC, 236-240).[63] Universals are often valued above impulses. But the individual must make choices based on unique situations not on those disconnected from action or of expected outcomes (Dewey, HNC, 254-265).[64] Holding to an "ideal" prevents the individual from the immediacy of the present and holds to understanding in the not yet experienced future (Dewey, HNC, 274).[65] According to Dewey, universal morality as an ideal fails because of its timelessness, its remoteness, and its alienation from the continued activity of "everyday affairs" indulging fixed meaning to complex habit-impulse relationships (Dewey,HNC, 280, 281).[66]

Dewey would hold that using fixed morals to judge individual action is retrograde yet maintaining prescience and immanence, not responsive to immediate reality. In a sentence, not only can the student-individual not receive valid direction in correction, but due to the ineffectual nature of experience past, must continue to do characteristic of self until some habit changing impulse moves the student-individual to habit replacement. In consideration of school discipline, such dissuasion prevents school authority from exercising their ability to provide for a conducive environment for learning. The One becomes destructive of the school's educational purpose to preserve the respect among the school community which strives to uninterruptedly educate all students. If schools found the authority to teach, there is still the issue of the individual or student and the development of a meaningful and distinctive selfhood. The unlawful citizen could maintain an unacceptable if not dangerous activity until the possibly lethal habit was replaced.
Dewey's individual is never to be defined but ever embroiled in the continuing process of becoming an individual, which may prove to be Protean or of an otherwise questionable identity. Thus the consequences of undesirable behavior may not be rightly judged even if definitive motivation could be reliably determined, although according to Dewey it cannot (Dewey, HNC, 43).[67] Dewey's reasoning was that we could not know motive which is invested

in the future for its interest and though it may be seen in the future, the reason for the resolved issue may only prove to be speculative. When authority of speculation is suspended, " [t]hen as the present merges insensibly into the future, the future is taken care of." (Dewey, DE, 64,65).[68]

Impulses which cause habit change and are vital to the individuation of the child, if properly attended by "liberated impulses" may stir habits that could otherwise find "stagnation" (Dewey, HNC, 170-171).[69] This living interaction, however, of habits and impulses is the constitution of Dewey's becoming of individuality. But if eruptive impulses are stifled, even though not directed to a particular habit, this can result in undesirable effects on the individual. Impulses act on objects to change habits, and, when this action is not allowed, the individual may develop pathologies or fantasies under this unfulfilled "inherent pressure" (Dewey, HNC, 140,141).[70] Repression may force "the impulse into disguise and concealment" yielding "evil" and "rebellion" through neglect (Dewey, HNC, 164-166).[71] When impulses are not allowed to act as intermediaries to "conduct," they may become "side tracked to find their own lawless barbarities or their own sentimental refinements" (Dewey, HNC, 169).[72]

Dewey would relegate social disruption to unrealized impulses. The student-individual must be allowed to act on impulses, to be experimental in conduct. To do less could possibly be contributing to waywardness or sickness. There should be concern that the individual might disregard the communal nudging and strike out for self while dissembling group interests, a possibility which could compromise the authority of people in community to coalesce in common belief and practice. Time, situation and environment are at least in part given blame for habits and behaviors not in the best interest of the group and resulting from the lack of direct control of individualism in its formative stages. Dewey gives the individual a weak claim of no clear attributable responsibility in the final determination; at least the individual is presented as less than critically responsible. When impulses challenge the inhering practiced habits, then actions are changed in a process that may last a lifetime. If guilt does not reside in individual action, then it must be found in the lifelong dismissal of impulses that would render the extreme individual, ironically, more positively responsive to the community.

It has been suggested, and not for the first time, that Dewey's view of behavior imparts an impulsive nature to account for the more daedal nature of human activity. Life, it has been said, is so complex that to explain behavior by such a simple eruptive mechanism could not explain in detail that which is a more individual and interactive. And, it must be added, that the development of a child against expectations, if not by disciplinary brick walls, is analogous to developing musculature in a baby who is never offered any resistance to movement. A child under these conditions would not be given the opportunity to find resistance to behavioral alternatives. Dewey himself held that children needed adults to guide them, but did he mean to let them struggle in a world for which their understanding is limited and their potential undoing of others may result from an empirical exploration of their environment while an adult merely facilitates the experimentation? Certainly Dewey did not intend this. One would imagine that he found no suitable way to reconcile his gift of individual philosophical autonomy given freedom despite the potential for extremism preying selfishly on the freedom of the Many. It is a difficult appeal to the voluntary will of the prisoner who has been set free to stay in the cage once the door is opened wide. There is a strong impulse to excess when specific terms of release are not specified in detail.

There is the idea that impulses must be advantageous for all in order that it find approval in action. Dewey held his idea of individual freedom against his own recognition of the reality of extreme abuse, against selfishness and habitual stagnation. Kant's understanding that a society of good men would work toward good ends of cooperation was shared by Dewey (Dewey, HNC, 44).[73] Today we see the idealism of Kant and Dewey, the emergence of idealism, that in principle Dewey would have rejected, but could have been a bone of contention with which he would wrestle throughout his days. Dewey would find the goodness in ultimate service of the individual to the group possibly inconsolable by extreme individual opportunism. Dewey found his defense of individualism run amok in asserting that immediate effect is insufficient and must be seen in time, if at all. Good behavior is irrelevant for the individual who is only atomic to the collective; only group progress and collective civility is good. The teachers and the students in school care and deserve better than the hope of true community, when individualism can be controlled thus learning and socialization of students can proceed unimpeded. The individual citizen must find membership while stifling self.

Human nature does not bear the burden of individuation at least not the traditional view that individuals behave in patterns based on self interest and survival. Dewey would allow experience at the "margin of liberty" to explore the eruptive impulses that must challenge habit replacement without the benefit of directing behavioral patterns (Dewey, RIP, 208).[74] Expression of altered behavior patterns whether antisocial or not must be allowed to be attended by group approval. Consequences for anti-group habit adoption do not appear to have punitive value as judgment could not be justified based on the growth process natural to individuation. Any consequences would only be applicable at the time, and, as the individual is beyond any event to which consequences might be assigned, the levying of punishment is not practical or defensible. Accountability is dubious; punishment is virtually impossible, and alteration of non-sociable behavior is at best a long-term process, if even possible short of death, the end to the ever-changing individual.

Man garners his greatest meaning from society. Although habits are patterns of activity which are individual; "[t]he individual is a social product" of this habituation who can " only be understood in relation to his culture and its institutions." The dualism of individual and society is really unity. Habits are shared through relationships which is their "locus." "Except to the biologist, what a man is literally depends upon what other people are..." (Hook, 118,119).[75]

The individual is the one that experiences in time, "locus" and situation. The customary practices of culture are activities of moral habit. The summation and modification of these habits by individuals are both physical and moral (Dewey, HNC, 32-41).[76] The collectivity of habitual activities is not primarily communal even though individuals adopt habits within a common environment. Common habits are replaced, presumably as the environment makes need and as individual habits may need to be replaced (Dewey, HNC, 58).[77] In Dewey's view the "inflexibility of old habits is precisely the chief cause of their decay and disintegration" (Dewey, HNC, 130).[78]

Though Dewey's understanding of individuation has not been assimilated in detail, it has been absorbed into the larger culture and pedagogy in more subtle ways. It is ironic that the support of organized judicial challenges to modify communal action under the law, in effect, has given freedom and the right of individual experience precedence over the greater will of the society and called it just. No doubt Dewey would have principled difficulty with this contemporary practice of insuring individual freedoms over communal authority. Society and the schools are having great difficulty with this practice. The mindset that a student-individual's freedom to comportment as willed among a group whose wishes are not necessarily those of a majority nor, for that matter, a minority of the group, is both unreasonable and clearly counter to Dewey's principles concerning individual and group habit formation and replacement. The legal fall out from such practice for which schools must contend raises the bar of attainable freedom for the individual in the street and within the school whose goals for community and academics will be compromised. Dewey's individualist is repeatedly enthroned over a kingdom of Many with every loss of community and school authority, resulting in the individual subjugating all to the authority of the One. Dewey claimed that individual freedom must yield to the "organization" without which their can not be "objective freedom,"

> In order to arrive at these agreements, individuals have to make concessions. They must consent to curtailment of some natural liberties in order that any of them may be rendered secure and enduring (Dewey, HNC, 307).[79]

Yet the impulse-habit foundation of individual growth calls on the free individual to give up the developmental promise of what solely satisfies self through voluntary "choice" in habit selection and replacement. But freedom cannot be found wanting for experimental individuation. "Choice is an element in freedom and there can be no choice without unrealized and precarious possibilities." "In...use of desire, deliberation and choice, freedom is actualized " (Dewey, HNC, 306-313).[80]

Dewey seems to have cast his bread on stormy waters. On the streets are we to let individualism have its way without regard to Others? In the schools are we to depend on the young, uncontrolled and self-focused to take a mature view of others and are we to look to the student-individual to determine whether we will be granted the freedom to learn and teach Others? Or are we to allow the student-individual to act experimentally on impulses that break to the surface and hope that those resultant actions will not adversely affect anyone? Although Dewey clearly did not see the inept, inexperienced young running the schools as student-individuals without concern for others, he seems a bit lost in this dichotomy of self experimentation and the consolation of Others. With such concerns, is there any wonder that progressive education has created unworkable behavioral policies and insufficiently guided student-individuals? Even if the bulk of the student body, caring and sensitive to the needs of others, were to behave so as to make a solid academic and social commitment to their school community, the student-individuals, though in trivial numbers, could and do bring down academic institutions by their freedom to selfishness and desires deliberating their own wants and skirting consideration of group cohesion .

Dewey's collectivist authority, loose as it may be, allowing for change but doubtful from what change and to what next, as with the transcendentalists waiting for the eruption of impulse which will inform each individual in growth and new understanding, becomes a wide gulf breached between authoritative individual experience-based learning, or education, and a group authority loosely constituted of like mind-action members. The fallacy of Dewey's collectivity hangs up again on the lack of practical boundaries for native individualistic authority and a group centeredness which of necessity must be lacking in definite ends due to a potentially shifting purpose. The problem is compounded when the general collective purpose is not held even loosely by marginal or nominal group members who would set individual habit formation over that of group welfare. And there is but hope yet no reason to believe that the individual will eventually ascend to the common purpose if allowed superior authority. Dewey gives responsibility to the group for changing the environment and not forcibly the heart of the extreme individual nor any definitive prospect for his containment.

For Dewey order in the broader function of the school must recognize and must permit the unquestioned assertion of authority in the school. The individuation of the child must occur as the student submits to the authority greater than an impulse induced epiphany or outward expression; the student must submit mind and body not only to the authority of the lesson but also to the discipline of living with others. Order is required in both realms as a growing holism under the direct action of establishing habits. The democratic expression of self must be permitted by all, and through order and reason, with guarded allowance of impulse and habit formation, the school can then provide its essential service of academic instruction and civility. Under conditions of change or uncertainty about habit replacement, students must not be definitively judged and punished without certainty that unacceptable habits were not retained. Dewey felt this could never be known and so judgments and their consequences could not be brought against a student, since replacement of habits giving rise to native behaviors of an unacceptable nature could not be determined.

But reality in the public school is often harsh. Reality in the schools has not been diminished; reality in the classroom comes in stormy waves. Teachers and local school administrators face the welling tides of real experience immediate and recurrent. There is no certainty of authority to teach and protect children entrusted to the school. It is with a suspect authority to judge that education becomes strained to near meaninglessness (Dewey, HNC, 43).[81] These effects in the broader society may have even life-threatening outcomes.

In summary, only if actions become embedded in repeated action does habit become established in individual authority. Through impulsive actions old habits may change as needed, pragmatically, as empirically useful. Understanding who one is is established through an ongoing habit replacement as needed: consciousness is born in challenging habit. Pre-suppositions from authority outside the individual may bring judgment and consequences for judged action but this only represents a lack of understanding. There are no ends, what are called ends are merely means to more means, and therefore consequences may not be levied justly against an individual who is merely seeking "self-interest." Authority is individual; it is flexible and not universal. Nothing is above the impulse mechanism of habit formation. Character is only to be judged at the end of life, when there is no more action. For consideration of character, all actions must be known, and, since Dewey's epistemology is one of uncertainty, whose morality is particular, accusations against the living are untenable and against the dead are up for debate. There are no real heroes and authority is in the lap of the collective, without coercion, freely given to the assembly. Yet for the group as well as the potentially prodigal group member, any relationship must not be seen as fixed lest the individual becomes stagnate in imposed authority. To coerce to behavioral standards is to threaten rebellion in the One. The student-individual has no master but self. No school, attempting to operate under such constraints, has any certainty of maintaining a suitable teaching environment or has the reasonable expectation that students will seriously pursue studies and show civility to peers. Both knowing as learning and morality arise from inside the student-individual to work out action as each One decides. So for the citizen who has a habit of defiance and violence; he must be allowed to express his character, un-lauded and un-judged.

Chapter 8
Pedagogy

> Every moment instructs, and every object; for wisdom is infused into every form.
>
> - Ralph Waldo Emerson, *Essays*[1]

> It will never be known what acts of cowardice have been promoted by the fear of not looking sufficiently progressive.
>
> - Charles Péguy, *Notre Patrie*[2]

Dewey's pragmatism was to consider society a laboratory in which individuals would unite behind group purpose, in fact, multiple group purposes for multiple groups. He put his philosophy to the test in the late nineteenth century as he directed the University of Chicago's Laboratory School, The Dewey School, as it was to be called. Using his experimental approach to pedagogy, pragmatism in practice became a laboratory for empiricism. Although writings and lectures would greatly outlast his short stent directing classroom services, Dewey's educational theory would be drawn on by generations of followers. The Dewey school practice would endure, as it would come to be understood and practiced by his acolytes in striking contrast to that of traditional educational practice and often less faithful to Dewey's intentions.

In his 1916 book *Democracy and Education*, Dewey called for a public program of education in America which would promote true democracy or "social continuity of life. " Such a school system would serve "the constant reweaving of the social fabric." Education would not be a product but an on-going pragmatic process of united epistemology and morality. Dewey's educational vision, however, would not stop at the school house door; education was to be a collective practice in which individuals communicated as they learned together thus "enlarging and improving experience." "Formal education," by tradition had been held tightly to abstraction and academic rote, while understanding, education proper, was "indirect," an on-going "process" within the community. "Communication is a process of sharing experience til it becomes a common possession" (Dewey, DAE, 3 - 11).[3]

Experience was to replace the tradition of rules and rote as the unflinchingly prescribed *modus vivendi,* agreement among conflicting views, of modern education. Perhaps rote learning, which Dewey so deplored as a singular teaching method, was objected to for its pressing of ideas on others as much as the staid educational ritual which is identified with direct instruction and abstract learning set apart from experience. Educational methods, unrelated to individual knowledge of life, were dry and uninteresting to the students. The memory of facts would be no more than experiencing by proxy and, therefore, would not be true experiential learning. And so, assuming facts apart from experience would be giving primary authority to the Other and relegating learning to proxy. Individual authority taken from individual experience must trump borrowed facts, for learning could not be depended on to be "trans-experiential," since experiential knowledge was unique to set, setting, self and situation (James, TMOT, xliii).[4]

Learning could not be reliably transferred with authoritative impress, dedication and obligation. Knowing would be obtained through a process of communal evolution. The wide meaning that Dewey took from his own understanding of education did not ultimately consist in mere individual authority, although given. Doctor Dewey thought quite idealistically that group context might arrive at parity without coercion. He held out hope that collectivity would result in equality and shared learning. To realize true democratic community, "physical proximity," a mere gathering of group members would not suffice, only "social continuity of life." The practice of community would become educational through the formation of relationships such that all authentic interaction would tend to empower a broad view of communication. Community would be more than the result of individuals serving as "part of a machine work." Dewey believed that the group, especially an educational community in its true sense, was to contribute to the prevention of a generational disconnect and the loss of social stability. In maintaining a chain of relevance among the generations, he felt that education could be critically poised to aid in addressing issues of the school, community and even the greater society (Dewey, DAE, 2-5).[5]

In "My Pedagogic Creed," Dewey ensconces "the school as the primary and most effective instrument of social progress and reform" (Dewey, MPC).[6] While this may seem to be in conflict with statements concerning the less than primary importance of education, a correct understanding probably reflects the recognition that if institutional democratization could be accomplished, school could reliably implement that "necessary condition" for change which could result in the establishing of a requisite true democracy which Dewey considered foundational to that "condition." In Dewey's words: "The conception of education as a social process and function has no definite meaning until we defined the kind of society we would have" (Dewey, DAE, 29-49).[7]

"Education proceeds ultimately from the patterns furnished by institutions, customs, and laws. Only in a just state will these be such as to give the right education" (Dewey DAE, 103).[8] An acceptable pattern of democratic rule must afford the governance of society while conducive to and supportive of true education. Dewey optimistically believed that although such a society was not in fact currently in place in America, a truly democratic nation could be pragmatically constructed (DAE, 113,114).[9]

Here he leaned away from his understanding of the pragmatic present to take an idealistic and inconsistent peak at the future. Dewey's pedagogy has never sustained a broadly cast and reasonable program for attainment of a true democratic education. Dewey contended that through community and formal education, rightly seen, America could become truly democratic. For education's part it would need to provide through the state all the needs of America's children with the social education provision being subject to the capacities of individual children. Moral teachings of the home were to be supplemented by the educational community. Dewey saw the modern instructor, unlike the traditional teacher of his day, as a facilitator who would encourage the child but would in effect be just another learner offering direction for the child's growth determining how "the disciplines of life shall come to the child" (Dewey, MPC, Article Two).[10]

Democracy would flow liberally from the facilitation of equality. "Common subject matter" and "specialized social environment," he believed, were the keys in uniting races and cultures and would "look after nurturing the capacities of the immature" as they grew. The society is made of many societies. Social education through "diversity" would exert greater communal meaning by providing a learning environment which would in turn tend to effect a change in the educational process. Once again: "We never educate directly, but indirectly by means of the environment." "[U]nworthy features of the existing environment" would, in this process of change, be eliminated by "[s]election," in "weeding out what is undesirable" but additionally by a "simplifying" and a building to complexity through an understanding of civilization, which is not "remote" nor "invisible"(Dewey, DAE, 22-27).[11] Dewey, unlike many of today's schools, would not allow detrimental influences of the environment to enter the school without screening first for the "undesirable."

The practice of democratic principles would thus be infused into a curriculum in which all might find their place, while the process of education was to arise from an interaction of objects within the individual's environment. The environment, he maintained, works unconsciously; it is "subtle and pervasive." The school would tend to offset the " unconscious" environmental pressures by positive "conscious" instruction. Dewey would emphasize "language," "manners," "morals" in action, "good taste" and "æsthetic appreciation." "The effect of a tawdry, not arranged and over-decorated environment," Dewey wrote, "works for the deterioration of taste, just as meager and barren surroundings starve out the desire for beauty." The "deeper standards of judgments of value are framed by the situations into which a person habitually enters "(Dewey, DAE, 20, 21). [12] It would seem that Dewey had a reasonable vision of school "æsthetic" and "diversity" but would not be able to sustain a serious philosophy of learning with respect to adult direction, which, by orality or print, becomes "comparatively foreign to everyday life" (Dewey, DAE, 22, 23).[13]

Learning, so he maintained, is multidirectional involving a free communicative exchange among teacher and students. "The educative process is the result of meaningful sharing" (Dewey,

DAE, 6).[14] The proper learning and social environment to infuse a "vital impulse" must be met by employing that which appeals to the "interest" of each student. "Interest represents the moving force of objects...in any experience having a purpose" (Dewey, DAE, 152, 153).[15]

It should not be assumed that Dewey was anti-intellectual, only that in its dry form teaching may do more to alienate students than any hard academic lesson material given experientially to the interest of students. Dewey's original understanding of practical instruction has been seriously dated by contemporary technological advances. Experiencing technology, in educational terms in Dewey's day, amounted to the anachronisms of hand sewing, cooking or construction; such examples are pedestrian when compared to the hyper-technological present and an ever-changing innovative modernism of ubiquitous and unstoppable techo-culture. The timeless principle of hands on "manual training" was his unswerving approach to instruction, learning as experience in doing (Dewey, MPC, Article Three and Article Four).[16] Watching a screen would not be acceptable to Dewey for hands-on does not end in abstraction or in interactivity of predetermined outcomes. The child cannot under such circumstance self direct.

Today's classroom technology, ironically, far in advance of anything Dewey could have imagined such as computer simulation and learning-from-a-distance, may have replaced direct experience in the laboratory by substituting eyes-on for the hands-on conception of real life experience. Such technology's might have been considered by Dewey to be little more than abstractions, having no immediate bearing on real life or community, merely individual learning, or pseudo-learning in the fullest sense, and, if license is not taken next, "a mangled fragment, a poor substitute for the living whole from which it is extracted." And yet Dewey considered abstract concepts and ideas unavoidably necessary in purchasing technological or even practical meaning. When for each individual, one experience borrows from another, it is "the only way in which something enlightening can be secured" (Dewey, RIP, 149-151).[17] Community is obviously the linking requirement for individual experience to transfer individual effects. Otherwise it is difficult to adequately resolve the meaning of this apparent contradiction especially when seen in light of the accompanying statement: "Every concrete experience in its totality is unique; it is itself, non-reduplicable" (Dewey, RIP, 150).[18]

This would be true, in its proper interpretation, whether we are concerned with duplication by One or by Others. Perhaps the sharing of the learning as communication, the foundation of communal bonding, is the context in which to properly understand the otherwise non-transferable nature of experiential learning. Technology of his day was a vital part of his pragmatism but began what was to be seen by many as an attempt to turn education into a job training program for many willing as well as reluctant students. Dewey felt that the best place for such hands-on training, if it must be had by the young, was the schools rather than embarking on a Faustian bargain by outsourcing to business and industry, although this did begin to happened before Dewey's death. Dewey expressed that there could be a "danger" in emphasizing specialization directed toward "future pursuits." Dewey saw education finding ends in such special training and limiting educational possibilities. His look to the future even future ends is difficult to resolve with his pragmatism of the present and his understanding of uncertainty (Dewey, DAE, 369).[19]

> Put in concrete terms, there is danger that vocational education will be interpreted in theory and practice as trade education: as a means of securing technical efficiency in specialized future pursuits... Education would then become an instrument of perpetuating unchanged the existing industrial order of society, instead of operating as a means of its transformation (Dewey, DAE, 369).[20]

He talked of "transformation" for progress and change not only for society but also for the individual in communal context. "[E]very person shall be occupied in something which makes the lives of others better worth living, and which accordingly makes the ties which bind persons together more perceptible - which breaks down the barriers of distance between them" (Dewey, DAE, 369).[21]

This vocational education training with which Dewey was concerned had ramifications beyond the student-trainee being locked into a job for which satisfaction or even appropriateness would not reward, but that the mechanical nature of the ultimate job experience could remove that satisfaction of work done and send the individual on a pursuit of monetary ends. Accrual of things may make serial replacement of goods the ultimate occupational purpose in life yet may leave the growth of the individual outside the educative process. Furthermore, the unhealthy stress of material acquisition on individual to individual relationships does not often serve the building of community (Dewey, DAE, 371-374).[22]

Materialism would tend to disrupt interest in individual change. By extension we come to see job training as a habit which for growth of the individual must realistically be replaceable as needed. To grow through habit replacement is the process of gaining knowledge through experience and through "change of conditions," "novelty." Without habit replacement, work becomes mechanical and the individual is mislead to stray from work and become less attentive to any problematic change which might arise and to solutions to any problem (Dewey, DAE, 395).[23]

Dewey's concern for the ongoing education of Americans brought to ground the prospects of the daily life of the worker. The "greatest evil" is that there are people working in jobs that they are not right for, but continue to work for the sole purpose of gaining more money. "While too often the individual has no concern with occupation beyond the monetary return it brings: ...neither men's hearts nor their minds are in their work." Those that rise above other workers, those advantaged in "worldly goods" "over others," "are stimulated to pursuits of indulgence and display; they try to make up for the distance which separates them from others by the impression of force and superior possession and enjoyment which they can make upon others." " It would be quite possible for a narrowly conceived scheme of vocational education to perpetrate this division in a hardened form" (Dewey, DAE, 370, 371).[24]

Dewey's leadership through his influence in words was notably absence regarding the imposition of trade education in the public school. It would seem to have contributed to that travesty of pedagogy the promotion of learning levels which would become code for the classism in modern education: some to leadership and some to labor. A true democracy in education would allow anyone the chance to rise above their station. Each citizen has a limited capacity but no one should be prevented from growing to their fullest. Dewey felt that all persons should enjoy complete freedom of opportunity in learning and in all of life's work. An elitist or working class distinction, a classism, an oligarchy, imposed on the citizenry was not acceptable in any understanding of democracy. Differing paths to educational opportunities and the limited potential for educational advancement was, in Dewey's mind not true to democratic principles clearly defined and implemented (Dewey, DAE, 130-145).[25]

It was not only his concern for a democratic pluralism and freedom of the individual to change that Dewey proposed reconstruction of American public education. A practical education must have access to practically considered sources of educational media. For Dewey the tradition of "textbook" education was meant for preparing the children of the elite, "only one class of people," for a life devoid of practical necessity. It is curious that the ideas of books and facts, which Dewey would limit in the younger students' classroom, may have also been seen as a limitation by external authority. Transmitting facts and vocabulary by rote, as practiced within the curriculum for some and not others, could also be considered to deliver the certifying authority granted to those destined for leadership. The minds for these leaders are exercised, while the hands of the laborers to be are given to bodily service.

It is easily inferred from Dewey's challenge of democratizing the public school that his sanctioning occupational course work in the schools was to allow all students to experience manual training. It would seem that the consideration of individual capacity had left him with the inevitability of the two classes with only a spattering of higher capacities finding their way to the upper class for learning and leadership. Dewey gave a mixed message about education. Yes it was social, this cannot be denied, but it was also academic and here his view on limiting books early in education would push him deeper into the tradesman's camp. He showed a strong disaffection for the broad spread use of books at all levels in the school, and considering that he was a scholar and an author of many books and innumerable articles, he wanted those directed to leadership to experience the hand work of those who might be relegated to labor. Yet Dewey did not seem to recognize the advantage for the future laborer by having been exposed to the studies prescribed for the elite. But while Dewey wanted all to rise as far as they could through education in a democratic America, pluralism, he agonized, was being relegated to a caste existence for a lower class unable to count on an education and an upper class which would be allowed to escape from the drudgery of labor.

Selfish youth would not grow into a population which would permit educational democracy. Yet by holding low expectations for these children while entertaining the remote possibility that some of their numbers might find a leg up through education to a higher station in life, Dewey armed only with a method and not a detailed plan, idealistically wishful that some of these children would succeed in procuring a better education and thereby a potential position in leadership, and by keeping with the optimistic view of individual capacities to learn, was convinced that his hope for education and true democracy were attainable in American society. Each child would, however, do what he or she could do, by the estimation of abstract progressive education metrics probably resulting in the pigeon-holing of students into a determinate future, categorized and contained. Dewey was willing to acknowledge in his pedagogy the authority of the individual, free of coercion. The student-individual then and since has been placed clearly at the epicenter of education living out freedom whether destined to labor or to the more mundane life of relative leisure. Each student was to find his or her way by experimentation.

He hoped that the child through a true democratic education would become an element of the true democratic school. Dewey's understanding of the child did not involve human nature as traditionally held, that is, a fixed behavioral innateness. The child would grow and adapt, he believed, and he had optimistic expectations that the child would find a comfortable fit within the community. Through the process of social growth within one or more associative groups, Dewey felt that individual behavior within the group would ultimately result in most falling into acceptable limits of support for group purpose. This he was sure would be possible without the imposition of coercive enforcement. He held as axiomatic that "authority and freedom do live in a happy and fruitful marriage" (Hook, JD, 152).[26]

Without experimental evidence to support such marital co-existence, Dewey set in place an assumption that has not only come true in practice but has become one of modern public education's mayor problems. The authority for the school does not reside in the people that man the school. A remote administration does not and cannot know the particular problems that it faces, only the school staff knows. The lack of definitive authority for the school is also the result of the students who believe that they have personal rights that trump those of the school. This is the legacy of an indefinite authority. As someone suggested, it was more than the fact that Dewey had said little about how this "marriage" was to realistically occur, since he had ignored detailed descriptions. For someone who was reservedly skeptical about the fixed outcome of any process, as a function of the uncertainty of knowing, Dewey did little to show the unity of the continuum of individualism and the group. The child in time would forsake the selfishness of childhood and become a mature community member. This meliorist position would not prove to work on student-individuals finding their own way into the group anymore than societal groups finding aberrant individualism being ultimately and dependably absorbed into society and assuming group purpose.

Education, Dewey tells us is a "reorganization of experience which adds to the meaning of experience, and which increases the ability to direct the course of subsequent experience." In this process of experience one may "intend consequences instead of just letting them happen..." (Dewey, DAE, 90).[27] Controlling the environment was essential to Dewey's schema of instruction. Education is a response to the environment: as surroundings and situations change, then one, we must hope, will appropriately responds to those changes. The process of "growth" would thus be invoked through the changes. "In directing the activities of the young, society determines its own future in determining that of the young." Society depends on our "directing the activities of the young." But controlled guidance is required, since the "primary condition of growth is immaturity," which Dewey saw as "positive," "a power," "and by potentiality potency, [and] force" (Dewey, DAE, 49).[28]

In effect we are to allow the young to change the environment with the result that the young infect society with "immaturity." This may explain why the student-individualist have taken over much, even most of the school's authority. But even Dewey felt that the child needed more controlling guidance than the child-centered proponents were able to assign, but agreed that the student was the soft wax on which to write life's foundational experiences. Dewey's understanding of learning methodology is best visited in application. The students were to have opinions about the subject material and express those opinions. But a history of educational understanding was misguiding public schools. Dewey looked to Locke's woeful attempt to fill the empty mind as the expressed intent of the schools, to train the mind to think by rote and repetition. This seemed to Dewey only a way to write on the wax but not to organize and find relationships among the ideas which could become the actions of life-changing experience. Dewey saw in Locke's abstraction of knowledge a duality, the mind working without the body, a passive exercise not engaging the whole student (Dewey, DAE, 71-80).[29]

The optimism of early twentieth century America was not lost on Dewey, but in the final analysis of his understanding of democratic education there must be a fair appraisal of his educational principles. Any claim that this was a school lacking hard academic curricula, however, is not well founded for academics had a hands in action as a foundation. Dewey hoped that passive learning would eventually be replaced by learning activities in which hands-on methods would give life to the school.

And yet to Dewey the failure to educate was not that there was just head knowledge, facts, in the curriculum, but that there was to be found a failed commitment to the community. To see a child educated to selfishness was to allow a student-individual to disregard the greater good of the school community. Coercion was not a possibility to control the individual, any Hobbesian "coercive" control to alleviate fear within the school would not be acceptable to Dewey since individual freedom could be compromised by forcing group authority. If only in theory, Rousseau's Emile would not be permitted to run free in school halls but controlled in the name of protecting the rights and safety of others in the school. Education would have to find a median position not defined by solipsism or by the constraints of coercion which would allow neither usurpation of student or student-individualist freedom nor the free practice of student-individualistic license. Consideration of the rights of all students, the potential for danger for the school community has become a critical concern to the safety of the modern public school.

Dewey speaking from the past correctly represents the remote administration's scapegoating, throwing the responsibility for school failure on the backs of teachers, when the culture has taken over by incursions against school administration. Dewey would invoke a softer form of empiricism in which the process was merely emphasized rather than being hoisted up on the altar of information. The answers were to be always forthcoming but the attendance to the process spoke to useful answers to questions raised everyday. In shifting the emphasis from the competitive to the cooperative, Dewey thought that all men could be raised to higher levels of life easing the sole appeal to individualism. The Many so controlled could find education's goal of cooperation and realize community within the school and without.

Like the history of reform ideas from colonial American times it could be maintained that neither success nor failure could be judged given the unattained true democratic requisite and the inability to sustain the course of reform. It is on this point also that Dewey's ideas could never be empirically rebuked, and it is the reason, assuming evidence of failed ideas would challenge theory and practice, that his magically socializing concept of education continues to haunt the public school. Dewey would guard himself and his ideas from empirical failure by his unreserved caution that only by true freedom within a truly democratic society would such a society be able to produce a truly democratic educational program (Dewey, DAE, 106).[30]

The progressive education movement from the late nineteenth century continues to assert its ideas even in todays public schools. Much of it was promoted as a Dewey-inspired educational reform while often moving away from his ideas. The 1918 publication of the *Cardinal Principles of Education,* a government framework for streamlining education for college-bound and labor-bound students in public schools, was an attempt to set students on the most appropriate path to a life of meaningful work in response to the demands that industrialization was making on American labor and democracy (Gov. pub.,1918).[31] Before the war Dewey was "sympathetic" to "socialism" or better Social Democracy which was "reformist in character," but after the war he turned to Progressivism which avoided the ideas of a "great apocalypse," and he never embraced Marxism which advocated violence to correct social problems or "[a]narchism" advancing the "social pathology" of the One (Hook, JD, 162, 163).[32] He did believe in "economic organization" by "socialization of the basic instruments of production...so that the liberty of individuals" "might" be supported although such dichotomous beliefs suggest that both individual freedom and the betterment of society can be accomplished through "socialization." (Hook, JD, 157, also the section on "The Good Society").[33]

Dewey felt that the progressive education movement would serve this end and would be "continuous" with the "tradition" already in place (Hook, JD, 163).[34] But even Dewey did not want to toss out the baby with the bath water, however, he believed the progressive trend would denigrate the past, tradition, while only experiencing the present and looking to the future. He wrote:

> It would be difficult to estimate the harm that has resulted because the liberal and progressive movement of the eighteenth and early nineteenth centuries had no method of intellectual articulation commensurate with its practical aspirations. Its heart was in the right place. It was humane and social in intention. But it had no theoretical instrumentalities of constructive power. Its head was sadly deficient ...Too often the logical import of its professed doctrines was almost antisocial in their atomistic individualism, antihuman in devotion to brute sensation.This deficiency played into the hands of

> the reactionary and obscurantists (Dewey, RIP, 100,101).[35]

He referred to these men as "professional philosophers" who found "appeal" in transcendence, dogma and lack of "experimental verification" (Dewey, RIP, 100,101).[36] This must all be weighed against the loose position with which Dewey saw "both the past and present," since for Dewey the lessons of the past were of value as long as they might be extracted for benefit in the present.

Progressives made the child elemental; Dewey saw the child as a barometer of community. Schools are conformed to motives far removed from original educational purpose. Students and teachers are numbers. Progressive education not only brought occupational training programs to the schools but the exactitude of micromanaging each student's progress often amounting to little more than a reductionist paper trail. Incursions into education by the hyper-emphasis on documented instruction and objective exit testing has made the departments and boards of education the ultimate providers of easily managed curricular sanctions. Even in the child-centered progressive classrooms, as Dewey decried the pedagogical context of educational instruction of many of the Progressive schools, he pointed to lackadaisical and *ad libitum* instruction without intellectual caring, while allowing student-individualism to shamelessly call the shots in the classroom.

Present concern should be that over seven decades later a failed progressive format for education is being pawned off on the American public and compromising the education of public school children without there being an effective challenge raised to failed results. Dewey recognized the failure. The progressive goal of integrating labor and leadership education in the school has failed and the message has been distorted from educating all students as a social function of schools to educating each student and bringing the focus on the individual student while not delivering the exemplary education that all children should be afforded.

Unfortunately today as in Dewey's time the child-savers are still pandering to childish attitudes both in the schools and in the larger culture. Many communitarians want the child to be educated without seemingly wanting or being able to be given direction and organization skills which children need for the protection of their legislated right to receive an education and move on to responsible citizenship. The cultural expectation for rights protection has been that the student will be allowed personal extremist behavior while less concerned about the child receiving a superior education. Instead the guarantee of an education has become merely the meeting of minimal academic standards. Responsibility for action needs to be focused squarely on the student by the school for learning and discipline. Pluralism should recognize and address collective differences in order to insure the progress of all student's self-improvement. Dewey's goal of a true democratic school should be realized.

Chapter 9
Unity

> Philosophy is...the last and highest term in pure contemplation. Whatever may be said for any other kind of knowledge, philosophy is self-enclosed.
>
> - John Dewey, *Reconstruction in Philosophy*[1]

Dewey drew a flexible philosophical framework for his pragmatism. He saw philosophy not as dichotomous or dualistic as did Plato and Descartes. The history of philosophy, as Hook tells us of Dewey's view, has accredited truth using "arbitrary definitions of philosophy" "ruling one another beyond the pale with arbitrary definitions of what philosophy is" still with "so little agreement as to what these truths are." "What is called truth is only that which hides intentions and has become "but a name for the elaboration of personal prejudices masquerading as impersonal axioms." (Hook, JD, 28, 29).[2] Life is unified. Hegel had shown Dewey that duality misrepresents the unity that pervades life (Hook, JD, 13).[3]

Arming an inherited pragmatism with residuals of Kant and Hegel, Dewey attempted a unique reconstruction of philosophy for a unified daily life.The unifying framework would be a process for living everyday, making every decision and carrying out every activity. Dewey would propose a unification of philosophy which relied on intelligent decision making in real time for guiding action. The range of separation and disunity in philosophy, even conflict, was seen as unacceptable in a true democracy supportive of daily life. Of the dualities which Dewey addressed were some of the following: body and mind, discipline and interest, duty and interest, ends and means, experience and knowledge, habit and knowledge, humanism and naturalism, individualism and the world, individualism and institutionalism, intellectualism and practical studies, method and subject matter, nature and nurture, objective knowledge and subjective knowledge, practical and theoretical, thinking and experience as well as doing and knowing. Although this is not a complete list by any means it does suggest a preponderance of issues among disparate domains infused with rationalism and experimentalism.

Such dichotomous pairings would be subjected by Dewey to a method of inquiry, the methodical process taken from science, which would show unification in the real world. Whenever questions are asked the trustworthiness of truth is scrutinized and "evaluations are made." Seeing that all problems arise in the world, Dewey would find worldly answers to unification of apparently antithetical issues. Why not ask questions from all fields of inquiry in the same way, as one would pursue all question in the world? (Hook, JD, 41, 42).[4] Hook explains.

> Long before the logical empiricists, Dewey had shown that most of the traditional problems of philosophy were pseudo problems, i.e., they could not be solved even in their own terms... Dewey went on to inquire what the genuine conflicts were which lay at the bottom of fruitless verbal disputes (Hook, JD, 44)[5]

And yet the resolution of opposition does not always come without turmoil or even violence in real life situations.

Dewey saw no point in "epistemological controversies," say, "over the priority of sensation or reason, subject or object," Resolution of problems involving science and morals could serve to reduce one to another as an ever renewed struggle between two attitudes contending for exclusive mastery over social life - radical and progressive on the one hand, the conservative and traditional on the other." He was convinced that understanding could be achieved among divergent areas of inquiry among "contending parties" by utilizing a scientific approach to resolution. Surely in "problems of social change" both "sensation and reason" must be entertained (Hook, JD, 44, 45).[6] So science and morals, both concerns of daily life, could be addressed in the same manner (Hook, JD, 42).[7]

Dewey felt that duality would in effect compromise real-world experience. Sidney Hook comments that philosophical epistemology and the "social disciplines" have had less success than even religion in finding unity. He attributed this to the failure of philosophy to know what "constitutes" philosophy's "subject matter." Hook claimed that Dewey's "scope of intellectual interests is so comprehensive" that his system of thought, organizes and "expresses a philosophy of life" "in the grand tradition." It is in this sense of systematic methodology, of united considerations of all life and living, that Dewey fashioned his philosophic unity (Hook, 27).[8]

One of Dewey's common themes was the holism of rationalism and action. The unification of the body's actions and the mind's thoughts does not permit dualism. This "makes a concrete difference to the world." The ability to create is driven by plans, or ideas which have meaning, as they are laid to "solve a problem" (Hook, JD, 60, 61).[9] Mind and body put to pragmatic action experientially defeat the Cartesian fallacy of body and mind separation. Rationalism could not justify action in the physical world but depended on its codependent interaction of the brain and body. Hands and plans working together, and to this end Dewey was convinced, activity would meet the demands of a modern democratic culture. The body-mind separation is also associated with "outward" and "inward", "knowing and doing," "theory and practice," mind as an "end" and body as a "means" to that end. Most deal with the active and the passive. Although thinking is an internal and passive process, Dewey counseled that the idea is the evidence of the external thing. To have the idea is to put it into physical terms and descriptions. The inner and outer worlds, emotion and intellect respectively, look in different directions. One to the outer world from which we gain our understanding and the other, emotion, to the inner world of the personal (Dewey, DAE, 391).[10]

Active learning and thought can not find separate meaning from the physical world no more than body and mind. The union of knowing and doing would be anchored in resultant activity. Kant attempted to unify by universals and failed with each new action by One being the hoped for good of all, but the empirical world changes, situation and environment change, thus changing both the objective and the moral world. This is not unity. Unity must come from reasonable action and understanding through experience.

Kantian rationalism does not work, Dewey maintained. "The object thought of and the outcome never agree" (Dewey, HNC, 252).[11]

Thought here is an antecedent plan to action. Or put another way: that which is in good confidence, which is willed for all, categorically willed, is not necessarily commensurate with the outcome of active experience among objects. Dewey claimed "the intrinsic continuity of ends and means" and "the essential unity of method and subject matter" united broadly in "the material of existence." By "intelligence" "one would perceive and test the appropriateness of behavior. " not in thought/act separation but in cooperative unity (Dewey, DAE, 377).[12]

Inseparability of agents and actions is not possible within Dewey's unification. Events in experience are incapable of being reduced to actions separate from the actors. Dewey explained that when you eat you do not separate the food from the activity of eating; the act of eating is destroyed in concept without the unity of both the food and the one eating being inseparably linked (Dewey, DAE, 195).[13] Dewey saw man as part of nature working to make a better world amongst a "contingent and precarious nature of existence...We live in a world which is an impressive and irresistible mixture of sufficiencies, tight completeness, or, recurrences which make possible prediction and control, and singularities, ambiguities, uncertain possibilities, processes going on to consequences as yet indeterminate" (Hook, JD, 216).[14]

Dewey's understanding of integrated epistemology flows from a holism which includes the thing known and the knower. The thing known is never known apart from the one that knows that thing. There is a sense in which knowing may be mental or internal, yet the idea of internalized knowledge carries with it the requirement that the external must exist and must be in the thought process itself (Dewey, DAE, 390).[15]

Knowing is singular, joining internal and external domains. It is on this internalization of the physical world that Dewey advocated extensive hands-on-learning theory. Thoughts disconnected from their objects are but dreams, each is in truth mutually dependent on the other. No less inseparable are our thoughts, whether capable of being predictive of resultant activities and our doing. It would seem that education has suffered historically at the hands of remoteness creating disunity as theory bearing no intended remediation. History, or reflection, tends to "distinguish between our own attitude and the objects toward which we sustain the attitude." "When a man is eating, he is eating food." We incorporate into every experience " a single continuous interaction of a great diversity (literally countless in number) of energies" (Dewey, DAE, 195-219).[16]

The complexity of the union of man and nature are agreed to by man's experience in the physical world. Union is firm if not evolutionary, changeable and uncertain.

> In truth, experience knows no division between human concerns and a purely mechanical physical world. Man's home is nature; his purposes and aims are dependent for execution upon natural conditions...This philosophy is vouched for by the doctrine of biological development which shows that man is continuous with nature, not an alien entering her processes from without (Dewey, DAE, 333).[17]

But knowing and doing must find their union through an ongoing, changing understanding of immediate requirements. "Unity is something sought; split, division is something given, at hand." Epistemology and Morality must be sought in "a normal development of a life process" (Dewey, HNC, 185).[18] Conduct and epistemology brought together may be united by knowing since both realms are of interest and occur in the natural world (Dewey, HNC, 182-185).[19] The result is unity as both "connect the theory of knowledge with an empirically verifiable theory of behavior" which in turn will produce a unity of understanding (Dewey, HNC, 183).[20] But a more basic problem of union loomed in consideration of culture and society. What of the groups which hold incompatible understandings ?

"The strife of systems [of institutions and of concrete problems] appears as a manifestation of the strife of cultures, of the struggle of different groups within the same culture, and of visions born of personal differences within groups (Hook, JD, 30-35).[21] Hook writes that Dewey believed that "the unity of the human being'" is to be found in "interpersonal relationships which are found in the realms of the social." A true democracy, Dewey believed, could only be established when the dualism of leadership and labor were no more, when each individual could move freely in a truly united democratic society, where the individual of membership had no limiting rank (Hook, JD, 118).[22] Concessions by group member's on "personal differences" may strain this cohesiveness, for the individual and the community are often found to be indefatigably opposite as forces in modern culture. But Dewey's claims of pragmatic solutions in resolution of duality often looks longingly, expectantly, to the future and, therefore, could not on a timely basis meet the critical requirement of pragmatic scrutiny, the present.

For experience may be empirically undertaken and unification may only be argued authoritatively and objectively in the present. The ideal that duality of the extreme individual and the group will find social convergence through melioristic forces is no more than a blind hope and is indefensible in keeping with Dewey's requirement of presentism. The transcendence from present time and the rationalistic idealism of hope for the convergence of group membership, is romantic, transcendental of the present. Merely given the name pragmatism, hosting tolerance for the present and a loose dependence on individual response is not enough to dethrone transcendence for meliorable impulses which look longingly toward a common purpose. Even in reflection, reaching back would be dispatched since it would also deteriorate unity out of time and "inevitably distinguish between our own attitude and the objects toward which we sustain the attitude" (Dewey, DAE, 195).[23] On this Dewey had extra-experiential expectations for one phase of attitudinal unification or "synthesis." "We are striving to unify our responses, to achieve a consistent environment which will restore unity of conduct" (Dewey, HNC, 183).[24]

It is for Dewey a "paradox and mystery of the theory of knowledge" that there is an ongoing expectation of knowledge within the experiential nature of " unity and difference." Dewey's "paradox" would give rise to a knowable unity when the "theory of knowledge" became "connected" with an empirically verifiable "theory of behavior." Behavioral response when unified will "achieve a consistent environment which will restore unity of conduct." Looking to outcomes is "ideal." (Dewey, HNC, 183). [25]

Expectation in phase or full portion is rationalistic, short of practice, transcendent in this respect, religion or transcendence, must be seen as unacceptable within Dewey's proclaimed pragmatic unity. Hook describes religion as: "the unification of the self through allegiance to inclusive ideal ends which imagination presents to us and to which the human will responds as worthy of controlling our desires and choices," that is "the unity of all ideal ends." Dewey only admits to ideals of "intelligence and democracy." Instead of religion unifying only "faith ... that makes us sensitive to the common needs of our common lot and gives us the courage to strive continuously not only for our own betterment but for that of our fellowmen" can unite. Man must become united with the Many and not under the idealism of religion which is "inclusive" and controls (Hook, JD, 219, 220).[26] The unity of society must come from outside of any religious, supernatural, or non-organic banner. Dewey saw unity in human interaction as a hoped for possibility consistent with the pervasive optimism of the young country, all be it, not in line with his idea of presentism and the immediacy of process. Dewey was to define unity as synonymous with "synthesis" whereby individuals converge in "responses, to achieve a consistent environment." This process of cooperation in "striving to unity" in the "environment" "will" "restore unity of conduct" (Dewey, HNC, 183).[27] Pragmatism suffers on this point in its dependence on prognostication rather than on the living data of experimentalism. The environment becomes Hegelian as elements within the environment struggle to find a dialectical equilibrium.

What would be considered "alien" by Dewey would be any influence which would have its binding based on a non-earthly unity, a metaphysical, unity. The present, the immediate theater of experience, could not be punctuated by a separation of the present and a remote future, for the separateness of the metaphysical took away progress "requiring the cooperation of organism and environment as the "ground as well as the legs" in "[w]alking." Dewey would consider "alien" any actions which would take the individual out of the pursuit of earthly unity. The removal of metaphysical ideas to a unified understanding of all ideas and events without categorical assignment, using methodology of common inquiry, allowed Dewey to view all daily considerations with singularity (Hook, JD, 14-16).[28] There were no cultural and educational distinctions, no cognitive and behavioral issues, for instance, only one way to understand the whole of the world in unity which would be attained through a pragmatic methodology of inquiry that best served the individual and the entire membership's interest enabling the immediate answer to all inquiry and immediate understanding. Time found its unity in a communal present, one given to change with event and environment. Unity in a perpetual alteration of life and perspective. Unity with Dewey stands low against the raging methodology of inquiry and change when unity as universality is considered, the so-called "intrinsic goods." "So-called intrinsic goods, whether religious or esthetic, are divorced from those interests of daily life which because of their constancy and urgency form the preoccupation of the great mass" (Dewey, RIP, 171).[29]

It was in the unity of many issues of duality that he based his theory of educational practice. Dewey offered a way of unifying all aspects of classroom experience into one methodological approach which addressed the two major classroom concerns, learning and behavior, or "knowledge" and "moral growth." Usually separated in theory, "knowledge from activity," Dewey found unity in extending beyond the classroom the goal of learning to overcome in an educational scheme where learning is the accompaniment of continuous activities or

> occupations which have a social aim and utilize the materials of typical social situations. For under such conditions, the school becomes itself a form of social life, a miniature community and one in close interaction with other modes of associated experience beyond school walls. All education which develops power to share effectively in social life is moral... Interest in learning from all the contacts of life is the essential moral interest (Dewey, DAE, 418).[30]

"[T]he unity of the human being" depends on "the quality of interpersonal relationships which are found in the realm of the social" (Hook, JD, 118).[31]

Education was united through a "social continuity" (Dewey, DAE, 29).[32] The unity of the larger society was seen as an educational process in which the constant reweaving of the social fabric could sustain the unified community. "Society is conceived as one by its very nature." Yet denoted as the "de jure," official, and the "de facto," in reality, community is often seen as "ambiguous." The diversity of membership in a group or memberships in multiple overlapping or separate groupings must permit equal representation, "a plurality of societies, good and bad." Dewey ends up sanctioning groups in broad strokes.

> Society is one word but many things...Men band together in a criminal conspiracy, business aggregations that prey upon the public while serving it, political machines held together by the interest of plunder are included. If it is said that such organization are not societies because they do not meet the ideal requirements of the notion of society, the answer, in part, is that the conception of society is then made so "ideal" as to be of no use, having no reference to facts; and in part, that each of these organizations, no matter how opposed to the interests of other groups, has something of the praiseworthy qualities of "Society" which hold it together. There is honor among thieves, and a band of robbers has a common interest as respects its members. Gangs are marked by fraternal feeling, and narrow cliques by intense loyalty to their own codes. Family life may be marked by exclusiveness, suspicion, and jealousy as to those without, and yet be a model of amity and mutual aid within (Dewey, DAE, 94,95).[33]

Groups are seen as societies, to not consider society in the smaller context. In the larger context, isolation of individuals within the authority of the group would prevent the development of members by failure to inter-activate alliances across groups and societies.

An "ideal society" can only be established through rationalism. We must test our productive thoughts against inseparable existing society, practiced society. Dewey, citing Plato, defines the "slave as one who accepts from another the purposes which control his conduct." It is not accepting the general standard that promotes the unity of collectivism and society. In "isolation" is made "rigidity and formal institutionalizing of life, for static and selfish ideals within the group." Dewey seems to give the authority to the One. "The peculiarity of truly human life is that man has to create himself by his own voluntary efforts; he has to make himself a truly moral, rational, and free being" (Dewey, DAE, 94-99,102-104).[34] Dewey thought that the Platonic view that each person could be pigeon-holed was a failure to see "that each individual constitutes his own class, there could be no recognition of the infinite diversity of active tendencies and combinations of tendencies of which an individual is capable" (Dewey, DAE, 94-99,102-104).[35]

In the physical world man is not remote; man lives in a physical world, and is "continuous with nature." Lessons learned in the physical world are not just math or science but all subjects are at least overlapping on their margins. All knowledge is interrelated (Dewey, DAE, 333, 334).[36] There is a "close interdependence" of all subject matter." Learning is a process of hybridization much like multiple group associations may be interrelated through common members. Learning is multifaceted and united. "It [education] should aim not at keeping science as a study of nature apart from literature as a record of human interests, but at cross-fertilizing both the natural sciences and the various human disciplines such as history, literature, economics, and politics" (Dewey, DAE, 334).[37]

Apart from the various resolutions of duality, one stands out as an ignominious gall on Dewey's philosophy in that the individual and the group could not be seen as separate. Was the individual one with the collective, if she did not submit to it purpose? Dewey never stopped referring to those individuals who took an extreme position toward the group by holding up self over the good of the Many. The extremist was merely a physical element within the group that did not seem to find its purposeful membership in a group but subsisted in inconsolable solipsism.

Dewey did not believed that the individual and the community were to be considered as separate issues. The reality was that the extreme or radical individualist was a dualistic element which could not be exorcized from group association nor from Dewey's thoughts and was to becomes an Achilles heal of Dewey's communitarian pragmatism. Dewey looked idealistically to the reclamation of the extreme egoist in an ongoing evolutionary process of repatriation. The group would possibly absorb extremist individuals into the council of the Many. Dewey's pervasive recognition throughout his writings of this cut-and-run individualism is an indication that such individuals could find a comfortable oneness with the Many. Dewey refocused or doubtfully shifted to the tending of ourselves and held out for self-realization and the creative process of individual recreation.

> Let us perfect ourselves within, and in due season changes in society will come of themselves is the teaching...But when selfhood is perceived to be an active process it is also seen that social modifications are the only means of the creation of changed personalities (Dewey, RIP, 96).[38]

Dewey never explained how direct methodology would bring the errant into unity. Those "changed personalities" must result from "social modification" resulting from intelligent activity and a change in social environments.

> The intellectual variation of the individual in observation, imagination, judgment, and invention are simply the agencies of social conservation...When the social quality of mental operations is denied, it becomes a problem to find connections which will unite an individual with his fellows (Dewey, DAE, 347).[39]

Freedom may be found among individuals in society where diversity and change are permitted.

> A progressive society counts individual variations as precious since it finds in them the means of its own growth.

> Hence a democratic society must, in consistency with its ideal, allow for intellectual freedom and the play of diverse gifts and interests in its educational measures (Dewey, DAE, 357).[40]

Dewey's solution to this dilemma was to promote inclusion thus ultimately avoiding extreme and selfish individualism in confrontation. Give the group the freedom to join into community purpose with individuals having overwhelmingly self-centered goals and focus and given freedom to be their own individuals, unrestrained, then membership would through daily contact work to change egoistic members who would recognize the failure of exclusive self-interest. Former recalcitrants may then seek assimilation to the group and its purpose. But what Dewey may have seen as mere paradox of unity, of purpose, is the crux of tension that plagues society in general and contemporary public education as well. Without disciplinary intervention, the extreme individual is unlikely to move to communal union but maintain a radical view of changed group purpose. Constraints to insure this tact would be relentlessly vilified by Dewey who denied coercion as policy since it impinged on individual freedom. Remember that Dewey had proposed that "control" would be the result of both individual self-restraint in combination with that of the process of extreme individual reclamation which must be left to the nebulous evolution of the group and its purpose.

The Unity of morality and knowledge are both tested on this point. Dewey maintains an idealistic view of individualism in which One, adrift from the group purpose, may return without coercive intervention. This is based on an irrevocable fact: that one who knows will do. This is an impossible and unreliable judgment based on the reality of individual violent acts in society and of public school disruptions. The justification for postmoderns is that if a person acts in an immoral way, on individual judgment, then the problem is the forsaking of, using Dewey's term, "intelligence." Inextricably linked in a societal machine, the unity of action moves to properly understand culture as its laboratory, as the school bares the weight for society. Dewey writes that "the work of intelligence" is in the "revising and readjusting habits [of behavior] even the best of good habits, [which] can never be foregone." Intelligence is ongoing and marks a moral process in which time is "the essence of the moral struggle." The ability to understand and do are inextricably linked. Intelligence is linked with behavior and its progress (Dewey, HNC, 51, 96, 97).[41] Those that hold to a fixed morality prevent the application of knowledge being applied to gain advantage for the elevation of the group. Working together as one simple machine, epistemology and morality, unite us in thought and deed. Dewey's understanding without definitive methodology removes this duality from theory and places it in the center of daily life, left to the existentialist, the One, to authenticate himself in knowledge and moral judgment.

Having given the goals of daily life over to theory, Dewey ushered in precursors to existential and postmodern theory. Dewey could not shake the idea that the young had the right to academic and civil freedom which was in his time already amending the philosophic soil of America. His contribution of order, form and methodology in education has proved of great value as well as his commitment to collective learning modes, but the vagueness of rightful boundaries of authority in theory ironically had no dependable, practical application in the real school. From the Dewey School to the progressive school movement, historically his ideas have stirred up educational issues drawing on German idealist educators and American-grown transcendentalists. Dewey's pragmatism has come to support a view that all that may be considered educational or societal building must unify, and, yet, averaging goals and behaviors has had disastrous results in society and in the school. The enlightened science of knowledge and morality has been given by Dewey to the individual through experience and now in the twenty-first century there is a need and a search for a workable authority. If by experience the One is given the right to choose authority, the group will be at most secondarily considered.

Perhaps a unity of ideas brings us to the prescience of latter philosophical movements of the twentieth century. Dewey's emphasis on experience and uncertainty presaged the appearance of two major philosophical movements of twentieth century. Existentialism arose as a European phenomenon but Dewey had previously claimed certification of the individual to an ongoing self-defining experience predating the existentialists through his general views on the reliability of thought. Postmodern philosophy released the individual to find an undisputed authority for which others could not reliably question. To release the individual to a self-defining existence where ultimate authority inheres, is the modern formula for lawlessness and failed schools.

Dewey led American public education into modernity under the influence of German idealism, a limited absorption of transcendentalism, Kantian and Hegelian carry-overs, uncertainty, the primacy of experience and the hope that America may one day in intelligent action install true pluralism and equality of education for America's young. He also organized and formalized lessons and gave the modern teacher a group as well as an individual pedagogy. But the duality of education has not been defeated. Some are exposed to rigorous learning and some are exempt. Some are given the opportunity to become intellectually piqued while others are not and are to find only a life in labor without opportunity to knowledgeably decide on a life path. Educating beyond material ends has all but been labelled a traditional view of learning. Yet maximizing education for all students could enable more through academics to find a better future, a better job and a better understanding of the world in which each must navigate. The defeatists claiming that some just cannot learn is no justification for bringing educational judgment on even one child, certainly more than those that are of diminished capacity, for a life of relative drudger and unemployment in bad times. Give a child a sound, exemplary education and the resultant adult may be able to better cope with vocation and all of life's thought provoking challenges. Dedication to a unity of mind and body must direct an equal education for all children and a guarantee for all citizens.

It is not possible to summarily discount all of Dewey's ideas without finding some contributions useful. Community is a natural human affiliation that cannot be denied in principle nor ignored in practice. Certainly the school must provide order and equality in its dual roll of instructing and civilizing the young. Dewey's epistemology has had a tragic effect on Western society as a way to avoid certain obvious truths and responsibility, but, at the same time, his application to instruction, although light on fact-based content qua fact, provides a much more educative and open arena for learning more broadly. This stands in contrast, an ironic turn, when the new objective testing standards are considered. The latter being narrow and un-educative and tending to squeeze out the opportunity for considering concepts in learning, for the student should be able in writing to justify an understanding beyond but using the factual knowledge obtained from a deep study. The impact of Dewey's understanding of morality in society and on the school, however, cannot be justified, if for no other reason, than the loss of concern for others. The Individual is becoming only self-seen and self-justified in all that he or she does.

Conclusion

Both in concert and in conflict, Dewey was influenced by more than a home-spun pragmatism, rather he found inseparable influence in the romantic and transcendental hopefulness of America. Decades before Dewey was to begin finalizing his philosophical version of pragmatism, American education was feeling the influence of romanticism, an absorbed idealism which like pragmatism would also bring optimism to an expanding American frontier as a wave of pioneering zeal which would advance individual self-reliance and embolden a nation's confidence. The deism of influential founding fathers drew from an Enlightenment era as from John Locke who would reckon man set adrift, left alone, responsible to help himself. Certainly Dewey had seen the self-resolve and such self-dependence in the nurturing community of his youth. Such determination must surely have grown and infused his understanding or compromised it. The idea that individuals would bend to the wishes of the group is wishful and a group that is constituted in that manner must suffer unity.

An argument for authority to be awarded either the One or the Many might go something like this. The organizational integrity of the group, its meaning and purpose, depends on at least deferral to group purpose. A cohesive group must be identifiable through its membership, of which each member must elevate group purpose above that of the primacy of individual membership, or otherwise lower action in pursuit of core resolve. Both the One and the Many must find a felicitous resolution of wants and needs in order for there to be a consensus of practical purpose and dedication to that purpose. Dewey's central fallacy is that in practice, a workable unified purpose must garner influence and support of at least a critical number of united members or factions, while failing to find this support may result in friction which could derail or dilute or destroy the purpose of the group without an evolving understanding induced by errant influences within the group. A workable empiricism requires a confluence of directed actions and at least passive judgments for the evolving benefit of the collective purpose. Passivity has given Dewey's ideas a break in their inculcation of the modern American mind and body.

Dewey's fallacy or bind involves the unification of individuals into and through an understanding of communal daily experience. The failing of his philosophy is in allowing autonomous freedom for the individual, awarded out of fear of oppression, yet unrestricted by practical example, and the group who must without coercion bring the extreme individualist into compliance or wait out the confluence of the One into the Many unified in body and mind. With this acquiescing or winning-over of the One must be assumed a self-balancing and refocused representation of the individual leaving primary concerns of self to find dedicative purpose in membership.

It is by non-coercive, auto-balancing adherence to group purpose that the group or community will not be compromised and sullied. Even if evolution of makeup and purpose are given the One must not destroy in unification with the group a positive influence of assimilation. One must see community in the idealism of faithful belief that its collective impact will redirect the individual from individual parochialism and selfishness to a dedication to the good of the group. Society too often suffers from lawless separatism and very little hope and time repairs this division. Teachers and local administrators have experienced the effects of such fallacious practice in school operations, awaiting the student-individual to join with the educational program of the school. Recidivism marks the failure of the polis to rehabilitate the criminal for society. Such optimism, such idealistic hopefulness, has not been seen come to fruition to any noticeable extent in the classroom, but has typically resulted in continued rebellion, as in the larger society, when rebellion very often continues to pursue its course. Dewey would feel the bind as he would come to see the individual and the group as ultimately and usually separable. When conflicts arise, marrying agencies and removing the bind temporarily from consideration, a Darwinian understanding of social progress may be realized in examples of concomitant consequences of coercion, death and enslavement.

Authority is now under the temporal hold of empiricism. The authority of individual experience challenges the rules of society.

Dewey's influence, on this point, is particularly damaging to the school culture in the vagueness and the extent to which it inadvertently challenges the authority of learning and student self-discipline versus rights. Reflecting on student-individual actions and not being able to establish salient authority for making judgments and for assigning consequences to undesirable actions, disciplinary action invoked by school officials becomes difficult to justify and often impractical when attempting enforcement. Evidence of disciplinary infractions in the school must be found inconclusive against the claims of any individual accused of misbehavior, since the individual accused is the only one, according to Dewey, who may have primary authority in the event. This has been made real to us in court cases where defendants have managed to walk on the weight of supposed individual rights which were allowed to trump the proof of accusation. Even the victim claiming wrong doing may not override the claim of rights leaving neutralized evidence to be dismissed in judgment. Now no one has authoritative perspective of the event. Yet another witness could support either side but the opposition view makes a valid challenge to the majority opinion.

All narratives are doubtful, if not in the immediate dispute, then in time even the arguments of all sides could wane in authority. For as we have learned of Dewey's rigid requirement for knowing authoritatively, this requires immediate primary agency and with time still is subject to revaluation. Individual experience is authoritative, albeit temporal, yet as authoritative as that of any accusing local school staffer in behavioral disputes. Hard evidence does not meet Dewey's requirement of primary agency and is not acceptable even if closely observed and honestly judged, without bias, and only in real time first-hand can experience be known. The axiology of experience may even seem to reside in its impermanence.

Into the school and the nation was to creep the worth of the individual as the experiential authority. Optimistic understanding of the individual was to linger in modern progressive education, even overly asserted in the perennial wakes of failure and unreality. Rousseau had placed innocence in the heart of the "noble savage" and Dewey could not seem to get the recognition of collective authority to displace it. Man in the collective had more or less by default become canonized along with the group.

Dewey's justification of community and experience in faithful purpose, the activities of life rather than the musings on an inner world, the activities of an outer objective world, must stand as religious not in speculating an internal god-like religion of self but a communally secular belief and faith in a realistically collectivist humanity. Both seemed to take a similar view of giving to others, while Dewey saw experience and responsibility at least to some extent through the lens of his early upbringing. Although helping one another would contribute to the collectivity of the group, Dewey would have seen the work of the group to provide for any needs of members as a function of carrying out group purpose in an almost Kantian dutiful act removed from emotion and feeling. To serve the group is to serve individual needs. This was in keeping with the elemental nature of the One within the Many and is as close as the two entities struggling for authority might find common ground in this skewed utilitarianism. Even if this is sufficient explanation of hierarchical authority sorted out among the One and the Many, Dewey never gives detailed explanation of how this might work in the school or society. It might even seem that for fear of charitably tainting a gift with self worth, Dewey is giving in to motive which he denied existent and further affirmed in the case of thought-action brought to fruition. For why cannot a need that is seen be a need pragmatically attended by donation; must there be reflection on the individual giver for motivation for giving?

Again, Dewey was grown in a century of Emersonian optimism lacking sufficient order to affect the stabilization of "opportunities of present life." Dewey would not "thrown to the wind" all "consistency" in an undisciplined exertion "against all organization and all stability," but like Emerson and the other transcendentalists, Dewey did not pursue "fixity" and rigidity either (Dewey, HNC, 100).[1] Dewey would find for order for the Many and to the their purpose. Like Emerson he would take the mechanism out of man to free him from being "only the tender of a machine," "into spiders and needles" and try to find some natural meaning in experience (Dewey, HNC, 144).[2] Dewey opposed rigidity in the extreme, yet the opposite extreme also was to be feared in its excess. Lives lived "under the guise of a return-to-nature dream of romantic freedom" nor "a continual source of improvised spontaneities and novel inspirations," "in which all life is plastic to impulse" "which stands in defiance of organization and institutions" would not provide the "steady reorganization of custom and institutions" which Dewey felt was possible through "utilizing released impulse" intelligently for saving the individual from romantic "ideals." Habit replacement Dewey agreed was present in the child for "renewing of habit rendered possible by impulse," but never stops in the adult, for "if it did, life would petrify, [and] society stagnate." Dewey favored a controlled response to behavior in which the child's or the adult's [i]nstinctive reactions" could be "woven into a smooth pattern of habit" and not in "superficial" and "rigid habit" expression (Dewey, HNC, 100,101).[3]

Dewey proffered ideas which were to come to engulf public education while lingering in the American psyche until it declared itself more broadly after his death. He had a vision of what a truly democratic America could be. Dewey's pragmatism cost society much. The loss of certainty, individualistically derived morality, the unification of conflicting elements of experiential life, and the inauthentic transferability of knowledge derived from experience, have left a pall on society as it has been absorbed over the last century in practice and failed lives. It has brought the public school to it knees as Dewey failed to explain and prove how without coercion, in Hegelian becoming, the One would even want to become the defender of group purpose.

Key to Text References

BGAE - *Beyond Good and Evil* (Niezsche)
COPR - *Critique of Pure Reason* (Kant)
DAE - *Democracy and Education: An Introduction to the Philosophy of Education* (Dewey)
ECHUTOM - *Equiries Concerning Human Understanding and the Principles of Morals* (David Hume)
E - *Essays, First and Second Series* (Emerson)
E - *Ethics* (Dewey and James H. Tufts)
HNC - *Human Nature and Conduct* (Dewey)
HWT - *How We Think* (Dewey)
JD - *John Dewey: An Intellectual Portrait* (Sidney Hook)
MPC - "My Pedagogic Creed" (Dewey)
NA - *The New Atlantis* (Francis Bacon)
P - *Pragmatism: A Name for Some Old Ways of Thinking* (William James)
POMAL - *Principles of Morals and Legislation* (Jeremy Bentham)
QFC - "Quest for Certainty," Gifford Lectures (Dewey)
RE - *Essays in Radical Empiricism* (William James)
RIP - *Reconstruction in Philosophy* (Dewey)
THN - *A Treatise of Human Nature: An Attempt to Introduce the Experimental Method of Reasoning into Moral Subjects* (David Hume)
TMOT - *The Meaning of Truth* (William James)
TNOT - *The Nature of Truth* (Harold H. Joachim)
TTOMS - *The Theory of Moral Sentiments* (Adam Smith)

Bibliography and Notes

Chapter 1: Soil and Seeds

1. Hook, Sidney, *John Dewey: An Intellectual Portrait* (Cosimo Classics, originally published by John Day Company, New York, 1939). p. 10. The opening chapter quotation showing Hook's acknowledgement of Dewey's philosophical radicalism.
2. Ibid., pp. 11, 12.
3. Dewey, John, *Democracy and Education: An Introduction to the Philosophy of Education,* Text-Book Series in Education (Originally published The MacMillan Company, New York, 1916). pp. 279-281.
4. Hook, Sidney, *John Dewey:An Intellectual Portrait,* pp. 5, 8.
5. Ibid., p.13.
6. Dewey, John, *Democracy and Education: An Introduction to the Philosophy of Education*, pp. 376, 377.
7. Hook, Sidney, *John Dewey: An Intellectual Portrait,* pp. 13-15. Instinct, impulse and action move together in a process whereby one's understanding of self is revealed from childhood.
8. Dewey, John, *Democracy and Education: An Introduction to the Philosophy of Education*, pp. 405-418. There is no doubt that Dewey was to maintain an individual view of action probably in regard to Kant's categorical imperative and its dutiful consideration of self as the instrument for the guidance of others. Dewey never found a way out of this philosophical bind. The one making actionable decisions for others does not guarantee benevolence.
9. Dewey, John and James H. Tufts, *Ethics* (Originally published by Henry Holt and Company, 1908), pp. 176, 177. Rumor has it that Dewey was to rid philosophy of authority for it had been invoked over him in his youth by the rigors of educational routine. Although he actually used a classical Greek phase on rare occasion in his writing, he could not recommend classical education as its languages seemed a diversion from leaning English.
10. Dewey, John, *Democracy and Education: An Introduction to the Philosophy of Education*, pp. 28, 29. This is a justification for

community and using a rationalization, for which he was opposed, to give the benefit of the doubt to the individual as a communal animal while still being "interested" in the goals of self.

11. Ibid., p.28. The individual however is not expected to get along without some over seeing and should only be directed with his or her full agreement.
12. Ibid., pp. 28, 29. The individual is to suppress his own "natural impulses" although we will see that if others suppress his impulses he may not have a normal development and could manifest 'pathologies." Dewey was not an admirer of authority which becomes quite evident in later chapters.
13. Ibid., pp. 28, 29. The control of society cannot be a result of the voluntary compliance whether with the help of each citizen or not for chaos would ensue. The best example of this can be seen in the public schools where student defiance is viral.
14. Hook, Sidney, *John Dewey:An Intellectual Portrait*, pp. 5, 8, 14, 15. Dewey was to never lose his idealism as it is to be seen in his melioristic view of a future he would reject for presentism.
15. Ibid., pp. 5, 7, 12, 15.
16. Ibid., pp. 7, 8, 13. Dewey was right about communal learning being "genuine learning" where the group has to negotiate, disagree and work toward consensus.
17. Ibid., pp. 5, 8. Natural dialectic was a group effort in processional reconfiguration of communal and actionable attitudes about purpose.
18. Ibid., pp. 14, 15.
19. Ibid., p. 13. With the loss of intuitionalism was a possibility of dependable knowledge and certainty.
20. Ibid., pp.5, 8, 9, 10.
21. Ibid., pp. 15-17.
22. Dewey, John, *Democracy and Education: An Introduction to the Philosophy of Education*, p. 350.
23. Ibid., pp. 350-353. Dewey was to find as Ferdinand Tönnies that understanding of mere society and real-life society differ.
24. Dewey, John, *Reconstruction in Philosophy* (Originally published by Henry Holt and Company, New York, 1920), pp. 86-88,182,187,188,166. Inclusiveness and "hedonism" appear to be incompatible.
25. Emerson, Ralph Waldo, *Essays: First Series*, II. "Self-reliance (Originally published by James Munroe Company, 1847).

26. Hook, Sidney, *John Dewey: An Intellectual Portrait*, pp. 8-11.
27. Ibid., p. 22.
28. Nietzsche, Friedrich, *Beyond Good and Evil,* In: *The Complete Works of Friedrich Nietzsche*, vol. 12, trans. Helen Zimmern (T.N. Foulis, Edinburgh, 1911), p. 9.
29. Bacon, Francis, *The New Atlantis*, Bacon thought he saw the "Finger" of God in the working of nature.
30a. Dewey, John, *Reconstruction in Philosophy*, pp. 35, 50, 82, 89.
30b. Dewey, John, *Democracy and Education: An Introduction to the Philosophy of Education*, p. 312.
31. Dewey, John, *Reconstruction in Philosophy*, pp. 81-83. The thought-action union was to deny that involuntary action could not be certified as operating with only action. The idea of the combined influences of both thought and action was to reside in the repetitive action invoked by habit formation.
32. Ibid., p. 98.
33. Ibid., p. 83.
34. Ibid., p. 51.
35. Dewey, John, *Democracy and Education: An Introduction to the Philosophy of Education*, pp. 309-323. Dewey's idea of epistemology was an impracticality with questions standing against any fact that was supposedly known. It was more skeptical than affirming when seen in a societal issue where acting on this principle was to find no direction of purpose.
36. Dewey, John, *Reconstruction in Philosophy*. pp. 100, 163, 164. Common sense was the result of preconception and anticipation of acceptable understandings.
37. Ibid., p. 100.
38. Dewey, John, *Democracy and Education: An Introduction to the Philosophy of Education*, pp. 382-384. Dewey felt that philosophy by itself was a close system. Ideas had to be made useful and "concrete" in order to be more than mere speculation.
39. James, William, *Essays in Radical Empiricism,* "The Experience of Activity" (Longmans, Green and Company, New York, 1912). James' empiricism was based on experience. "The principle of pure experience is also a methodical postulate. Nothing shall be admitted as fact, it says, except what can be experienced at some definite time by some experiment; and for every feature of fact every so experienced, a definite place must be found somewhere in the final system of reality. In other words: Everything real must be experienceable somewhere, and every kind of thing experienced

must somewhere be real." It is curious that postulation is a preconception without experiential foundation.

40. Hook, Sidney, *John Dewey: An Intellectual Portrait*, pp. 8,9.
41. Ibid., pp. 9, 25-27.
42. Ibid., pp. 25, 26.
43. Dewey, John, *Human Nature and Conduct: An Introduction to Social Psychology* (Originally published by Henry Holt and Company, New York, 1922), p. 100. Dewey saw a need for consistency while Emerson wrote: "A foolish consistency is the hobgoblin of little minds, adored by little statesmen and philosophers and divines." from his essay "Self-reliance," referenced above.
44. Dewey, John, *Human Nature and Conduct: An Introduction to Social Psychology*, p. 144.
45. Ibid., pp. 100, 101. An assumption that must be made with regard to Dewey's ideas is that the agent of action must be "intelligent," an assumption that hinders application.
46. Hook, Sidney, *John Dewey: An Intellectual Portrait*, pp. 6, 10.

Chapter 2: Empiricism

1. Dewey, John, *Democracy and Education: An Introduction to the Philosophy of Education*, p. 401.

2a. Ibid., pp. 311, 312.

2b. Dewey, John, *Human Nature and Conduct: An Introduction to Social Psychology*, p.50.

3. Ibid., pp.19-22.
4. Dewey, John, *Democracy and Education: An Introduction to the Philosophy of Education*, pp. 71-74.
5. Dewey, John, *Reconstruction in Philosophy*, pp.35, 81-90. Sensation was the potential for destabilizing habits, for their replacement. It is that which leads to thought which when lead by activity may bring about replacement of patterned behavior.
6. Dewey, John, *Quest for Certainty*, Gifford Lectures Series, 1928-1929, Chapter V. Ideas at Work.
7. Dewey, John, *Reconstruction in Philosophy*, pp. 87-91. Certainty is difficult, if not impossible, it could be argued, if there is

no foundational context of thought by which to make sense of empiricism.

8. Dewey, John, *Reconstruction in Philosophy*, p. 23.
9. Ibid., p.83. Hume held to the particularity of events, yet Dewey could provide little more authoritative sequence to events as each must be seen as replaceable, thus any connectivity must be questioned not on the basis holistic meaning but on the doubt concerning particularity.
10. Ibid., pp. 89-91. Dewey tried to avoid the question of knowing by hiding its value inside experience where it could be sheltered by an argument for practicality.
11. Dewey, John, *Human Nature and Conduct: An Introduction to Social Psychology*, pp. 40, 41.
12. Hook, Sidney, *John Dewey: An Intellectual Portrait*, pp. 13-15.
13. Ibid., pp. 13-17. Although we are told that Dewey was the philosopher of the "plain man" there is very little that the plain man could garner in the form of practical advice for daily life. Dewey, in attempt to be inclusive, as Hook has claimed, had very little specific advice in the form of practical application.
14. Ibid., pp. 13, 14. Ridding philosophy of dualism does not answer the problem of confronting them in daily life. To the secular individual, life and death are irresolvable through synthesis since any resolution produces only death. The temporality as opposed to the finality of death do not seem to have a practical dialectic for the living or the dead.
15. Dewey, John, *Democracy and Education*: An Introduction to the Philosophy of Education, pp. 341-344. Although the individual is responsible for experience, truth is only realized in communal connection.
16. Dewey, John, *Reconstruction in Philosophy*, p. 163. It is hard to imagine that Dewey does not imagine having a genie in the works that can average group goals like numbers so as to fit each member and his or her "special cases" to the satisfaction of the changing group. It would seem that the "confusion" would result from not knowing the group purpose as it flexed with the "consequences."

Chapter 3: Pragmatism

1. James, William, *Pragmatism: A Name for Some Old Ways of Thinking*,"The Dilemma in Philosophy"(Longmans, Green and Company, New York, 1907), pp. 15, 27, 30, 33. Opening chapter quotation.
2. Dewey, John, *Human Nature and Conduct: An Introduction to Social Psychology*, pp. 242, 179. Dewey, was drawn initially to pragmatism by James's version and not that of Charles Sanders Peirce. It was pragmatism, yet it was Sanders who conceived of this purely American philosophy. Sanders changed the name of his pragmatism to pragmaticism to recapture his philosophy, but it would continue to be referred to as pragmatism. James' and Dewey's more "radical" version would be the form in which the philosophy would be persistently represented.
3. Dewey, John, *Reconstruction in Philosophy*, pp. 21, 110, 111.
4. Dewey, John, *Human Nature and Conduct: An Introduction to Social Psychology*, pp. 238, 240, 241.
5. Ibid., pp. 290, 291.
6. Dewey, *John, Democracy and Education: An Introduction to the Philosophy of Education,* pp. 112, 115, 116. The idea of education for Dewey is greater than the formal education process, and becomes the centerpiece of his pragmatic philosophy. Education is found in every experience. To not have a true democratic society, therefore, was to not have democratic education, freedom of experience.
7. James, William, *Pragmatism: A Name for Some Old Ways Thinking*, pp. 40, 41."The Function of Cognition." James wrote this and continued with scientific theory, writing, "Beautiful is the flight of conceptual reason through the upper air of truth." "[E]very crazy wind will take her, and like a fire-balloon at night, she will go out among the stars"... always terminate (unlike most of our concepts) in definite percepts. James saw that philosophers were "dazzled" by the grand experience of science, when the day to day is mundane.
8. Ibid., pp. 56, 57.
9. Dewey, John, *Democracy and Education: An Introduction to the Philosophy of Education*, pp. 279, 281. Meaning to Dewey was, for all it could be to his understanding, truth. That which had immediacy (quickly, before it lost meaning) was to give meaning but without

fixed measure and only with regard to the situation, setting, subject, and time at hand.

10. Ibid., pp. 280, 281. Any situation could be considered instrumental in some action, therefore, epistemology and morality could be consider the same by the process by which they found meaning.
11. Dewey, John, *Human Nature and Conduct: An Introduction to Social Psychology*, pp. 245-247.
12. Dewey, John, *Democracy and Education: An Introduction to the Philosophy of Education*, p. 221. Mr. Thomas Gradgrind held to progressive economics and production levels. The understanding was in the numbers and facts unlike Dewey. For example, if a hurricane were to kill only five of the two thousand people on an island then, by Gradgrind's thinking, the natives' were successful in preserving their greater numbers and therefore their economic production levels. The loss of individual life was minimal and the group survived. Gradgrind and Dewey might not have been too far apart on this issue - except for the details. The group was preserved intact and their productive purpose was relatively unaffected by the loss.
13. Ibid., p. 416.
14. Bacon, Francis, *The New Atlantis*. In one of several "We have..." sections, in which Bacon describes the assets available to make life better through inquiry, that ends the book, *The New Atlantis*.
15. Dewey, John, *Reconstruction in Philosophy*, pp. 28-30.
16. Ibid., pp. 31, 36, 37. Like Bacon, Dewey saw the collective not the individual in a struggle with Nature, a task for which man alone was unequipped, but capable of progress in a communal effort.
17. Ibid., p. 38. Dewey would have wished that Bacon had applied thinking about man's addressing the needs of man by "uniting" "contemplation" with "daily experience" and not looking to the future but tying thought to action.
18. Ibid., pp. 116, 117.
19. Ibid., pp. 31-33.
20. Ibid., p. 47. Dewey rejected the evolution of supernaturalism which he saw as having its origins in scholasticism.
21. James, William, *Pragmatism: A Name for Some Old Ways of Thinking*, p. 50. Socrates and Aristotle offered ideals for which to strive in daily life. Locke took his perception of earthly activity as objective reality in action, while Berkeley had lofty supernatural ideas about the immaterial universe and its activity. Hume had little hope of making much sense out of the most simple sequence of

events finding no necessary cohesion among them. They each saw themselves in some respect as empiricists, but failed in fulfilling Dewey's understanding of pragmatism.

22. Ibid., pp. 51-61.
23. Ibid., pp. 45, 46.
24. Emerson, Ralph Waldo, *Essays, First Series*. "Nature." Dewey common ground with Emerson on the need to consider thought and so called motive as a function of an actionable outcome.
25. Hook, Sidney, *John Dewey: An Intellectual Portrait*, pp. 13-15. Truth and falsity in Hegel's view were irrelevant in that change and resultant understanding are the direct result of a struggle for survival alone. The resultant surviving entity is the meaningful one apart from any need to designate truth or falsity.
26. Dewey, John, *Human Nature and Conduct: An Introduction to Social Psychology*, pp. 44, 45. Uncertainty precludes judgment.

Chapter 4: Epistemology

1. James, William, *Pragmatism: A Name for Some Old Ways of Thinking*, pp. 191. 198, 207. Lectures V. and VI. Opening chapter quotations.
2. Hume, David, A *Treatise of Human Nature: An Attempt to introduce the experimental Method of Reasoning into Moral Subjects*, bk. 1. Of the Understanding, pt. 4. Of Sceptical and Other Systems and section 6. Of Personal Identity (Originally published by John Noon, London, 1739). p. 252.
3. Dewey, John, *Democracy and Education: An Introduction to the Philosophy of Education*, p. 246.
4. Tennyson, Alfred Lord, "Ulysses" In: *Poems by Alfred Tennyson* (Originally published by Edward Moxon, London, 1842).
5. James, William, *The Meaning of Truth*. "Preface" (Originally published by Longmans, Green and Company, New York, 1909), p. xli-xliii. James account of his exact understanding of objects and judgment is as he presents in his discussion that "objects are independent of our judgments." If judgment is a doubtful imposition on the physical world then those objects of concern would not be tied to the judgments for which they are spoken.

6. Dewey, John, *Democracy and Education: An Introduction to the Philosophy of Education*, p.161.
7. James, William, *The Meaning of Truth*, p.134.
8. Dewey, John, *Democracy and Education: An Introduction to the Philosophy of Education*, p. 397.
9. Hume, David, *Enquiries Concerning Human Understanding and the Principles of Morals*. sec. 1: "Of the General Morals," (Clarendon Press, Oxford, 1902), p. 3.
10. James, William, "Preface," *The Meaning of Truth*, p. xxxvii.
11. Dewey, John, *Democracy and Education: An Introduction to the Philosophy of Education*, p. 343. Dewey believed that could be no deductions taken from experience that leads knowledge, without any assumptions from thought or hidden patterning of action.
12. Ibid., p. 161. It seems that for all the not knowing in the process of knowing with a the lack of timely assurance, that Dewey finds obdurate faith in its future prospects.
13. Dewey, John, *Human Nature and Conduct: An Introduction to Social Psychology*, p.207.
14. Dewey, John, *How We Think*, p.100. "Lack of provision for experimentation," Chapter VII: Systematic Inference: Induction and Deduction.
15. Ibid., p. 200. "and to prior systems of experience," Chapter XVI: Observation and Information in the Training of Mind. Our senses teach us to reason from the world, books merely teach us by proxy, as a result, we come to believe the insights of others from the fixed pages.
16. Ibid., pp. 176, 177. "The Abuse of Linguistic Methods in Education," Chapter XIII: Language and the Training of Thought.
17. Ibid., p. 176.
18. Ibid., pp. 29-44. Chapter III: Education As Direction.
19. Joachim, Harold H, *The Nature of Truth*, Chapter I: Truth as Correspondence, sec. 1 through 3.(Originally published by Clarendon Press, Oxford, 1906). pp. 7-12. A mind may have "apperception" of truth, conscious thought. This would be to Aristotle correspondence of truth which he saw as "judgment or inference."
20. Ibid., pp. 17-24, sections 5 and 6. pp. 16, 17. Correspondence-notion of truth is necessarily merely a "symptom of truth," that which is "external" to the truth in which oppositional encounters might be addressed more broadly.
21. Ibid., pp. 17-24. sections 6 through 8.

22. Ibid., pp. 16-22. Joachim holds that truth is not a personal affirmation but must dwell "in finite experience" outside of the mind as well as within and finds fault with apperception and broadly considered forms of truth.
23. Dewey, John, *Reconstruction in Philosophy*, p. 157.
24. Dewey, John, *How We Think*, p. 1, 4. Chapter One, What is Thought?, (section) I. Varied Senses of the Term (Thought). Four Senses of thought from the wider to the limited and Thought induces belief in two ways.
25. Joachim, Harold H., *The Nature of Truth*, pp.64-68. sec. 21., (i) The Coherence-notion of Truth, Chapter III: Truth as Coherence. Joachim says, "What is true, is true not because but in spite of the immediacy of the experience in which it is sometimes revealed." Immediate experience may show truth but it must exist outside of experience and therefore the mind.
26. ibid., p. 66. If it is "conceivable," "[a]nything is true" according to coherence-theory. If we think carefully, "clearly and logically" through our conception then it is "conceivable." To be conceivable is to unify the "elements" of conception into "a single concrete meaning." Dewey has said that truth is meaning. This leaves us no closer to a workable and decisive understanding of coherent truth.
27. Dewey, John, *Reconstruction in Philosophy*, pp. 108, 109.
28. Joachim, Harold H., *The Nature of Truth*, pp. 66-68. sec. 22. and 23., "(i) The Coherence-notion of Truth," Chapter III: Truth as Coherence. Coherence- theory, for Joachim, has a greater relevance for science and philosophy where hypothesis and foundational principles or premises, respectively, provide the structure for argument.
29. Dewey, John, *Reconstruction of Philosophy*, p. 100. Confusing is the idea of common sense. Sophia Rosenfeld has written an excellent book on the subject: Common Sense: A Political History. This is well worth reading and may even justify Dewey, to some extent regarding the not so monolithic nature of common sense.
30. James, William, *Pragmatism: A Name for Some Old Ways of Thinking*, p. 171 "Pragmatism and Common Sense," Lecture V. This harkens to the Platonic categories of positions within the republic and the Kantian reasoned universal responses to duty. Each of these "orders" imparts meaning merely by their suggestion.
31. Ibid., p. 186. The "tricks" would be easily brought to mind as "routine" to account for sensational input.

32. Ibid., p. 182. Berkeley probably thought common sense a weapon of the learned materialists, an atheist's speculation. Berkeley's immaterialism was to oppose the materialists by denying them substance.
33. Ibid., p. 193.
34. Dewey, John, *Reconstruction in Philosophy*, p. 100. Chapter IV: "Changed Conceptions of Experience and Reason."
35. Ibid., pp. 100, 101.
36. Dewey, John, *Human Nature and Conduct: An Introduction to Social Psychology*, p. 36. Common sense relies on fixity and the idea that their are clear ends to experience and consequences, but for Dewey only uncertainty arose looking for ultimate ends when they were merely means to future means. In this sense Dewey did embrace the future despite his protestations to the contrary. There is no reason to expect ends merely a future of continuing means, possibly an unending number and without surety. It would seem in some sense that Dewey was pawning off on the future of means a transcendence of possibilities.
37. Ibid.
38. Dewey, John, *Reconstruction in Philosophy*, pp. 159, 160. It would seem that the "seat of authority" rests with the unverifiable, since knowledge of truth is non-transferable, and therefore must be subject to the parochialism of individual belief.
39. Ibid. pp. 36, 32, 33. Subjecting truth to interrogation provide verification without a justified statement of intention, an hypothesis or premise, by which to judge the experiential outcome.
40. Dewey, John, *Reconstruction in Philosophy*, p. 35.
41. Ibid.
42. Hook, Sidney, *John Dewey: An Intellectual Portrait*, p. 85. The young have a quite truncated view of the past and a limitation in looking for prospects in the future. Presentism would produce stagnation in the young having only present sight and little encouragement to think about the prospects of their future.
43. Ibid., 84. Dewey seemed to find support for his belief in the changeable and undependable nature of science by crawling to the idea of relativity which he believed had discredited the Newtonian view of the world and its mechanics.
44. Dewey, John, *Reconstruction in Philosophy*, p. 64. The Jewish law came about to place limits on "personal will," yes, but also to offer physical protection.

45. Dewey, John, *Democracy and Education: An Introduction to the Philosophy of Education*, p. 261.
46. Ibid., pp. 264, 266, 268. Pure science must follow the same methodology as applied science. Much of the former is the instruction to application, not always immediately, but in reserve for the future.
47. Ibid., p. 331. Science was to be collectively held, yet not the instrument of governance.
48. James, William, *The Meaning of Truth*, pp. 89, 90. Chapter III: "Humanism and Truth."
49. Dewey, John, *Democracy and Education: An Introduction to the Philosophy of Education*, pp. 146, 147, 393. Preconception establishes the possibility of cause and effect measured in the experience of the One.
50. Dewey, John, *Reconstruction of Philosophy*, pp. 29, 30, 110, 111.
51. Hook, Sidney, *John Dewey: An Intellectual Portrait*, pp. 53-58. Consensual theory of truth is given by Hook as a way to establish knowledge which is wrapped in group purpose and action, yet not necessarily allowing for opposition for change.
52. Dewey, John, *Reconstruction in Philosophy*, pp. 32, 33.
53. Ibid., pp. 32, 33, 117.
54. Dewey, John, *Democracy and Education: An Introduction to the Philosophy of Education*, p. 51.
55. Ibid., p. 313.
56. Kant, Immanuel, *Critique of Pure Reason*, pp. 7-9. "Of the difference in analytic and synthetic judgments." Introduction. Kant gave perception credibility by offering the experiential knowledge of an object such that the object, as the object itself, was to become understood in the mind's processing by the "spectator" or the "participant." Dewey took the spectator' authority away for the failure to make the knowable actionable as did the participant.
57. Ibid. Transcendental Aesthetics (German use: The critique of taste). Part First. pp. 21, 33. Through the *a priori* and *a posteriori*, initial thought and action, Dewey united his understanding of knowing as thought, from a Kantian construct, separating individual experiences.
58. Dewey, John, "My Pedagogic Creed," Article Three, In: *School Journal*, vol. 54, January, 1897. History is not for Dewey a transferrable record of facts and events, but rather a meaningful insight into the "progress" of man and his preferences for relationships among one another.

59. Dewey, John, *Democracy and Education: An Introduction to the Philosophy of Education,* p. 169. Dewey, of all people, felt that the dependence on words to negotiate "difficulty" was obscurantist. His own use of words at his Dewey School were regarding hands-on, actionable activities. He did not begin children in his school in books necessarily, but waited until they were interested in reading and writing. When the school closed in the middle of a child's education, some students may have not attempted to learn from books and had missed out on an early start in academic reading and learning.
60. Dewey, John, *How WeThink*, pp. 181, 174. I. Individual Meanings: (b) a sign preserves a meaning. Chapter Thirteen: Language and the Training of Thought. Dewey embraced communication but realized that despite their tendency to misrepresent we were obliged to use orality. Dewey felt that his ideas were difficult to explain because of verbal inadequacy. Words were problematic for clearly communicating ideas.
61. Dewey, John, "My Pedagogical Creed," Article Three, In: *School Journal*. Literature is but an "interpretation of social experience," for musing but unable to affect the change in the lives of others. For to be taught by the written word would be controlling the student, changing his or her understanding of life even without necessarily recognizing the influence.
62. Dewey, John, *Human Nature and Conduct: An Introduction to Social Psychology*, pp. 236, 237.
63. Dewey, John, *Reconstruction in Philosophy*, pp. 138-140.
64. Dewey, John, *Democracy and Education: An Introduction to the Philosophy of Education*, p. 169.
65. Ibid. p. 311. "Reason, universal principles, *a priori* notions" are the thought processes that must be completed by actionable events, in order to prove meaning, not assumed or given by authority of "august names."
66. Dewey, John, *Human Nature and Conduct: An Introduction to Social Psychology*, p. 304. Dewey felt that to interject ourselves into other's lives was to possibly enslave them by the weight of charitable care or advice.

Chapter 5: Morality

1. Emerson, Ralph Waldo, " Compensation," In: *Essays: First Series*.
2. James, William, *Pragmatism: A Name for Some Old Ways of Thinking*, " Notion of Truth." Lecture VI: Pragmatism's Conception of Truth, p. 222.
3. Dewey, John, *Human Nature and Conduct*, pp. 223-225. Dewey gives the authority for morality, not to a god, but to the individuals who are the active participants in immediate experience.
4. Ibid., pp. 18, 19. The individual shares the blame with the group to which he or she belongs. The actions of the One receive blame as does the group. Individual morality is not judged purely on the actions of the One; all bear responsibility.
5. Ibid., p. 22. Man changes the environment and the environment changes man. This becomes the reasoning behind the drift of knowledge as the surroundings and the current understandings attain to new prominence in the world. Man will be changed, his heart will react to the new influences, between the impulses to which he responds and the environment in which he must live.
6. Ibid., pp. 138, 139. The Individual with the authority of thought-action cannot be completely trusted. Only within the group will the One find direction and redirection, although each has the changing potential through impulse-directed habit. Authority even in regard to "altruism" is in the hands of the One, but not without concern.
7. Nietzsche, Friedrich, *Beyond Good and Evil,* p. 90. (Originally published by T. N. Foulis, London, 1906) trans. Helen Zimmern.
8. Ibid., p. 293. Dewey would have it both ways: the One may serve the good of the group, but the risk, and the caveat, is not to be raising One's own currency in the bargain.
9. Ibid., 292, 293.
10. Smith, Adam, *The Theory of Moral Sentiments*,"Of the Sense of Duty," pt .III. Chapter 1. Of the Foundation of our Judgments concerning our own Sentiments and Conduct and of the Sense of Duty. Chapter 1: Of the Principle of self-approbation and of

self-disapprobation.(Published by Alex Murray & Sons, London, 1869), p. 113.

11. Dewey, John, *Human Nature and Conduct: An Introduction to Social Psychology*, pp. 44-57.
12. Ibid., p. 46. Assessment of a man may only be ventured posthumously. But this still does not solve the problem of assigning to one's life good or bad or mixed value. Each person must have the authority to apperceive according to their own impressions.
13. Ibid., p. 47.
14. Ibid., p. 136.
15. Ibid., p. 47. Even those who seem to exalt greatness may have common or even undesirable points of character.
16. Ibid. A good may serve as the means by which a subsequent means may be an unwanted "consequence." Furthermore, one person's good may result in a "consequence" which is not good for another person. Therefore, individuals and groups are hardly capable of designating heroes or failed humans. Without judgment, all are merely human, not exclusively responsible for their flaws or their strengths in carrying out group purpose, which is always subject to change.
17. Ibid., p. 5. Although the ideal of group purpose is held up by Dewey as partial justification for the group, "conformity" is the opposing force in the process by which individuals and therefore groups grow and change over time.
18. Dewey, John, *Reconstruction in Philosophy*, p. 17.
19. Dewey, John, *Human Nature and Conduct: An Introduction to Social Psychology*, p. 64.
20. Dewey, John, *Democracy and Education: An Introduction to the Philosophy of Education*, p. 411, 412.
21. Ibid., pp. 28, 29. "Control" can only mean individual and groups are conjoined in personal direction and leadership.
22. Dewey, John, *Human Nature and Conduct: An Introduction to Social Psychology*, p. 278.
23. Ibid., p. 286. Dewey's social democratic views place the group blame of individual misbehavior on the business and industrial controls. The individual is literally made bad in personal action by the influence of business money and materialism.
24. Dewey, John, *Ethics*, p. 37.
25. Ibid., pp. 36, 37. Those impulses of change that are to bring identity to the individual are curtailed by the imposition of the purpose of business which has fixed goals and activities.
26. Dewey, John, *Reconstruction in Philosophy*, pp. 50-51, 98, 99.

27. Ibid. p. 100. The instrument of acceptable change was the evolving environment in which people live and are changed, not the influential force of authority external to the group and personal change.
28. Bentham, Jeremy, *Principles of Morals and Legislation*, Chapter 1: "Of the Principle of Utility," section XIII. (originally published by Clarendon Press, Oxford, 1907), p. 3.
29. Dewey, John, *Human Nature and Conduct: An Introduction to Social Psychology*, p. 43. Uncertainty would not allow intent or motive to move independent of action.
30. Dewey, John, *Reconstruction in Philosophy*, p. 139. Any exercise of "external authority" is a stopgap solution, an unacceptable solution, to urgency. The evolution of activities should be allowed to work their way through the environment to people and their groups.
31. Ibid., pp. 139-141. Thwarting impulses in young individuals, prior to their attaining growing and identifying habits may produce pathological conditions. Dewey felt that those habits that had been inculcated by parental authority were not necessarily healthy, that children needed to create an identity based on their own impulse-induced habits.
32. Ibid., p. 143.
33. Dewey, John, *Democracy and Education: An Introduction to the Philosophy of Education*, p. 184.
34. Ibid., pp. 343, 344.
35. Ibid., p.279. This statement is as logically fraudulent of information as the statement "my computer is invaluable." Invaluable does not mean that one cannot render value assessment, but it can be an abdication of verbal authority to clearly express value. To agree that the term "invaluable" is self-explanatory is to allow the assumption that my computer could not be replaced or that a cheaper computer owned by my neighbor who also says his computer is invaluable has the same monetary value as mine. In fact, I may claim that my computer is invaluable but on the first sign that it will not allow me to do what I need to do with a computer, it will be replaced as will my neighbor's less expensive but equally "invaluable" computer. To claim something is invaluable is to not claim that it is intrinsic-ally incalculable in relative value, that in its usage "invaluable" is not expected to decisively render information in that its value great or not is indeterminable from the description. Dewey is play a shell game in order to avert judgment in the matter, resulting in word trickery and dishonesty possibly while rendering a lack of clarity to his goal of inclusivity.

36. Ibid., pp. 279, 280.
37. Ibid., p. 309.
38. Ibid., pp. 351-353. At risk of being overly Freudian, it is difficult to imagine, on thorough inspection of Dewey's understanding of authority, that he had no traumatic experience with dicta during his impulse-driven childhood.
39. Dewey, John, *Reconstruction in Philosophy*, p. 186.
40. Ibid., pp. 183-186. Arriving at Maturity, if we can assume Dewey's intent, is the end point at which one finds independence from the domination by society, yet his ongoing fear is this independence that drives the individual, the extreme individual, beyond group inclusion and purpose.
41. Bentham, Jeremy, *Principles of Morals and Legislation,* p. 313.
42. Ibid., pp. 349, 405. How is Dewey's idea of individual authority not hedonistic in its origins and possibly in its ultimate consequence?
43. Dewey, John, *Democracy and Education: An Introduction to the Philosophy of Education*, p. 309. Experience is a unifying feature of pragmatism since it returns moral authority to the individual, yet it cannot be transferred to others or other cultures. It would seem we are all masters unto ourselves without the benefit to others in our care for them for want of being accused of selfishness. Dewey would see societal institutions handling our charity in order that it be done without chance for egoistic self-reward to the giver. This is certainly a motivation for government to do the charitable work, extricating persons from the evil's of condescension and back patting as well as the direct responsibility to others.

Chapter 6: Individualism and Society

1. Protagoras was affirming that truth is what every man wants to believe it to be. Opening quotation.
2. Dewey, John, *Reconstruction in Philosophy*, p. 207. Communication is necessary but it is merely the babbling of a "dumb" and "brute animal." When the group is in receipt of this "communication of experience," it may be trans-formed into group wisdom.

3. Dewey, John, *Democracy and Education: An Introduction to the Philosophy of Education*,p. 354. Intellectual freedom seems a bit chancy and dependent on the fortuity of an appropriate "situation."
4. Ibid., p. 355.
5. Ibid., 52, 53.
6. Ibid., 94, 99.
7. Ibid., pp. 102-105.
8. Ibid., pp. 106-110.
9. Ibid., p. 134.
10. Ibid., p. 143.
11. Ibid., pp. 151-158.
12. Dewey, John, "My Pedagogical Creed," What Education is, Article One, In: *School Journal.*
13. Dewey, John, *Democracy and Education: An Introduction to the Philosophy of Education*, p. 353.
14. Ibid., pp. 342, 343.
15. Ibid., p. 357. Subjectivism for Dewey is willed action of the individual; he sees it as objective when the willed action is accomplished by the group.
16. Dewey, John, *How We Think*, pp. 127-129. It was Darwin which gave Dewey his understanding of change and the influence of the environment in this change, but the categorization lead to conformity, antithetical to change. Pigeon-holing was not a way for commonalities to be recognized individually but to subject the individual to an uncomfortable fitting.
17. Dewey, John, *Human Nature and Conduct: An Introduction to Social Psychology*, pp. 220, 221.
18. Dewey, John, *Democracy and Education: An Introduction to the Philosophy of Education*, pp. 2, 3.
19. Ibid., pp. 312, 313.
20. Dewey, John, *Reconstruction in Education*, pp. 197, 198.
21. Ibid., p. 196.
22. Ibid., p. 209. Education is fulfilled in social function. If all of life is educative then this is the highest achievement for the individual, to be found in the purpose, the changing purpose of the group or groups.
23. Dewey, John, *Democracy and Education: An Introduction to the Philosophy of Education*, pp.71-73.
24. Dewey, John, *Reconstruction in Philosophy*, pp. 198-200.
25. Dewey, John,. *Ethics*, p. 68.
26. Ibid., p. 80.

27. Ibid., pp. 357-359. The individual that is "unreal" and "Impossible" is the extreme individual who looks to self and not the relational purposes of the group.
28. Dewey, John, *Reconstruction in Philosophy*, p. 207. Without the replacement of habits the individual would forfeit the "freedom to change."
29. Dewey, John, *Human Nature and Conduct: An Introduction to Social Psychology*, p. 321.
30. Dewey, John, *Democracy and Education: An Introduction to the Philosophy of Education*, p. 267.
31. Dewey, John, *Human Nature and Conduct: An Introduction to Social Psychology*, p. 303-313.
32. Dewey, John, "My Pedagogic Creed," Article Three, In: *School Journal*. Dewey sees the group or society as a living growing entity, while the individual is yet another "object" in the environment, albeit an organic elemental entity of the group.
33. Dewey, John, *Reconstruction in Philosophy*, pp. 194, 185.
34. Dewey, John, *Democracy and Education: An Introduction to the Philosophy of Education*, pp. 89, 90. Growth would be the result of the individual in the process of "random change" becoming an instrument of environmental "reconstruction and reorganization of experience" just as the individual was changed by the environment.
35. Dewey, John, *Reconstruction in Philosophy*, pp. 196-198.
36. Ibid., p. 207.
37. Dewey, John, "My Pedagogic Creed," Article One, In: *School Journal*. The interdependence of the One and the Many is for the very survival of individuality and society.
38. Ibid., pp. 118-120, 213, 231.
39. Dewey, John, *Human Nature and Conduct: An Introduction to Social Psychology*, p. 231. Motive is inseparable from action and is only known, if known at all, as a consequence of so-called motive and action working together.
40. Ibid., pp. 118-120, 213, 231.
41. Dewey, John, *Democracy and Education*, pp. 52, 53.
42a. Dewey, John, *Reconstruction in Philosophy*, p. 207.
42b. Dewey, John, *Democracy and Education: An Introduction to the Philosophy of Education*, pp. 130, 131, 259, 292, 293.
43. Hook, Sidney, *John Dewey: An Intellectual Portrait*, pp. 118, 119. Very few would argue the point that we are not formed, to some extent, by the environmental personalities of our early years.

44. Ibid., p. 125. Educative rote instruction, Dewey felt, would lead to hardening of the individual by "dogma," and competitive division among those in the learning community.
45. Ibid., p. 11.
46. Ibid., pp. 49, 50.
47. Dewey, John, *Democracy and Education: An Introduction to the Philosophy of Education*, pp. 351-357.
48. Ibid. Fixed knowledge does not respond to the changing environment robbing individuals of freedom and democracy.

Chapter 7: Individuation

1. Rousseau, Jean-Jacques, *Emile or On Education*, Book 1, p. 41. Opening chapter quotation.
2. Lewis, C. S., *The Abolition of Man*, Chapter 3, p. 78.
3. Hook, Sidney, *John Dewey: An Intellectual Portrait*, p. 11.
4. Dewey, John, *Reconstruction in Philosophy*, pp. 197, 198.
5. Ibid., pp. 208, 209. The thought that the individual by trial and error, experimentation, would come to find self-empowerment possibly in the extremes of experience cannot be a comfort to society. Encouraging the One to follow impulses and fall short of murder, rape and terror, is not always going to happen. What did Dewey have in mind to prevent felonious outcomes from this practice?
6. Dewey, John, *Human Nature and Conduct: An Introduction to Social Psychology*, pp. 2, 89. In Dewey's understanding, the "better" children would be the ones that think for themselves setting aside their parents direction and would no doubt be those children with fewer pathologies, for not rejecting the impulsive irruptions to new habits that challenge parental rearing.
7. Ibid., p. 64. The inference is that the young have more in the way of innate wisdom than the adults who move the children to "custom," to conformity. This is reminiscent of Socrates belief that knowledge is intrinsic to man which he supposedly demonstrated affirmatively by asking a slave about mathematics. The slave answered his questions but with inordinate leading on Socrates' part. The Platonic idea of knowledge was to be modified by the Neo-platonists who claimed that the child may have innate knowledge even divinity. Voltaire felt that, if the child had knowledge, it must have been lost at birth; this was

based, no doubt, on the unwise behaviors of neonates. Divinity was not an option for Voltaire, for he was an atheist; therefore, the child being divine held no merit. Aristotle and Voltaire both held that the child was a blank tablet, which would subsequently be written on by life. Aside from this issue, it is possible that Voltaire may have been a source for Dewey's idea of uncertainty.

8. Ibid., pp. 89-93.
9. Ibid., pp. 105n.
10. Ibid., pp. 254, 255.
11. Ibid.
12. Ibid., pp. 255, 256.
13. Ibid., pp. 89, 90.
14. Ibid., pp. 96, 97. Training (possibly thought of apart from true education) "molds" children and does not take advantage of the impulse-habit system of individual change.
15. Dewey, John, *Reconstruction in Philosophy*, pp. 196-207.
16. Dewey, John, *Human Nature and Conduct: An Introduction to Social Psychology*, p.105.
17. Ibid., pp. 196, 197.
18. Ibid., p. 105n. Impulses that "rush us off our feet" do not seem to proffer calm for reason, and the fact that the impulses are "undirected" appears to be much like Darwinian evolution, without guarantee that change though fortuitous will be beneficial, as changes in the environment change us for good or bad.
19. Ibid., pp. 155, 156.
20. Ibid., pp. 154-156.
21. Ibid., p. 156.
22. Ibid., pp. 156, 157.
23. Ibid., pp. 156, 157.
24. Ibid., pp. 91, 92.
25. Ibid., p. 95.
26. Hook, Sidney, *John Dewey: An Intellectual Portrait*, p. 11. Compulsion is "irrational" producing its effects immediately without "thought," "study" or "consideration" but arises from our "deeper intuition." The metaphysical characteristic of intuition which Hook had claimed Dewey had lost arose in our ontological drives. Habit formation has value but compulsion does not contribute authoritatively to habit.
27. Dewey, John, *Democracy and Education: An Introduction to the Philosophy of Education*, p. 62.
28. Ibid., p. 15.

29. Ibid., p. 5.
30. Ibid., p. 22.
31. Ibid.
32. Ibid., p. 85.
33. Dewey, John, *Human Nature and Conduct: An Introduction to Social Psychology*, p. 24.
34. Dewey, John, *Democracy and Education: An Introduction to the Philosophy of Education*, p. 90. Education in the broader sense is indirect as we adapt and change with changes in the environment.
35. Ibid., pp. 92, 93.
36. Dewey, John, *Human Nature and Conduct: An Introduction to Social Psychology*, p. 25. Intending consequences is close to motive for action, which Dewey denied since only consequence can reflect on motive. Without motive in a legal setting, there is no need for clemency; however, since the group, society, is in part responsible for the activities of the accused, there is no compete responsibility attributable to the felon. We are all, to some extent, guilty.
37. Dewey, John, *Democracy and Education: An Introduction to the Philosophy of Education*, p. 16.
38. Ibid., p. 24. The best environment would be that of a true democracy.
39. Dewey, John, *Human Nature and Conduct: An Introduction to Social Psychology*, pp. 98, 99.
40. Ibid., p. 183.
41. Ibid., p. 105.
42. Ibid., pp. 170, 171. Thought places constraints on habit.
43. Dewey, *How We Think*. p. 14.
44. Dewey, John, *Human Nature and Conduct: An Introduction to Social Psychology*, pp. 182-187. A unification of habits arises in the same environment, the same group.
45. Ibid., pp. 172, 173. Thought is the necessary impetus for actionable, patterned behavior.
46. Ibid., p. 175. The "philosophical fallacy" is the "easy answer" which leads to "supposition."
47. Ibid., p. 74.
48. Dewey, John, *How We Think*, p. 118. Dewey was not a skeptic in the sense that the Pyrrhonists were, but he agreed with the Stoics that claims of a finality of understanding would not be very often in the interest of truth.
49. Dewey, John. *Human Nature and Conduct: An Introduction to Social Psychology*. pp. 106, 109.

50. Ibid., p. 240. Procrustes would adjust his guest to his bed by cutting off parts that overhung. If he had a guest that fit the bed, then he would move the guest to another bed and make his adjustments. He was never going to be denied his cutting. All men are unfit. Procrustes was always right.
51. Ibid., p. 25. 49.
52. Ibid., pp. 25-30.
53. Ibid., p. 30. Dewey claimed that thought follows acts: ideas are merely " thoughts of ends," and ends are the means required to act until new habits are formed.
54. Ibid., pp.34-36.
55. Ibid., pp. 34-38.
56. Ibid. Character cannot be deduced since it is only the habit replacement of a lifetime that can lead to an assessment of character. Acts of acceptable character can reveal the nature of the individual at that moment but necessarily against a backdrop of prior good, bad or mixed natures.
57. Ibid., p. 195.
58. Ibid., pp. 193-198. The extremes of passion fix progress in individual becoming and interrupt by new habit formation.
59. Ibid., pp. 224, 225.
60. Ibid., p. 134.
61. Ibid., p. 34-38.
62. Ibid., pp. 228-231. Each act must become a means to new acts which may give a hint at character which is only competed at death, and then only by individual evaluation.
63. Ibid., pp. 236-240.
64. Ibid., pp. 254-265.
65. Ibid., pp. 274. An "ideal" fixes the process of becoming.
66. Ibid., pp. 280, 281.
67. Ibid., pp. 43.
68. Dewey, John, *Democracy and Education: An Introduction to the Philosophy of Education*, pp. 64, 65.
69. Dewey, John, *Human Nature and Conduct: An Introduction to Social Psychology,* pp. 170, 171.
70. Ibid., pp. 140, 141.
71. Ibid., pp. 164-166. One would have to question whether "rebellion" as the result of repression within the group context, say, terrorism for instance, would not be "evil" but could be merely group purpose.
72. Ibid., p. 169.

73. Ibid., p. 44. Dewey would not embrace Kant's categorical imperative, since it would represent a loss of individual freedom.
74. Dewey, John, *Reconstruction in Philosophy*, p. 208.
75. Hook, Sidney, *John Dewey: An Intellectual Portrait*, pp. 118, 119.
76. Dewey, John, *Human Nature and Conduct: An Introduction to Social Psychology*, pp. 32-41.
77. Ibid., p. 58.
78. Ibid., p. 130.
79. Ibid., p .307. The controls mentioned earlier are to be acquiesced to as accommodating the welfare of the group. Yet, does the conformity threaten to quell the appropriate replacement of habits?
80. Ibid., p. 306-313. If choice is accompanied by "precarious possibilities" should we desire freedom or fear it.
81. Ibid., p. 43.

Chapter 8: Pedagogy

1. Emerson, Ralph Waldo, *Essays: Second* "Politics" (Originally published by James Munroe Company, 1847), p. 193. Opening chapter quotation. Dewey could have agreed.
2. Péguy, Charles, *Notre Patrie*, 1905. Opening chapter quotation. Péquy wrote and died in this period of progressivism, killed during WW I.
3. Dewey, John, *Democracy and Education: An Introduction to the Philosophy of Education*, pp. 3-11. Although experience is not trans-experiential it is the glue that holds the group together, the binding commonality through communication.
4. James, William, "Preface," *The Meaning of Truth*, p. xliii.
5. Dewey, John, *Democracy and Education: An Introduction to the Philosophy or Education*, p. 2-5.
6. Dewey, John, "My Pedagogic Creed," Article Five, The School and Social Progress. In: *School Journal*. p. 33.
7. Dewey, John, *Democracy and Education: An Introduction to the Philosophy of Education*, pp.29-49. According to Dewey democracy is the requisite for true education.
8. Ibid., p. 103.
9. Ibid., p. 113, 114. Pragmatic freedom for Dewey could exist in what he considered a true democracy.
10. Dewey, John, "My Pedagogic Creed," Article Two, What the School is, In: *School Journal*.

11. Dewey, John, *Democracy and Education: An Introduction to the Philosophy of Education,*. pp. 22-27.
12. Ibid., pp. 20, 21.
13. Ibid., pp. 22, 23.
14. Ibid., p. 6.
15. Ibid., pp. 152, 153, "My Pedagogic Creed," The Nature or Method, Article Three and The Subject Matter of Education, Article IV. In: *School Journal*. A "vital impulse" must be provided the proper learning environment under which a relevant "interest" may be given to the student which will in turn drive learning.
16. Dewey, John, "My Pedagogic Creed," Article Three and Four, In: *School Journal*.
17. Dewey, John, *Reconstruction in Philosophy*, pp. 149-151. It is hard to imagine that Dewey would embrace today's techno-learning and computer curricula as a hands-on approach to learning.
18. Ibid., p. 150.
19. Dewey, John, *Democracy and Education: An Introduction to the Philosophy of Education*, p. 369.
20. Ibid.
21. Ibid.
22. Ibid., pp. 371-374. Dewey recognized the disabling of community under the impress of materialism.
23. Ibid., p. 395. Materialism may prevent the replacement of habit, as work becomes only an avenue to gaining possessions.
24. Ibid., pp. 370, 371.
25. Ibid., pp. 130-145.
26. Hook, Sidney, *John Dewey: An Intellectual Portrait*, p. 152. Dewey felt that most group members would join into common purpose. This would be in keeping with a melioristic view of the world.
27. Dewey, John, *Democracy and Education: An Introduction to the Philosophy of Education*, p. 90.
28. Ibid., p. 49.
29. Ibid., pp. 71-80.
30. Ibid., p. 106. Dewey ideas of pedagogy would be protected from failure by them not being possible, according to his claim, unless a truly democratic society were to be installed.
31. __________, *Cardinal Principles of Secondary Education* (Government Printing Office, Washington, 1918).
32. Hook, Sidney, *John Dewey: An Intellectual Portrait*, pp. 162, 163.
33. Ibid., p. 157.
34. Ibid., p. 163.

35. Dewey, John, *Reconstruction in Philosophy*, pp. 100, 101. Dewey came to question the application of his pedagogic ideas by calling out some progressive programs that were not teaching academically nor civilizing the young but pandering to their immaturity.
36. Ibid.

Chapter 9: Unity

1. Dewey, John, *Reconstruction in Philosophy*, p. 111. Opening chapter quotation.
2. Hook, Sidney, *John Dewey: An Intellectual Portrait*, pp. 28, 29.
3. Ibid., p. 13.
4. Ibid., pp. 41, 42.
5. Ibid., p. 44. Why not view opposites as extremes of the same thing, thesis and antithesis resolvable or unified in synthesis as in the union of body and mind ? This was a take-away from Hegel that Dewey could embrace in an earthly context.
6. Ibid., pp. 44, 45. There was no reason to find conflict in issues of knowledge, since each view is experiential and non-transferable. Both opposing views could hold to their understanding of an issue and both be equally meaningful.
7. Ibid., pp. 42.
8. Ibid., p. 27.
9. Ibid., pp. 60, 61.
10. Dewey, John, *Democracy and Education: An Introduction to the Philosophy of Education*, p. 391.
11. Dewey, John, *Human Nature and Conduct*, p. 252. Our perception of an object is not the object but an apperception. Like Kant the assumed and the real find union in our understanding. Our intent in thinking of an object does not match the reality of the object since our attempt at conjuring materiality does not produce thought equivalence.
12. Dewey, John. *Democracy and Education: An Introduction to the Philosophy of Education*. p. 377.
13. Ibid., p. 195.
14. Hook, Sidney, *John Dewey: An Intellectual Portrait*, p. 216.
15. Dewey, John, *Democracy and Education: An Introduction to the Philosophy of Education*, p. 390.
16. Ibid., pp. 195-219.

17. Ibid., p. 333. Dewey like Emerson lost a son and came to see Nature as hard and fearfully made. Man may feel alien in nature at times but is an inextricable element of the natural world.
18. Dewey, John, *Human Nature and Conduct*, p. 185.
19. Ibid., pp. 182-185.
20. Ibid., 183. Dewey saw epistemology and morality as the same, since morality was a form of information. Acceptable behavior was the result of having been taught (in an academic manner). Man would do as he should, if he were taught. Dewey did not dwell on the idea that those who knew might still do "evil" things. Dewey saw in their sameness unification.
21. Hook, Sidney, *John Dewey: An Intellectual Portrait*, 30-35.
22. Ibid., p. 118.
23. Dewey, John, *Democracy and Education: An Introduction to the Philosophy of Education*, p. 195.
24. Dewey, John, *Human Nature and Conduct*, p. 183
25. Ibid.
26. Hook, Sidney, *John Dewey: An Intellectual Portrait.* pp, 219, 220.
27. Dewey, John, *Human Nature and Conduct*, p. 183.
28. Hook. Sidney, *John Dewey: An Intellectual Portrait*, pp. 14-16.
29. Dewey, John, *Reconstruction in Philosophy*, p. 171. Dewey sought unity not the universality of the "intrinsic good" which does not pertain to daily living but is driven by the need for "constancy and urgency." Unity would embrace differences. Universality would not flex and would stand outside of experience.
30. Dewey, John. *Democracy and Education: An Introduction to the Philosophy of Education*. p. 418. 30.
31. Hook, Sidney, *John Dewey: An Intellectual Portrait*, p. 118.
32. Dewey, John, *Democracy and Education: An Introduction to the Philosophy of Education*, p. 29.
33. Ibid., pp. 94, 95.
34a. Ibid., pp. 94-99.
34b. Ibid., pp. 102-104.
35. Ibid.
36. Ibid., pp. 333, 334.
37. Ibid., p. 334.
38. Dewey, John, *Reconstruction in Philosophy*. p. 96.
39. Dewey, John. *Democracy and Education: An Introduction to the Philosophy of Education*, p. 347.
40. Ibid., p. 357.

41. Dewey, John, *Human Nature and Conduct*, pp. 51, 96, 97. To know is to do. This is Dewey's idealistic view of man and behavior.

Conclusion

1. Dewey, John, *Human Nature and Conduct*, p. 100.
2. Ibid., p.144.
3. Ibid., pp. 100, 101.

Index

A

82; freedom of, 83, 142; and individual action, 83; utilitarian, subjectivism, Mill, 88; immediate, in the classroom, 88; jurisdictional, 90; and Kant, 91; student-individual, 93, 117, 122; and Bentham, 93; Dewey's denial, 95; temporal, 95; in daily life, 95; and Locke,100; of group, Dewey, 101; and democracy, 109; what is too much?, 109; justifying, 109, 110; unearthly, 109; of tradition, 108; adult, 111; of habit, 118; to action, 118; of immediate action, 123; of speculation, 124; of the people, 125; communal, 128, 129; certainty of, 130; suspect, 130; certifying, 140; lack of definitive, 142; boundaries of, 161; workable, 161; undisputed, 162; argument for, 165; of learning, 167; collective, 168; struggle for, 168; hierarchal, 168

Authoritative(ly), institutions, 6; dubious behavioralism, 8; creativity, 26; negotiations, 38; agency, 38, 83; experience, 39; uniquely, 50; transferable, 56; control, 63; dictation, 87; critique, 90; group, 92, 110; individualism,107; student, 108; identity, 108; action and habit, 108; meaning, 109; individualism and group, 129; learning 134; in the present of,153; disputed 162 perspective,167; knowledge, 167; experience, 167;

Autonomy (autonomous),and others, 77; authority, 92; spirit, 98; philosophical, 126; freedom, 166

B

Bacon, Francis, and method for investigating the physical world, 25, 26, 46; utopian of knowledge, 25; and God's own hand, 26, 46; and theist, 27; utopian, 46, 47; man over nature, 46; modern thought, 47; sense of communal good 47; Dewey on application to science, 47; application of science as perfect, 47; and pragmatic conception of knowledge, 47; interdependence of science and society, 47; and the creator, 47; scientific method, 48; experimentation and facts, 48; experimentation and presumption, 48; idea of methodology, 48; inquiry, 66

Behavior(al), communally acceptable, 5, 21; dubious authority, 8; and habit, 30, 70, 81, 88, 100, 102, 120, 121, 125, 130, 160; and knowing, 31, 81; and sensation, 34; limits to 45; judging, 46; responsibility for acceptable, 78; destructive behavior, 78; as moral activity, 78; modeling good, 81; norms, 81; group influence of, 81; changeable,81; immediate authority, 81; and community control, 82; morally good, 84;

Index

extremist, 84, 88, 101; and pathologies, 85; and coercion, 86, 92; individual character and, 88; standards, Dewey, 88, 131; consequences, 88, 119; consequences and judgment, 88, 124; management by committee, 88; fit within the group, 89; expectations and consequences, 89; and "alternative possibilities," 89; judgment and mis-, 89; contentious, 90; authority in judging, 90; disputes, 90, 167; violations in, 91; assigning consequences, 91; authority, 92, 109; unacceptable individual, 94; and motive and thought, 94; and interaction, 100; total depravity, nature and, 106; universals and, 113; instinctive, 114, 117; child, 114, 126, 147, 169; and plasticity of learning, 114; and community, 115; individual, 117, 141; repetitive, 117; instinct, environment and , 149: acquisition of, 117; pattern, changing, 117; Dewey, habits and judging, 119; "ridiculed" for unacceptable, 119; and theory of knowledge, 120; self, will and, 122; impulsive nature of, 126; over-simplified explanation of, 126; irrelevance of good, 126; experience, habit and, 127; and group approval, 127; change of, 127; policies and progressive education, 129; innate, fixed, 141; test of appropriate, 152 theory of, 153, 154; and unity of conduct, 154; issues in a unified world, 156; unified classroom experience, 156; and intelligence, 161; averaging goals and, 161; claims of mis-, in school, 167; disputes in school, 167

Bentham, Jeremy, and utilitarianism, 61, 93; and a formal procedure for evaluation, 84; and the rule of morality and law, 93; and individual authority, 93; and man's responsibility for man, 93; and man's responsibility for self, 93; and egoism and hedonism, 93

Berkeley, Bishop George, 11; and immaterialism, 32; and nature of materiality, 34; essence and secondary characteristics, 34; antecedent to pragmatism, 49; and the truth of common sense, 64

Bind(ing) (philosophical),regarding the individual and group, 24, 25 166; in communitarian dedication, 25; Dewey's philosophical, 25; linguistic, 25; loose, 25; and connecting principles, 26, 35; inconsistent, 37; truth and a, 66; non- , universals, 92; and Dewey's inquiry method, 94; of persons 147; Dewey philosophical fallacy, 166; temporary, 166

C

Capacity education and developmental, 103; of plasticity, 107; limitations of intellectual growth, 111,

Index

116; education and, 144, 169; consequences of, 166

Coherence, of experience, 34; of narratives, 63

Coherent theory of truth, models and narrative, 62; and conflicting views, 63; Dewey and, 66

Collective, and duty, 17; goals of the, 17, 95; Dewey, progress of man and the, 21; good intentions, 21; unity, 24; One is a necessary element of, 24; rule over Nature, Bacon, 46, 47; earthly and responsible, 48; collective meaning for truth, Dewey, 55; resolution in context, 58; understanding, 63; and facts and concepts, 71; conduct, 82; and categorical imperative, 91; "intelligencies," 110; "habit," 122; the One and the Many, 123; and immediate need, 123; and the individual, 126; civility and group progress, 126; purpose and fallacy, 129; no heroes or coercion in the, 131; practice as education, 133; differences and pluralism, 147; individual and the, 158, learning modes, 161; purpose, 165; and good of the group, 166; Rousseau, Dewey and the authority of the, 167; Man and the, 168

Collectivist instrumental value, 86

Commonality, school and, 25; communal, 43; of truth, 63

Common sense, and "Scotch realism," 14; and an eternal teleology, 14; without method, 27, 64; as opposition to sense and thought, 27; and a fall back on routine, 27, 64; as rationalization, 64; Berkeley, for minds debauched by learning, 64; James, suspicion of, 64; Dewey, failed, fallen back on faith, 64; and rationalistic logic, 73; as non-individual, 74

Communication, Dewey accused of inadequate, 10; group influence winning over individual by, 81; and idealism, 89; individual subordinate except through, 97; society and true, 98; the group, purpose and, 104; as a common possession, 134; education and the broad view of, 134; foundation of communal bonding, 138

Communitarian(s), Dewey's philosophy as a merging of academic understanding and, 16; and conflict of individual and group interest, 25; without immediate judgment, 88; meliorism and goals of, 101; and the child, 146; pragmatism, 159

Community, Dewey's understanding of school, 9; in Dewey's youth, 14; Dewey, "Scotch realism," 14; Dewey's youth and religion, 15; Dewey, practical purpose of, 17; Dewey, interest in, 17; Dewey, group solidarity of, 19; Dewey and Hegel, 20; and agent of experimental inquiry, 21; authority of one's chosen, 23; individualism and , 25, 155; and the "general theory of education," 28; Dewey's school and pragmatic, 31; and

Index

apart from 80; can't reliably predict, 80; hope of establishing, 84; individual behavioral, 86; unacceptable, 88; acceptable judging of, 88; and behavioral expectation of students, 89; assigning behavioral, 91, 127, 167; Dewey's standards for, 94; violations and levying, 94; denial of, 107; aims and subjective, 107; as "meaning well," 107; selection of external, 107; pathology and, 116; intending, 119, 142; of negative habits, 119; habits not changed by, 121; as deterrent, 122; of undesirable habits, 124; of anti-group habit adoption, 127; time and, 127; uncertainty and, 130, 152; understanding and, 131; social progress and 166

Constructivist, theory of truth meaning and truth, 66; Dewey and, 66; and pure reasoning, 66; world and science, 67; non-individual, common sense and, 74

Convergence theory of truth, Dewey and, 63, 64, 66; as individual, 74; and truth, 74; and learning, 76

Correspondence theory of truth, as two factors determinately related, 60; and perception of the individual, 61; and truth, 61; limitations of, 61; and a plurality of meanings, 61; individual meaning and, 61, 74, 76; between subject and object, 62; and narrative, 62; as related to coherence-notion, 62; and Dewey, 63, 66; in progress toward commonality, 75; and the individual, 76

Curriculum, and the confusing context of truth, 66; and democratic principles, 136; for some and not others, 140; and commitment to community, 143

D

Darwin(ian), as a justification for change, 101; Dewey and advantage over others, 114; survivalism, 115; and conflicts, 166

Democracy (democratic), a pluralistic America, 10; *and Education*, 10, 32, 29; education for an informed, 13; society, Dewey's 15; public schools, true, 16; Dewey, society, productive and, 17; and the "general theory of education, 28; inconsistency of coercion and, 37; and pragmatics of education, 43; Dewey, philosophical framework for, 43; Dewey, science and, 68; collectivism and a true, 83; institutions, commerce and, 87; many meanings of, 87; formula for chaos and, 88; student-individual trumps freedom and, 93; ideal of better society for, 94; society, progressive and, 101; unity and growth to, 104; Dewey, community, and true, 108; "fixed learning" and, 109; and "collective intelligencies," 110; expression of self,

130; public program of education for a true, 133; community and true, 134; accomplishing institutional, 135; school and true, 135; society, school and acceptable pattern of, 135; and pragmatic construction of a nation, 135; from equality, 136; principles and practices of, 136, 140; provision of education in a true, 140; classism and 140; pluralism and, 140, 141; manual training and, 140; educational, 141, 143, 147; Dewey's hope for education and true, 141; reform requisite for true, 144; industrialization, labor and, 145; Social, 145; separation, disunity, conflict and, 149; hands, plans and, 151; dualism of leadership and labor, 154; unity in a 154; Dewey, ideals of "intelligence and," 155; ideals consistent with, 160; Dewey's vision of, 169

Derrida, Jacques, context and meaning, 71

Descartes, René, methods of investigating the physical world, 25 46; and mentally grasping the world, 26, 46, 91; Dewey, without action no authority, 26; "innate ideas," 26; and theism, 27; dualism of body and mind, 33, 154; idealist, 91; and apperception, 109

Dewey School (Laboratory School),Dewey's classroom practice, 9; educational philosophy into practice, 31, 133; enduring practice, 133; ideas enduring and derivative, 161

Dialectic(al), method of resolving practical understanding, 16; Hegel to Dewey, and history to nature, 20; Dewey's pragmatic writings, 98; equilibrium, Dewey, 155

Discipline (disciplinary), judgments, 46; lack of definitive knowing and, 74; disasters, Dewey, 81; school, 84, 124, 167; without hard fixed rules, 88; importance of rules of, 89; constraints, 89; chaos, 89; dispute over school, 90; violation or student-individual rights, 90; student esteem in issues of, 90; and prime understanding, 91; what constitutes, 91; hesitant or mute on school, 92; Dewey and, 92; individual, 99; student, 100, 130, 147, 167; or is student a victim of the environment, 119; means, ends, habits and, 122; child's expectation of, 126; child, 136; intervention, 160

Disunity, and group purpose, 101; and mind without action, 117; of philosophy in a true democracy, 149; as theory, 153

Diversity, of individual talent, 99; of views and communal change, 103; social education through, 136; school, 136; and inseparability, 153; group, 157; and individual capability, 158; freedom, change and, 159

Dogma, of the past, 5; imposed by authority, 33, 73; teaching and, 38; pragmatism against, 49; and truth, 58, 85; tradition and, 59; and experimental verification, 64, 146; moral, 65; indurate, 73; and predetermination, 105; individual, 105, 108; group-held, 108

Dualism, Dewey, Hegel and, 16; "disjunctions, " "alternatives" and, 16; Descartes, of body and mind, 33, 151; Dewey and Kantian, 37; of individual and society, 127; of leadership and labor, 154

E

Education(al), and theoretical truths, 6; hanged in traditional public, 7; praxis of non-traditional, 8; an American view of public, 8; prophet of modern American, 8; Dewey and practical, 9; Dewey and the state of modern public, 9, 15; prominent theorists in, 9; Dewey and the theory of, 9, 133; Dewey pedagogy, 9; Dewey, unification of methodology, 16; Dewey, unity of philosophy and, 19; Dewey, as a mission, 20; Dewey, methodological critique for, 20; a system of communal, 21; without the group, 21; idealism and American, 22; Dewey's ideas and public, 23; Dewey's unfailing dedication to institutions of, 25; "general theory of," 28; and true democratic freedom, 28; as a laboratory, 28; Dewey's views on subjects matter in, 29; Dewey's ideas reside in public, 29; Dewey commandeered America, 30; Dewey's failed theory of, 30; theory went international, Dewey, 30; more practical than theoretical, 36; process of, 41; and pragmatism, Dewey, 42, 43; as social glue, 42; and the individual, 43, 101, 108, 109; the nature of the term, 46; Dewey's view of expansive, 47; Dewey's methodical and organized, 48; similarity of life and, 48; Dewey, community, truth and, 49; Locke, obstacle to, 52; Dewey, procedural uncertainty and, 52; Dewey, usefulness traditional, 59; truth, knowing and, 66; Dewey, methodologies and experimentation of, 67,68; Dewey, respecting both the social and, 71; Dewey, difficulties of a traditional academic, 71; Dewey, fixity and, 71; Dewey, words obscuring ideas in, 71; Dewey, knowing, truth and the nature of, 75; as a lifelong pursuit in the broadest context, 82; meliorism and a hopeful prognosis for, 87; with a moral context, 87; a way to a better community and world, 87; and emancipation from social dependencies, 87, 88; and violations of disciplinary rules, 89; and societal regeneration of the individualist, 94; and society and hard

Index

act within the 117; habits give control over, 117; as "medium" for change, 118; acting on impulse repeatedly drives habit within the, 118; education of the young, controls the environment, 117, 118; education, indirect through the, 118; different experience form different, 118; behavioral infraction and the, 119; advantage of an appropriate, 119; unification of responses by the individual is a sign of appropriate conduct in the, 120; unity in nature, mind, impulses in habit selection in the, 120; objects are media in the, 124; school discipline and a conducive learning, 124; variables in behavior, time, situation and, 125; student empirical exploration of the, 126; habits and common, 127; group changes in the, 130; expectation for a suitable teaching, 131; a"specialized social," 136; "diversity" and the learning, 136; indirectly educate by the, 136; eliminating unworthy features in the, 136; works unconsciously, 136; learning and the over-decorated, 136; vital impulse requires student interest abed proper, 134; Dewey and controlling the, 142; education is a response to the, 142; young allowed to change the, 143; the objective and moral world change with the, 151; unit of conduct by a consistent, 154, 155; equilibrium within the, 155; cooperation of organism and 155; time, the present, and the, 156

Epistemology, tolerance in issues of, 5; in Dewey's unified philosophy, 15; and Dewey's idea of change, 19; Dewey's complex, 20; and life, 27; is suspect, Dewey, 27; experimental and practical, Dewey, 27; of relationships, experience and usefulness, Dewey, 28; part of Dewey's empiricism and pragmatism, 31; of Dewey is compromised, 39; James and Dewey and irresolvable, 44; Dewey, as one - morality and, 45; school practice and a floating, 46; as pragmatic, 56; Hume, a sequence of issues, no resolution, 58; and coherence theory of truth, 63; and authoritative agency, 74; Dewey, selfish, 76; Dewey's, a misnomer, 76; and moral theory, 77; and relationships to others, 95; loss of authority in daily life, 95; Dewey, transitory, 110; Dewey's, uncertainty, 131; education an ongoing process of morality and, 133; Hook, and social disciplines less successful than religion, 151; Dewey, the knower and the known included in his, 152; and morality must be sought in a normal development of a life process," 153; and conduct united in natural world, 153; and fixed morality united us through one simple machine, 161;

Dewey's, avoids truth and responsibility, 162

Event(s), proof of unity of thought and action in the resultant, 23; radically tolerant, unanalyzed and fragmented understanding of the, 28; experience of sequence of related, 34; Dewey, not a world of isolated events, 35; order among real objects in interaction in the, 35; habituation and change among objects and, 36; Hegel, no prioritized 36; universality, time, situation and, 45; experiential knowledge, questioned on environment, time and, 45; Dewey, pragmatism requires the action of experience and, 50; life as experimental, changing with time, situation, agency and, 50; agency for understanding tim, situation and, 55; -horizon, a validating point for meaning and truth, 57; meaning full as it prepares for future understanding, 57; each issue non-transferable knowledge, 58; Hume and teleology of an, 58; Hume, merely random grouping of, 58; Dewey, difficulty in claiming viable knowledge, 60; narratives and the same, 61; correspondence and a limited recording of an, 61; Dewey, as action, 61; without truth serving as a private tool, 61; each narrative may correspond to the actual world, 61; perspectives of an, 62; not related through time, 66; Dewey, Hume, a skeptical history of, 67; verification of past, 67; seeing something happen is not knowledge of the, 68; Kant, preconception as a condition for an experiential, 69; Dewey, intuition and concept aid in perceiving the, 70; Dewey, combined thought and action in an, 70; is individual,70; predilection necessary to understand an, 72; Bentham, authority of determinative action in sequential, 84; observation only evidence not proof of, 85; as a material of thinking, 85; lost in fading history, 88; need for immediate interaction in, 89; alternative understanding of, 90; primary story of the, 90; perspectives prevent resolution of present or future, 90; student-individual and the details of a disciplinary, 90; primary authority in the, 91, 167; authority of past, 91; only specific changing objects and, 116; changing conditions and, 116, 156; agent beyond the, 127; equals action and actors, 152; without categorical assignment, 156; no one has authoritative perspective on the, 167

Evolution(ary)(evolving), of Dewey's pedagogy, 7; implication for Dewey's philosophy, 23; of pragmatic ideas, 42; action and societal, 57; communal understanding as equilibrium and, 63; of veracity, Dewey, 63; social needs under pressure of pressure of truth, 64; of experiential action produces communal meaning, 77; seventeenth century, "intellectual," 78; individual, the immediate seat of communal, 81; challenge to *status quo*, a force for societal, 84; in schools, the risk of disciplinary, 89; community, understanding of group purpose, 92; knowing through communal, 134; union of man and nature is, 153; process of repatriation of extreme egoist is, 159, 160; must not destroy unification, 166

Existential, (existentialism) (existentialist), Dewey predated, 20, 76, 161, 162; complexities, every changing, 116; the One, 161

Experimental(ly), constructed school, Dewey, 7; inquiry and the group, 21; individual, the agent of inquiry, 21; Dewey's epistemology as, 27; acts only useful, 36; as hands-on learning activities, 37; universals, laws and fixed rules must respond to, 45; daily life is, 45, 50; supernaturalism not an evolving, 49; approach and dubious pragmatism, 52; verification not possible with dogma, 64; thought is only a suggestion of, 70; the past and the reconstruction of history, 71; invention and the individual, 71; issues and uncertainty, 74; Dewey, and history in terms, 75; not rote or routine but act, 105; individual has authority, 110; student-individual must be allowed in conduct to be, 125, 129; freedom and individuation by, 128; laboratory as pedagogy, 133; evidence of authority and freedom, 142

Experimentalism, empiricism would point to, 38; daily experience and agency, 38; science, data and facts, 45; human understanding through, 48; dubious meaning in Dewey's pragmatic, 75; pragmatism and, 155

Experimentation, a necessity for knowing, 10; one of Dewey's two methodologies, 15; no dependably enduring, 46; facts of nature forced into form by active, 48; its own goal, not certainty, 50; individualized and non-transferable, 51; both meaning and truth emerge with active, 66; Dewey's pedagogy through, 67; growth of individual through active, 114; adults facilitate, children use, 126; dichotomy of consolation of others and self, 129; each student must find the way by, 141

F

Fallacy, Dewey's empiricism, 38; Dewey, universality as a, 120; Dewey's collectivity, 129, 165; Cartesian, 151;

with, 105; nature of the individual, 113; rules and habits remove, 123; old habits not, 127; authority is individual and 131; Dewey's philosophical framework, 149

Freedom, in community, individual freedom, 10; beyond permissible margins, 10; prelude to Dewey's ideas of individual, 16; forced compliance and loss of, 18; Dewey's pragmatism and individual, 22; through Dewey's "general theory of education," 28; dream of romantic, 30; student-individualism, 31; unchallenged individual, 55; flexibility of knowing and loss of individual, 73; willing for other compromises, 75; come to the knower by experience, 75; posited by individual, 77; imperatives to duty remove authority for complete, 83; universals strip away individual, 83; the group, individual and, 87, 92, 93; of individual trumps other, 93; student-individual and loss of, 95; charity and individual, 95; for an individual means growth, 97; favorable, effective thinking and, 97; Rousseau, Emile and, 99; and "ragged" individualism, 100; solitary experience does not promote, 100; of individual within group context, 100; Locke, and doing and knowing, 101; of individual authority and thought, 101, 109; of the individual and disruptive behavior, 102, and mechanical approach to individual, 103; lone nature of individualism would deny, 104; Dewey's individual would grow in, 105; self-defined, 106; Dewey's principle of individual, 106; student-individual and, 107; divisive individualism and self-, 107; with unity of mind and body, no need for, 109; individual intellectual, 109; individual responsibility and, 111; in classroom, individual allowed, 111; for the individual and Dewey's avoidance of specifics, 111; for the individual and potential for extremism, 126; of individual experience over societal will, 128; and experimental individuation, 128; choice is an element in, 128, 129; student-individual and learning, 129; all persons should enjoy complete, 140; democratic pluralism and, 140; student-individual, living at the epicenter of life in, 141; and authority, happily married, 142; of the individual and forced group authority, 144; of student-individual and license, 144; only true democracy can then be, 144; of individual and societal through socialization 145; in society with diversity and change, 159; in society with intellectual, 160; coercion an individual, 160;

academic and civil, 161; individual autonomous, 166; dream of romantic, 169
Free will, 102; Freud and, 116, 117;
Froebel, Friedrich, bringing idealism to America education, 22;
Future, Dewey's expectations of unity in the, 17; Dewey prophet of the, 20; Dewey. application not in the, 45; Bacon, man's utopian, 47; ends, means and the, 56; present events prepare way to the, 57; live in experience and look to a bright, 57; we walk in the present toward the, 57; knowing and truth in expectation of the, 57; Dewey, so fades the present and the future, 59; "Deliberation is not calculation of an indeterminate, 59; ours is the present not the, 59; Dewey, convergence and hope for the, 63; events in past, present and, 67; Dewey, tenderness for the, 70; experience cannot control for prospects in the, 75; Dewey, hopeful expectation for education's, 87; counseling guidance and the, 90; behavior, 90; group or individual good not determined for the, 95; the One, the Other and needs for the, 123; action not in past or, 123; "ideal" and the not experienced, 124; only speculation of the, 124; present emerges insensible to the, 125; Dewey's inconsistency with regard to the, 135; Dewey, "danger" in emphasizing pursuits of the, 138; Dewey, pragmatism and ends in the, 138; studies for laborers of the, 141; students, education and determinate, 141; society determines its own, 143; experiencing the present and looking to the, 154; separation of the present and a remote, 155; education and a better, 162

G

General theory of education, philosophy as, 28; only through democratic freedom, 28
Good will, Kant, optimism for man's, 17; for man Dewey adopts Kant's, 83
Group(s), preference, 13; purpose, 13, 17, 21, 23, 24, 38, 39, 51, 75, 92, 98, 101, 111, 133, 142, 160, 165, 166, 168, 169; self-seeking, 13, 158; interdependence, 19; solidarity, 19, 83, 95, 108, 110; authority, 21, 38, 43, 88, 92, 101,110, 129, 157; and individual, 18, 22, 24, 25, 38, 77, 78, 81, 83, 86-89, 92-95, 99, 101, 104, 106, 110, 119; 125-127, 142, 161; goals, 22; common determination, 23; unity, 25, 43; function, 25, pragmatism, 43; action, 45, 98; and truth 55; and tolerance, 74; and knowledge, 74, 75; activities, 87; values, 87, 89, 98, pluralism, 87; beliefs, 88; will, 88, 128, 154; and chaos, 88; and the young, 93; and meliorism, 94; harmony, 94; diversity, 97;

behavior, 100; dogma, 108; habits, 115, 127, 128; cohesion, 129, 134, 166; differences, 153, 154, 157, 158; freedom, 160

Group welfare, individual habit formation over, 129

Growth, Dewey's optimism about a young America's, 13; democracy and societal member's, 87; individual freedom means, 97; individuation depends on experience not, 100; individual, 101; of group without fixed standards, 104; extremist, fixed in habit without, 104; random change in identity not part of process of, 105; intelligent replacement of habit and "capacity for, 111; exploration and experimentation empowers the process of, 114; habit modification and growing and, 117; routine arrests, 118; "fixed-ends-in-themselves" halt, 123; consequences for individuation and, 127; impulse-habit foundation of individual, 128; group and individual, 129; child discipline of life and, 136; materialism and, 139; individual association and social, 142; appropriate response to change and the process of, 142; immaturity, the "primary condition of," 143; learning, behavior, "knowledge" and moral, 156; individual and progressive society's, 160

H

Habit(s), diverse philosophical schools and traditional intellectual habit, 23; the child and replacement of, 30; replacement, 30; rendered possible by impulses, 30; instinctive reaction into a smooth pattern of, 30; not "superficial" and "rigid" formation, 30; the true "stuff" of experience, 34; a term for ordering acquired elements of action, 35; formation and intelligent understanding of change, 36; "Genuine knowledge" and "practical experience" and, 57; of use, 58; Middle Ages, scholasticism and, 69; due to direct and repeated behavior, 70; behavior as knowledge and, 81; replacement of old and bad, 81; more appropriate, 82; consistent action and, 83; replacement with new, 89; replacement of old, less useful, 89, 116, 120; earlier individualism and, 97; understood in social terms, 99; replacement and bring extremists into the group, 100; and individual identity, 103; lone individual fixed in, 104; revision and collection of new, 106; and individual intellectual freedom, 109; "impulses and", 109; by intelligent replacement for life and "capacity of growth," 111; procession of experience and adaptive "capacity of growth," 111;

impulse the driving force for selection of, 114; inculcation of young with adult, 115; communal mechanism of individual brought to evaluation of, 115; impulses push to challenge, 115; "arrested and encrusted," 115; that are new will free man from the past, 117; and changing behavior patterns, 117; compulsion and, 117; replaced in time and situation, 118; calling out, 118; reduced to routine ways of acting, 118; reflection on and changing, 118; impulses modify or removed, 118; repeated action of impulses dries formation of, 118; arrived at individually, 118; rest with individual authority, 118; addiction and "bad," 119; not deliberately found, 119; "capricious," 119; formation and replacement as "continuous" reconstruction of experience, 119; pathology and forced, 119; individual, environment and, 119; school, its environment and, 119; challenging traditional and established, 119; may be destroyed by conflict impulses, 120; refreshing of, 120; and liberating powers, 120; thought, impulse and, 120; not patterned, will not change behavior, 120; that are "vital" and those in "stagnation," 120; and consciousness and conscience, 120; and war between impulses, 120; unity with impulses and resultant, 120; direct action, thought and, 120; Dewey, *tabula rasa* an, 121; individual is changed by new, 121; as dicta, self evinced by, 121; combination of, 121; as active means and ways of acting, 121; may become the "will,"121; analogy of good posture, 121; not changed by consequences, 121; ideas depend on, 121; and not and "end," 121; and act before the thought, 121; social customs and the collective, 122; and a lifetime - character, 122; means, ends and, 122; undesirable actions and, 122; student-individual and bad, 122; quelled replacement of, 122; and fixation on objects, 122; and fixed rules remove "flexibility," 123; universal morality, "everyday affairs," and, 124; and characteristic of self in student-individual, 124; lethal, 124; and "liberated impulses"and "stagnation," 125; individuation, impulse and, 125; and stifled impulses, 125; impulses acting on objects to change, 125; blame for behaviors and, 125; and impulses and process of a lifetime, 125; and approved action, 126; and experience at the "margin of liberty," 127; adoption by anti-group and individuation, 127; and the individual as social product, 127; relationships are the "locus" of, 127; customary practices of culture are moral, 127; physical and moral, 127; are individually yet commonly held within a common environment, 127; as the individual makes changes within the environment, 127; as inflexible, their decay and disintegration, 128; counter to formation and replacement of, 128; - impulse formation and satisfying the self, 128; problem of individual over the group, 129; order and establishing, 130; and judgment and punishment of student, 130; individual authority and, 130; impulsive action and pragmatic usefulness, 130; consciousness is born in challenging, 130; nothing above the impulse mechanism of formation of, 131; expression of defiance and violence, 131; replacement of novelty, 139; replacement and "mechanical" work, 139; and knowledge, duality, 149; "the world of intelligence" in "revising and readjusting," 160, 161; replacement as a lifelong process, 163

Hedonism, self and others, 92; Dewey, Bentham and, 93

Hegel, Dewey borrowed from, 8, 11; James Marsh and, 16; Dewey not a follower of, 16; Dewey and the dialectic and, 16; Dewey and universals and, 16; and Dewey's aversion to dualism, 16; Dewey, opposites and, 16; ideals, presumptive of consequences without expectations and predictability, 19; idealism and, 19; Dewey, idealism and, 19; Dewey, change and, 20; and historical approach to the ideal and the Absolute, 20; "knowledge never immediate or self-certifying," 20, 50; and a progressive metrology, 21; change, experience, objects in the environment, 36; and the "power of sheer survival," 36; not able to respond to "specific problems," 36; and absolutism and metaphysical understanding, 37; and methodology of uncertainty, 37; and unification and not dualism, 37; and history of knowing by individual experience, 37; and Dewey and individualism, 97; and Dewey and the unity of life, 149; and dialectical equilibrium of elements in the environment, 155; and Dewey's modern education, 162; and the process of the group drawing in the individual, 169

Helvetian, and "infinite perfectability"121

Herbart, Johann, Pestalozzi's student, 22; "recapitulation" of knowledge, 118

History (historical), Dewey's philosophy has, 13; of American schools, critical

world, 36; Dewey, nagging, 37; Dewey, hopefulness, 38; expectations and rationalism, Dewey, 41; knitting of One into the Many, 43; influences, Dewey, 55; communication, Dewey, 89; expectations and habit replacement, Dewey, 89; of categorical imperative, Kant,91; expectations and the mark of the group, Dewey, 94; near group harmony, Dewey, 94; speculation and change, Dewey, 105; hope of individual redemption, Dewey, 110, 160; hope for group unity without coercion, Dewey, 134; peeks at the future, Dewey, 135; methodology, no detailed plan, Dewey, 141; reclamation of the extreme egoist, Dewey, 159; hopefulness for rebellious students, 166

Idealized, mathematics without dimension, 72

Identity, of group or individual, temporal, 77; without intrinsic or terminal, 102; of person by society, 103; Locke, "passive," 103; mechanical assignation of, 103; and shadowy individualism, 104; science of human nature account for , 105; random change in, 105; public education's, 108; self-generated, 113; questionable, 124

Idolatry, passions into, 122

Inclusive(ness), Dewey, societal, 8; Dewey, philosophical, 13; Dewey, truth and, 58, 63; Dewey, conflicts and, 63; Dewey, collectivism and, 74

Inflexibility, of old habits, Dewey, 127

Individual(ism), old meaning, 5, 61; action, 6; and institutions, 7, 101, 108, 149; and pragmatism, 7, 14, 22, 41, 43, 48, 49, 55, 61; and authority 7, 50, 56, 60, 66, 71, 77, 78, 81, 83, 92, 93, 95, 101, 107; and community, 10; and freedom within community, 10; student, 10, 39; and learning community, 10; and group preference, 13; and self-seeking groups, 13; and Dewey, 14; and Dewey's philosophy, 15; and society, 17, 99, 145; and thought and action, 17; and duty, 17; solitary, 17; and others, 17, 129; and "public and common ends, 18; coercion and external authority, 18; as free and actionable agency, 19; and knowledge, 19, 20, 37; inquiry, 21; and nature and society, 21; and public concern, 21; and actionable experimentation, 21; and the group, 21, 23, 24, 38, 77, 78, 89, 87, 92, 94, 95, 98, 99, 100, 143; and education, 21, 43, 144; and utilitarianism, 22; selfish, 25, 27, 51; and rationalism, 26; and epistemology, 27; and "general theory of education," 28; and romantic ideals, 30; and self-expression, 31; and sole empiricist authority, 33; and uniqueness of experience, 34; sand "disconnection of meaning," 37; Dewey, and

Index

collectivist fallacy, 38; and immediate experience, 41; and Plato's authority, 42; and experience, 42, 51, 52, 55, 56, 57, 58, 61, 66, 71, 75, 77, 85, 89, 102; as an "organ" of society, 43; subjugation to state, 43; as an active element, 43; and Kant, 45; unique, 45, 56; and behavioral limits, 45, 107; Descartes and insulation, 46; and power over nature, 47; and instrumentalism, 50; and mechanism of change, 51; and perception and chaos to the group, 51; and actionable thought, 53; and conflicted truths, 55, 63; and truth, 56, 64; and intended action, 56; and unique experience, 58; and a claim to knowledge, 60; and judgment and perception, 61, 89, 90; and narrative, 61; knowing and judgments, 69; and freedom, 16, 73, 75, 77, 83, 92, 93, 97, 99, 100; and knowing, 74, 95; and abstract logic, 74; solitary, 76, 99; and character, 79, 80, 88, 102; and replacement of bad habits, 81; and behavioral control, 82, 88, 94; and extreme, 91, 98; Enlightenment, 91; and judgment, 91; and charity, 92, 95; and independence from tradition, 96; as "dumb" and "brute" animal, 97; in universal terms, 97; earlier, 97; incomplete and Plato, 97, 98; and Hegel, 98; and society, Rousseau, 98; and diversity, 99; and society and emancipation, 99; and the "good creator," Rousseau, 99; philosophical subjectivism and "practical," 101; for, and self-containment, Dewey, 102; Dewey, and flexible, 105; self-generated, 113; and associative life, 115; and control of, 125, 127; and time, 126; atomistic, 145; student, 146; and the world, 149; and institutionalism, duality, 149; cut-and-run, 159

Individuality, and learning and social activity, 21, James, pragmatism and, 48; "self-direction" and beaching the castes of workmen,82; trumps freedom and democracy of others, 93; Dewey, Plato and, 98; society and addendum to, 98; with elemental function in membership, 98; Plato, Rousseau and, 99; and "spacial distance," 102; as a potential threat to the group, 101; and extreme and disruptive behavior, 102; random change and process of "growth," 105; is created, only changed by society, 106; as loose cannon, 107; and group influence, 110; and its constitution, Dewey, 125

Individuation, Chapter 7 topic, and experience, 100; as an ongoing, active replacement of habits, 115; mechanism of, 117; impulses, habits and, 125; and patterns of behavior, 127; growth process natural to, 127; and assimilation into the culture, 128; and

and doing, 153; and Dewey's ideas of presentism, 155, 156; and narrative, 167; and primary agency, 167

Immaterialism, Berkeley's, 33; Dewey, objects beyond sensationalism, no, 34

Immorality, a challenge to tradition, as "bias and prejudice," 89

Impulse(s), forces of "instinct," "action" and, 16; to public ends, individual subordinates natural, 18; Nietzsche, philosophy a tyrannical, 24; all life is plastic to, 30; habits and impulses, 30, 109, 114, 115, 116, 118, 125, 130, 169; control of, 82; C. S. Lewis, benevolent, 113; is "indiscriminate," 114; rushes blindly into an opening of chance, 114; as an advantage over others, 114; Emerson and, 115; Dewey, action and, 115; as selfish, yet arising to group service, 115; "rushes us off our feet, 116; unresponsive to environmental needs, 116; a "law unto itself," 116; gives opportunity, 116; allows it expression, good or bad, 116; arises undirected to interact with the environment, 117; reflected on, as compulsion is irrational, 117; acting repeatedly on drives, 119; habits replaced by natural, 119; conflict with established habits, 119; in adult, habit replacement for life, 119; habits may be destroyed by conflicting, 120; replace less useful habits, 120; are a source of liberation, 120; liberates power, 120; and intelligence, thought and habit, 120; and thought, twins impeding habit, 120; drives man between "vital" and stagnate habits, 120; and thought and action, 120; habits and unorganized, 120; and habit replacement, 120; and "theory of knowledge," 120; and unity of nature and mind, 120; and habit replacement creates new habits in individuals, 121; student-individual civilized by eruptive, 122; universals often valued above, 124; habit relationships in"everyday affairs," 124; student-individual and habit replacement, 124; vital to individuation in the child, 125; liberated, 125; and habits, constitution of Dewey's individuation, 125; stifled, pathology may result, 125; repression, "evil" and "rebellion," 125; as intermediary to conduct, 125; unrealized to social disruption 125; student-individual allowed to act on, 125; dismissal of, 125; to excess without special terms of release, 126; and individual abuse of cooperation, 126; and "margin of liberty," 127; habit foundation of individual growth, 128; experiment with, 129; Dewey and transcendentalists, 129; problem with Dewey's theory of, 130; mechanism, nothing above it, 131; vital and appealing to student "interest," 137; common purpose and meliorable, 154; life is plastic to, 169; and romantic ideals, 169

Institution(alism), once authoritative, 6; roots of understanding of, 7; understanding of action, Dewey, 13; Dewey, effects on, 20; Dewey, rationality and social, 21; skepticism of educational, 25; duty of educational, 28; life, impulse and, 30; Dewey, social practice as, 36; and societal needs, 87; democracy and political, 87; culpable role of, 101; directly to blame, not extreme individual, 101; changes as external to self, 102; shifting of individual transgressions to 104; individuals rule over societal, 108; individual must find meaning in culture and its, 108, 127; student-individual destroy academic, 129; democratization of, 135; "Education proceeds from pattern given by," 135; and individual, duality, 149; and the strife of systems, 153; individual "rigid" in "isolation" and "formal,"158; romantic freedom "in defiance of organization and," 169

Instrumental(ism), of education in daily life, 7; Dewey's understanding of pragmatism, 9, 44, 73; to teaching and learning and Dewey's educational theory, 9; and Dewey and his students, 13; and Dewey' philosophical methodology, 15; theories only good as, 15; had value in solving problems through experience, 15; union of action and thought, 23; experience as useful, 26; the world intelligently changed as, 27; ideas, action, pragmatic issues and, 41; has value, 44; has meaning, 44; as predetermined as one choice over another, 45; thought to attendant action, 45; empiricism useful and amendable is, 45; individual action and application of, 45; scientific method, soldier of Dewey's, 47; science to Dewey was, 48; to usefulness, truth as an "approximation," 49, 50; individual authority of, 66; truth and, 74; Dewey, values are "intrinsic" or, 86; value, collectivist, 86; for social progress, the school as most effective, 135; of production, socialization is basic, 145; "liberal" and "progressive movement" of constructive power, no theoretical, 145;

Intolerance, as certainty, 95, 96

Intuition(alism), and "Scotch realism," 14, 113, 117; and Biblical history, 14; Dewey and, 20, 69; and common sense, 64; Kant, of pure thought, assumption in, 68; Kant, experiential event and, 69; and thought with action, 70; and *a priori*, 72; compulsion and, 117

Irrational, compulsion driven by, 117

Irreformable, American society, 15

Index

J

James, William, and an American view of man, 8; gave pragmatism its name, 15, 28; early link to the assumptions of pragmatism, 8,15, 49; a way that Americans would view life, 28; pragmatism, a variation of Dewey's, 28; " radical empiricism," 28, 118; welcomed Dewey as a peer, 28; magnanimous toward pragmatists, 28; pragmatism and reality, 41; and individual immediate experience, 41; and "alternations of flights and perchings," 42; definition of philosophy, 42; and valuelessness of understanding, 44; and testing of understanding, 44; and testing and an irresolvable epistemology, 44; and uncertain of science, 44; and laws as approximations, 44; science and language, 44; usefulness of science, 44; and loss of religious prestige, 44; and loss of religious metaphorical authority. 44; and pragmatism and individuality, 48; and "preluders" and antecedents to pragmatism, 49; fragmented pragmatism, 49; and "empirical attitude" and "concrete action," 49; and pragmatism "unstiffens" all our theories, 49; and pragmatism as instrumental, 49; and the hypothetical and action, 49; and truth and reality, 55; pragmatism diverges from Dewey, 57; Dewey's pragmatism a broader species, 57; and immediate experience, 57; experience and reality, 57, 58; and common sense, 64; common sense and resorting to categorical escape, 64; and common sense and tricks of human thought, 64; common sense and truth, 64; lack of faith in common sense, 64; and experience as process, 68; and truth and morality as expedient, 77; and passions, 122; and "trans-experiential knowledge, 134

Judge(d), public school pedagogy, 10; by fixed law and rule, 27; and group conflict, 38; by consequences, 38; flawlessly, 51; a faithful likeness, 62; by conceivability, 62; as *a priori* synthetic knowledge, 69; thought with action, 72; free of predisposition, 78; of individual character, 78, 131; acts and action, 84, 139; and the situation, 82; by collectivist instrumental value, 86; clearly, 88; misbehavior, 89; individual, 110; reluctance to, 120; old habits, 120; individual action by fixed morals, 124; undesirable behavior, 124; concerning habit replacement, 130; authority to, 131; and individual expression, 131; success or failure with true

K

Index

of physical and metaphysical worlds, 69; and idea of individualist perception of objects, 69; and *a priori* synthetic judgments, 69; and Dewey's idea of habit, 70; and action in time and space, 70; and morality, 80; and will and the "controlled self," 80; deontology, 80; and optimism of man's good will in action, 83, 126; and mechanical duty, 83; and unified life, 92; unification with universals, 151; and rationalism, 152

Knower, and experiential authority, 57; and known, 58, 60; and error in judgment, 61; and responsibility for knowing, Dewey, 63; authority for truth of knowing, 63; gains freedom by experiencing the known, 75; and the thing known, integrated epistemology, 152

Knowing, and experimentation, 10; and experience, 19, 27, 37, 50, 66; and doing, 19, 45, 95, 101, 1494, 151, 153; by neither mind or action apart, 26; uncertain nature of, 27, 37, 41; replacement of, 27; and behavior, 31; and sensation, 34; and Kant's noumena and phenomena, 34; practical, 34; and scientific method, 47; objective, 48; technique of, 48; meaning and truth, 49; fixity of, 49, 70; as temporary, stop-gap, 49; as "self-corrective," 50; and a pragmatic and changing world, 50; as transcendental, 51; by Dewey and Hume, 51; without guaranteeing causality, Locke, 52; subject to change, credibility, 52; and its methodology, 52; dependable, 52, 59; and truth are but an itch or whimsy, 56; lost in the past, 57; as indefensible, 58; and habits of use, 58; agency of 58, 74; from inductive individual experience, 58; as inclusive, 58; ongoing process of, 59; and immediacy and extended time, 59; and learning and retentive usefulness, 59; and meaning, 60; and truth must maintain a "systematic coherence," 62; and truth in the world of objects, 63; difference between meaning and, 63; authoritative control of, 63; and James and sensation, 64; defining, fixing, 63; constructivist approach to, 66; and Dewey on education, 66; and Dewey's "imagination," 67; "pure," 69; and science, "fixed and inflexible," 69; in thought with action, 69; and "*a priori* synthetic judgments," 69; and intuition, 69; and skepticism, 70; and its value out of time, 71; a traditional comfortable, 72; without action no, 72; loss of individual freedom with flexible, 73; only in the present may we have utility of, 73; and truth, specific delimitation, 74; and Dewey and obstacles to teaching and discipline, 74; and student individual interest, 74; transferable 74; and the very nature of

interaction, 102; individual action and, 105; and "human action," 105; education and the union of body and mind, 109; individual authority in, 110; through growth or tradition, 115; "recapitulation" of, 118; "theory of," 120; "character of," 120; by proxy and disinterest, 134; as abstraction, Locke, 143; failed without connection, 143; self-enclosed philosophy, Dewey, 149; and habit, dualism, 149; and experience, dualism, 149; objective and subjective, dualism, 149; internalized, 152; theory of, 153, 154; expectation of, 154; unified, 156; from activity, 156; is interrelated, 158; and morality unified, 160; and fixed morality, 161

Known, innately, things, 20; widely, Dewey, 20; by thought not substance, 34; fort meaningful effect, 37; languages for tolerant choice or expression, 44; Bacon, but not becoming fixed or possessed, 47; transcendental without thought value or expectation of meaningful outcome, 51; as temporary and arbitrary, 52; and "knower" separated in categories of things, 58; knower and whole knowledge, 60; responsibility of the knower for the, 63; apart from experience, 68; and transferability, 74, 75; by experience, 75, 167; modern student and the, 76; and only knowing individually, 95; as a word may be compromised, 118; and habits, Dewey, 130; and character, 131; acts of cowardice, Péguy, 133; and the knower inextricably linked, 152

L

Laboratory School see Dewey School,

Law(s), of logical positivists, 25; of individuals as subordinated y reason, Kant, 26; fixity of law, 27; Dewey's access to society through, 29; Dewey, condescension to, 37; only as an "approximation," 44; held to scrutiny, physical, 45; no universals or fixed, 45; of physical world subject to change, Dewey, 67; of physical world only given from outside the real world, 67; is assimilated to command or order, 67; as the ruling influence, 67; is regarded as self-evident, 69; in the school and judgment lost, 74; inferior to meliorism, 87; of questionable authority, Dewey, 89; and practices, hypocrisy, Dewey, 89; fixity, "bias and prejudice," 89; breaking, 91; and Jeremy Bentham, 93; Bentham, rule of morality and, 93; and certainty, 93; and culpability, 94; in the face of reason, 96; impulse and, 116; its authority in society,

Index

Locke, John, derivative of, 11, a method for investigating the physical world, 25, 46; and mind theory, 26; and sensation, 26; and theism, 27; experience acquired objective knowledge through the senses, 33; and sensationalism, 33, 34; empiricism and fixity, 34; and an objective materiality, 34; object-related realism, 34; not truly empirical due to "theory of mind," 34, 35; an antecedent to Dewey's pragmatism, 49; nothing but experience, 52; experience linked to ideas only by trial and error, 52; not innate knowledge, 67; a ghost of the Enlightenment, 91; authority of the experimenter, 100; freedom of doing and knowing, 101; *tabula rasa*, 103; as scribe (on the blank slate), 105; all experience written on a blank slate of mind, 121; as education filling the empty mind, 143; mind and body, duality, 143; man set adrift and left alone, 165

Logic(al), of "sensationalistic empiricism, 34; knowing and the blinded mind, Bacon, 48; of knowledge replacement, 48; rationalistic, self-certifying, 73; abstract, 74; reduced to individual opinion, 74, 86; and "Scotch realism," 113; not instinct, 117; of doctrines of liberal and progressive movement, 145

Logical empiricism, problems and solutions, Dewey, 150

Logical positivism, laws and universals, 25; would escape scrutiny, 48

M

Man, a purely American view of man, 8; wants to control life, 10; Kant, optimism and ultimate good of, 17; the basic element or democratic productive society, 17; Dewey, optimistic view of, 17; history, reason and, 21; and group and nation, 21; society modified by progress of, 21; Bacon, and utopian view of, 25, 46, 47; Bacon, God's provision for, 26; Emerson would take the mechanism out of, 30, 168; Dewey, philosopher of the "plain,"36; transcendence, the common, 42; made language, laws, 44; Bacon, inquiry into knowledge benefit, 46; and collective rule over nature, Bacon, 46; of letters, Bacon, 47; science servant of, Bacon, 47; over nature, not over Man, Bacon, 47; conquering nature, Bacon, 47; applied science to lose sight of, 68; fully in view of purpose when human exploitation set aside, 68; as "spectator" or "participant," 68; history, record of social life and progress of, 71; certainty, devotion to the ideal, 72; is slave who executes the wishes of others, 75; life is progress, 77; removed from

Index

abolished ends, 78; give a fish, charity, 79; receiving praise unworthily, Adam Smith, 79; ultimate good will, Kant, 83; man to move the earth, Bentham, 84; progressing into a better world, 87; his welfare and melioration, 87; education in the environment better, 87; independent, move out of moral context, 87; and private happiness, 93; knowing and civilization, 95; and conflict of experience, 95; the measure of all things, 97; and diverse groups, 97, 98; Dewey, Plato, and the individuality of, 98; and perfectibility of, 99; submerged in nature, 99; as a creature of nature, 99; economic, 101; and solitary purpose, 101; freedom and disruptive behavior, 102; as a variable, 102; a creation in the communal works, 103; can be elevated above nature, 103; for himself, 104; and natural science, 105; graced with will and intellect, 105; flex of redefinition, 105; part of nature 105, 152; "organic" in society 106; selects external consequences, evil, Dewey, 107; selects internal feelings, evil, Dewey, 107; capable of plasticity, 107, 114; can be socialized, 108; cosmology, a backdoor for, 108; needed for nature, 108; raised uniquely for himself, Rousseau, 113; better equipped to learn from experience better than animals, 114; and continual change, 116; freed by new habits, 117; and "perfectability," 121; with bad posture (analogy), Dewey, 121; garners greater meaning from society, 127; depends on what other people are, 127; and experience eating (analogy), 153; union of nature and, 153; home is nature, 153; continuous with nature, 153, 158; must become united with the Many, 155; has to create himself, 158; not remote to the world, 158; set adrift and left alone, Locke, 165; canonized along with the group, 168

Mankind, provision from God, 26,46; begins history submerged in Nature, 99; disunity, 101; graced with "will", "intellect" and "flexibility," 105; and "infinite perfectibility," 121

Mann, Horace, and the Common School, 8

Mathematics (mathematical), laws, 72; as whimsy, 72; and Dewey and the authority of numbers, 72; and a confusion of propositions and processes, 72; must be made experimental in inquiry, 72; with measured units, 72; reduced to individual opinion, 74

Meaning(s) (meaningful), Dewey prophesied of social, 7; Dewey, avoidance of decisive, 11; Dewey, doubts of final, 15; as instruments, 15, 44; Dewey, flexible use or language and, 22; Dewey, rejected formulaic, 27; through sequential

Index

Index

discussions "like fighting air," 44; James, religion useful and, 44; Hook, judgment of "truth and falsity," 50; Dewey, merging Kant;s worlds of physical and, 69; Dewey, and unity, 155; Dewey, separate from physical world takes away progress, 155; Dewey, singularity and, 155

Method(ology), Dewey's practical, 9; appropriate group, 9; Dewey's philosophical, 15; Hegel's dialectic as, 16; Dewey, of unity, 16; Dewey, critique for both science and education, 20; of "inquiry," 20, 150; Hegel's progressing, 21; Dewey, of instrumentalism, united, 23; Dewey, thought and action as unified, 23; machinations of the mind, 25; of Dewey's epistemology, 27; common sense without, 27; experiential learning, 31; Dewey, all problems by scientific inquiry, 36; Hegel' engine of, 37; authority and definitive, 38; Dewey, unclear, 38; of investigation, 46; Dewey, Bacon and empirical, 47; Dewey, applauded Bacon's, 47; Dewey, Bacon, in pedagogy and science, 47; Dewey, scientific, 47; Dewey, Bacon modern progenitor of scientific, 48; Dewey extracted from Bacon the idea of, 48; Dewey, education organized and, 50; Dewey, pragmatic, 50; Locke, experience and ideas but no, 52; of knowing, 52; of acquisition of knowledge, 60; of getting at truth, 60; no practical, intellectual, 64; categorizing as, 64; tolerance allowed in, 65; authority in society, 83; for finding a solution, 84; for deciding about behavior, 88; and replacement of habits, 89; and murder, 90; of inquiry of uncertainty, 93; Dewey and bind, 94; and relativistic morality, 96; judgment, conduct and, 105; as a model for order and inquiry, 114; conduct, self will and, 122; rote learning, 134; Dewey, not detailed plan, 141; Dewey's, learning, 143; hands-on, 143; Dewey, failed practical, 145; and subject matter duality, 149, 152; Dewey, taken from science, 150; Dewey, of unity, 151; of common inquiry, 156; of inquiry, pragmatic, 156; Dewey, of unity and universality, 156; Dewey, of mechanism of unity, 159; Dewey, without definitive, 161; Dewey's contributions, order, form and, 161

Metrics (measurement), of acceptable behavior, 109; abstract progressive educational, 141

Mind, Biblical and intuitional hold on the, 14; separation of body and, 16; opposites as integral as body and, 16; one's will denied, in one's right, 17; and general inquiry, 19; dialectic with individual into the community, 20; individual and community in "correlative," agreement in, 22; Dewey, "penetration" of the Culture's set of, 24; machinations of the, 25, 46; Locke, purpose-claim of, 26; Dewey, natural certified together, action and, 26; Descartes, dualism of body and, 33; dilemma of body and, 33; Locke and Hume, theory of the, 34, 35; finding meaning only in the, 35; Dewey, no more duality of body and, 36; as biological, 36; Authority would yield to subjectivity and, 37; knowledge unchanged, "Pure," 42; philosophy from "bias and prejudice," freedom of, 42; flourishes of science "dazzle" the, 44; truth already possessed by the, 48; and circle of traditional learning, 48; intrinsic experience and the rationalistic, 46; "The Agent of Reorganization, 58; Dewey, loss of specific knowledge of the, 59; and "interpretation" "weigh" on getting at truth, 60; truth may be created in the activity of the, 61; the judge, the judging, 61; thought goes through our, 61; mental separation from situation is the duality of body and, 62; Descartes, objects not conjoined in action with the, 62; unity of matter and, 62; Berkeley, debauched by learning, 64; science marks the emancipation of, 68; ideas are the life of the, 69; objects need foreknowledge to impress the, 69; in degrees, the self achieves, 85; self not separate from, 85; Plato, thought and the, 85; Descartes, only knowledge of the, 91; the individual thinks his own, 97; objects produce truth in the, 98; Locke, isolated objective world from the, 100; Locke, world and impression made on the 100; the individual as, 102; duality of matter and 109; intrinsic individual meaning, meaning of the, 109; individual holism as body and, 110; disunity of action without, 117; Dewey, school, laboratory for changing the, 118; habits of the, 119; "continuity of nature and, 120; unity found in nature and, 120; idea, action, will and, 121; and habit replacement, 122; student-individual, freedom and the, 128; student to the lesson must submit body and, 130; men's work, neither heart or, 139; hands of science, leaders exercise them, 140; Locke, to fill the empty 143; and rote and repetition, 143; Locke, duality body left out of the work of the, 143; duality, body and, 149, 151; unification body's action and thought of the, 151; as an end, 151; unity of body and, 162; passivity and American body and, 166

Misbehavior, judging, 89; figment of a biased imagination, 90; Dewey's reluctance to judge school, 119; and primary authority, Dewey, 167

Mistrust, of hypothesis, Dewey, 105

Montaigne, **Michel De,** individual as inconstant, 102; man in flux, 102

Moral(ity) (moralities), Dewey, tolerance in, 5; issue of protest, 5; particularity, 3. 13; drift of, 10; Dewey, unified philosophy including, 15, 23, 39; Emerson, and oneness with the physical world, 23; Dewey, no fixed, 27; in common senses without a method, 27; Dewey, as one, epistemology and, 45; dogmas, political and, 65; Dewey, theory of, 77; Dewey, individual working, 77; determined by group, 77; a communal glue, 77; standards for, 77; Aristotle "regulated" moral theory, 78; preselected ends in fixed, 78; beyond activity, 78; Predetermined forms of, 78; blame on grounds of, 78; behavior as activity of, 78; ego and concerns for others, 78; character, 80; uncertainty and bottom-line, 80; Hume, acts of, 80; Dewey, acts of, 80; "good", fixed, 80; Kant, and issues of, 80; and behavior as knowledge, 81; education, knowledge and, 81; definition alternative possibilities in which all activities are involved, 82; collective conduct and, 82; good of community, individual, 83; Kant, duty in action of, 83; actionable consideration, 84; and ethics unknowable, 86; Dewey, brings together both intellect and, 87; education has a context of, 87; man out of communal context is out of context of, 87; standard of meliorism in, 87; a group value, 87; of individual disavowable, 87; democracy has meaning of, 87; measuring the extremes of life's variance in, 88; no set standards of, 88; acceptable, 88; addressing issues of, 88; action and consequences, 88; issues not resolvable, 88; and disciplinary constraints, 89; tradition and, 89; responsible action and, 91; justifiable action, 91; plan for the One, Dewey, 92; Bentham, utilitarian understanding of, 93; education and, 93; judging of disputations of, 94; of a referent of communal action, 94; and salving of "savage breast," 94; goals and collectivity, 95; and uncertainty, 95; action the biased measure of, 95; and loss of knowing, 95; and usefulness, 95; certainty as intolerance, 96; relativistic, 96; fixity of, 101; internal changes in, 100; neutrality in individual, 104; Dewey, higher type of personal, 104; phenomenon changing, 116; and pathology, 116; universal, 124; fixed to judge individual, 124; habit, 127; summation of habit both physical and, 127; uncertain epistemology and particularity of, 131;

N

human, a function of society, 113; a set of behaviors but flexible, 113; individuals interacting community, human, 113; child becoming with exploratory, 114; begin good and a child's, 114; Dewey, culturally divergent behavior and human, 117; individualization proceeds toward "continuity" of "mind" and, 120; unity of mind and, 120; Dewey, individual, 121; behavior imparts an impulsive, 126; Dewey, "margin of liberty" and human, 127; Dewey, non-transferable view of child's human, 141; and nurture, dualism, 149; Dewey, man part of, 152; union of man and, 153; man's home is, 153; man continuous with, 153, 158; science as a study of, 158; individual, elemental, 168; dream of return to, 169

New Atlantis, The, Bacon, dreams of, 25, 46

Noumena, Kant's, 34; Dewey, into experience, united phenomena and, 34; as the thing in itself, 34; what lay behind action, 92

O

Object(s), Dewey, simplified view of world, with, 11; Dewey, the physical world of, 23; Dewey denied ideas apart from, 33; Locke's apperception and, 34; Dewey, and pragmatic realism, 34; Berkeley and the world of, 34; Berkeley, without "substance," 34; Dewey, fact of the 34; immaterialism and a world of real, 35; Habituation, intelligent understanding in and among, 36; Hegel, reality of, 36; experience, teaching manipulation of material and, 36; Dewey, rationalism and real world of, 45; Descartes, insulated individualism among remote, 46; and action, thought and activity, 56; not in consideration when outside realm where can be extracted, Dewey, 57; Dewey, ideas not apart from, 57; unique experience among, 57; preconceptions and useful, 58; "knower" and "known" separated into categories of, 58; passively observed, 59; Descartes, denied action enjoined with 62; unity of mind and matter ongoing with, 62; correspondence and change in 62; inseparable subject-, 62; truth and knowing in the world of, 63; no knowledge without use of, 69; of judgment not intrinsic values, 86; a scene of harmonious "truth," world of, 98; creators and teachers are the world of, 104; others and, 105; nature in space and time, a number of diverse, 105; individuals are environmental, 105; individual authority for knowing, 109; Dewey, transcending, 109; specific changing, 116; repeated activity drives habit formation at the hands of, 118; environment with change in, 118; action through relationships with, 121; become media of "means," 121; habits stayed on certain, 122; to change habits impulses act on, 125; infused into every form, 133; education and an interaction of, 136; interest, moving force of, 137; agreement of outcome and, 152; thought, antecedent plant to action among, 152; thoughts are dreams when disconnected from, 152; attitude and, 153, 154

Objective(ly), Descartes and, 26; Locke and Hume, knowledge, through senses, 33; material, preceded by consideration of observer apperception, Locke, 34; changing world and rationalism, Dewey, 45; character of knowing is, 48; Hook, absolutism not, 69; Kant, perception determines what we will know as, 69; forms and mathematics, 72; Locke, world isolated from the mind,100; flux of life and Nature, 111; freedom and the "organization," 128; and subjective knowledge, duality, 149; world and moral world and changes, 151; world and moral world with experience in the present, 154; Dewey, outer world and an inner world, 168

Optimism, Dewey, for society and school, 7; Dewey, grown in soil of, 15; Dewey, found in Kant, 17; idealists and, 22; retained in America, 22; Dewey, as meliorism, 23, 94; drives national, 30; Emersonian, 30, 168; Dewey, based on individualism, 56; Dewey, a tenderness for the future, 70; Dewey, Kant's ultimate good will in action, 83; Dewey, and democracy, 87; Dewey, Rousseau ill-placed, 99; Dewey, as idealistic hopefulness, 166

Organic and Organic society, utilitarian understanding of, 22; to society man is, 106; union of individuals, society, 106; activities, a balance of habits, 117; supernatural, non-, 155

P

Paradox(ically), science feared and welcome, 68; knowing 70; of not knowing as knowing, 70; as belief from experience, Dewey, 95; and the theory of knowledge, looking to ideals, 154; Dewey, of the individual and the group, 160

Passion, fortified against change,122; unresponsive to the moment, growing into idolatry, 122; fixation of, 122; waiting to subside in student-individual, 123; unaffected by idea or "Reason," 123; school unable to curb, 123

Past, dogmas of the, 5; knowing and truth lost in the, 57; a product of accidents, 66; history and narratives of the, 66; events and consequences, 67; and present events, 67; events dead and inert, 70; and facts and concepts, 71; wisdom biased, 73; learning from the, 73, 74; truths are preconceptions, 74; power of experience trapped by the, 75; and the cultural "rules of caste," 82; experience is misreading, 91; concept reliability of the, 98; without allowance for progress, 117; accepting the effect of experience, 117; Freudian, 117; new experience free from, 117; outmoded ways of the, 118; action not in the, 123; ineffectual of nature of experience of the, 124; denigration of traditional, 145; Dewey, extracted value of the, 146

Pathology, correcting student error may create, 85; impulse suppression may create intellectual and moral, 116, 125; coercion may produce, 116; from duress where habits are forced, 119; anarchism advancing the "social," 145

Pedagogy (pedagogical) (pedagogic) (pedagogue), Dewey's revolutionary, 7; of Dewey's lingers, 7; Dewey' philosophy and pedagogy, 8; ambivalence toward Dewey's, 8; Dewey's illustrious, 9; patch-worn public school, 9; Dewey, weight of dubious authority, 13; Dewey's unified philosophy included, 15; Dewey's practice of, 15, 68; Dewey, prophet and, 20; Dewey and sociological understanding, 21; Dewey's students of, 22; Dewey, health of his, 29; usefulness of Dewey's, 29; Dewey alive in todays ideas of, 29; and American understanding of, 29; Dewey, failed application of, 31; Dewey School at University of Chicago, 31,133; Dewey, of order, 31; bind of Dewey's, 37, 38; Dewey's uncertainty in the practice of, 38; Dewey's use of Bacon's methodology in his, 47; "My Pedagogic Creed," 70, 135; Dewey, language and, 71; obstacles to Dewey's, 74; uncertainty and failure of modern, 74; Dewey's knowing and truth in, 75; primary experience and Dewey's, 128; Dewey, and true democracy, 135; Dewey and classism, 139; Dewey and the authority of individual, 141; Dewey and progressive, 146; Dewey, individual and group, 162

Peirce, Charles Sanders, and an American view of man, 8; Dewey's philosophical basis, 15; and pragmatism, 28; and Dewey's and James' pragmatism, 41; and the process of science, 41; and belief that science has rules for action, 44; and final judgment, 70

Pestalozzi, Johann, and American idealism, 22

Phenomena, and sensation of the thing, 34; the haunt of everyday life, 34; Dewey united Kant's noumena

correspondence, 61; of meaning as communal understanding, 63; "moral meaning," 87; Dewey, favored over individuality, 98; democratic, 140; in America as a caste system, 141; should recognize and address collective differences, 147; "of society," 157; hope for true equality and, 162

Politic(s)(al), mavens and reformers, 9; Dewey found access to, 29, 158; truth for dogmas, moral and, 65; democracy, society, and the institutions of, 87; "Moral meaning" and individualist cultural groups of, 87; school board and, 91; public and the machine of, 157

Politico, idealism and ruling, 43

Postmodern(ism), understanding of individuals and institutions, 7; Dewey predated, shades of Derrida, 20, 71, 161; Dewey's pragmatism, existentialism and, 76; effect on society, 160; and the individual, 162

Power, coercion, "superior physical," 17; Dewey, of experience "in action," 19; Nietzsche, will to, 24, 105; Hegel, "of sheer survival," 36; Bacon, felt empiricism's, 47; Bacon, over nature, 47, 103; James, to "unstiffen all our theories" 49; to our own purpose, but our own, 58; given to the moment and its moment, 75; charity and, 79; of the one in need, 79; control and, 82; child's "instinct and," 99; child in possession of all his, 99; individual freedom as, 103; of human nature, 103; individual, 104; to learning, plasticity or, 117; over the environment, habits give, 117; impulses release habits which liberate, 120; of one's self-interests, 123; growth of immature young is, 143; liberal and progressive movements had no constructive, 145; education shared in social life is moral, 156

Practical(ity), Dewey's education produces, 9; Hegel, understanding and resolution, dialectic, 16; Dewey, purpose of community, 17; action not as duty, 17; problems and experiences of life, Dewey, 19; philosophy more flexible, 19; sensation, "emotional and," 22; understanding of individual and the group, a bind, 24; Dewey, epistemology, 27; Dewey, as a primary goal, 29; Dewey, guidelines not given, 31; empiricists, 33; rationalists, 33; meaning inspired after Plato, 33; fitted empiricism, 33; affairs, reality and empiricism, 34; principles as, 35; tools, acts, 36; education would become more, 36; pragmatism, uncertain and, 41; metaphysics not, 44; life and discovery, 45; character of knowing, 48; Dewey, experience, a great teacher, 52; an advantage in usefulness, 52; certainty not, 56; Dewey, knowledge

Index

129; group collective, 129; common, 130; Dewey, pragmatism a laboratory behind group, 133; multiple groups, multiple, 133; "interest," student moving force of objects in any experience having a, 137; replacement of goods as the ultimate occupational, 139; work and monetary, 139; individual expectation accepting of common 141; individual absorbed into group, 142; school and educational, 146; of man and natural conditions, 153; transcendence, meliorism and common, 154; slave accepts another's, 158; group membership and, 158; group membership and inconsolable, 158; solipsism and group, 158, 160; as paradox of unity, 160; individual influence and group,160; individual return to group and its, 160; members must elevate group, 165; individual wants and needs and group, 165; consensus of group, 165; Dewey's fallacy in a unified workable group, 165; friction destroys the group, 165, 166; individualism is destructive to group, 166; evolution of individual, 166; life and real, 168; Kant, duty and group,168; Dewey, order and group, 168; the One as the defender of group, 169

R

Radical, tolerant, unanalyzed, fragmented, understanding of events, 28; "radical empiricism," James, 28, 118; Dewey, experimentation influence would be, 38; Dewey, resolution of problems, progressive and, 150; individualist a double element, 159; individual in a group, 160

Rationalism, and empiricism, 26; Cartesian, 33; closes the door on the universe, 41; that is deductive, to empiricism that is inductive, 41; and idealistic expectation, 41; Dewey gave cognitive distance to, 42; dependent on transcendence, 42; not objective cannot allow a changing world of objects, 45; only attends to truth as a proposition, 49; pragmatism, empiricism and, 51; as a tradition guiding theory, 51, 52; as pure thought, 52; Dewey eschewed, 55; Dewey thought to remove from inwardness, 109; of the One, 110; disparate domains infused with, 150; holism of action and, 151; could not justify action in the real world, 151; of Kantian philosophy does not work, 152; "ideal society" can only be established through, 158

Rationalist(ic), empiricism and known objects, 34; Hook, individual experience authoritative no universal impressed the Western world, 51; the One and the Many, 52, 159; dubious, 52; doing what we want, 52; James's lecture, *Pragmatism*, 53; Dewey, measured by individual action, 55; ends become means with Dewey's, 56; Dewey's, much broader species, 57; experiential theory of truth, 65; declined rigidity of truth, 65; Dewey's, fantasy and daily life, 76; discipline in school and Dewey's, 84; society as a laboratory for empiricism, 133; Dewey, technology and, 138; future ends and, 138; Dewey, flexible philosophical framework for, 149; Dewey's unique form of, 144; meliorism and transcendence, 149; and prognostication, 155; Achilles heel, 159; and an averaging of goals and behaviors, 161; romantic and transcendental hopefulness, 165; romanticism and, 165; absorbed idealism and, 165; Dewey's, and cost to society, 169

Present, Dewey's philosophy of the present, 8; struggle for authority to teach in the, 10; Emerson's optimism, lacking opportunities, 30, 168; knower given experimental authority in the, 57; events, prepare for future understanding, 57; toward the future we awl in the, 57; Tennyson, "margin fades"as the, 59; not the future is ours, 59; Dewey, is all that is extant, 66; events past and, 67; the utility of knowing only in the, 73; wisdom of the past and needs of the, 73; Absolute truth is preconception, "dream," 74; for an uncontrollable future, losing the, 75; authority to know in the, 95; change is ever, 105; past experience and action in the, 117; actions give rise to means in the, 123; ideals prevent immediacy of the, 125; Dewey, idealism and the pragmatic, 135; Dewey and the hyper-technological, 137; Dewey, the future and the, 138; experience and looking to the future, 145; value of past in benefit for the, 146; progressive failures, 146; Dewey, duality and the, 154; unification, authoritatively and objectively in the, 154; transcendence and the, 154; losing tolerance of the, 154; the immediate theater of experience, 155; progress, remote future and the 155; time finds unit in a communal, 156

Presentism, Dewey's requirement, 154; and the immediacy of process, 155

Principle(s), of "coercion or compulsion," Dewey, inappropriate practice or misunderstanding, 18; "binding and connecting" and reason, 26; Dewey, usefulness without, 26; individual subordinated to reason, 26; Hume, chaos and, 35; experience within itself carries, 35; "vital and or, 50; mind stays outside of experience, 58; preconceptions, 69, 70; certifying logic of, 73; idealism, 154; expectation in phase or full portion, 155

Reactionary, Dewey, fixity is, 65; educational "deficiencies played into the hands of " "obscurantists" and, 145, 146

Reality, quotidian empiricism, 34; Hegel, physical among objects, 36; of entropy, 37; James, a personal philosophy allows people to experience, 41; James, the only literally true thing is, 55; James, falsity and, 55; outside of immediate experience, 57; of sameness, means and ends, 65, 122; no obscuring of perception, 71; thought often escapes from reality, 73; truth, a personal analogy by which to question, 76; of blame for individual extremism, 82; only actions in the present, 123; fixity and immediate, 124; Dewey, individual freedom and experience in, 126; in public school, harsh, 130; reality of society, 157; of individual as a dualistic societal element, 159; of individualism and group unity, 160

Reason(ing) (ed), Dewey's ideas beyond all propriety and, 9; history, in the progressive unfolding of man is, 21; negotiates relationship during experience, 26; by perception individual subordinated to, 26; Hume, no authority to experience but to, 26; common sense and, 27; Hume, to turn the world into "a heap of chaotic and isolated particulars, 34; sensationalistic empiricism and experience, 35; facilities of mind, 35; Hegel, not able to respond to "specific problems," 36; Dewey questions of traditional, 36; individual truth through, 37; of individual judgment may fail in action, 56; order requires an alignment of occurrences which are, 58; from a "significant whole," truth and know must maintain a "systematic coherence," 62; clear idea to our commitment to action, 65; constructionists employ "pure," 66; universal principles, 73; individual willing and judgments that are, 80; one must control impulse with, 82; Dewey, rejected Kant's *a priori*, 83; standards to find actionable meaning and, 84; may become suspended, 89; primary story events and resolution of problems that are, 90; laws and traditions and arguments in the apace of, 96; man a creature of, 99; Nietzsche, "will to power," rigidity of purpose but without, 105; expectation of harmony with Dewey's philosophy of unity, 107; and passions, Dewey, 123; One's self-interest and the rule of, 130; the school, order and, 130; "epistemological controversies " over the priority of sensation or, 150; "problems of social change" and "sensation and," 150

Rebellion,without coercion, only expectation is, 92; repression may yield, 125; coercive behavioral standards threatens, 131; optimism and unchanged, 166

Reform(er), colonial and early American, 9; wait for the One to self, 25; school an unworthy vessel with theories and, 31; validation of experience by, 33; only internal moralistic changes are of importance in general, 102; school, most "effective instrument of progress and change, 135; true democracy and the history of school, 144; inability to sustain the course of, 144; progressive education and Dewey-inspired, 144; Dewey, Social Democracy as, 145

Revolutionary,influence of Dewey's pedagogy, 7; Dewey's philosophy revolutionary, 23; "intellectual," 78

Rousseau, Jean-Jacques, ideas and Dewey, 11; and society, 98; Plato gave nature, 98; nature, 99; optimism, Dewey, 99; God and nature, 99; and "total depravity," 99; and perfection, 99; And Emile's freedom, 99; and society as necessity, 105; and Man and Society, 113; Emile, 143; and innocence, 167

Rule(s), no one should be judged by same, 27; become fixed, experience deserted, 42; custom fit experimental, 42; "the foot," 42; fixed universal laws should respond to experimental imperatives, 45; over nature, collectively, 46, 47; for action, our beliefs and reality, 49; no higher than individual intelligent experience, 50; of One, 51; not self-evident, 69; arbitrariness of foot, 72; without consistent agreement judgment is lost, 74; as a non-event, judgment, 82; of caste, 82; not hard or fixed, but within a changing environment, 88; Dewey's view of law and, 89; morality and, 89; of discipline and a right to an education, 89; infringement on a student-individual's unique experience, 90; Bentham, of morality, 93; and proof of culpability, 94; in society or school, individual self-, 107; individual, over societal institutions, inthroned in, 108; "procrustean beds of fixed,"121; of reason, 123; fixed habit and, 123; experience to replace tradition, 134; acceptable pattern of democratic individual experience, 135; challenges to societal, 166

S

Savage, breast and morality, 94; education, nature and the child, 99; Rousseau and the wise, 100; "noble," 167

Index

Index

Index

group offers direction and, 110
Subjective, Kant, duty in thought and action, 17; truth and Hume, 61; consequence, 114; and objective knowledge, 159
Subject matter, truth, time and, 66; for the "imagination," 67; as analogy or self-referent, 75, 76; and learning, no specific value or meaning, 76; in "My Pedagogical Creed," 105; democracy and common, 136; and method, dualism, 149
Synthesis, of antithetical influences, 64; of knowing in thought and action, 69; attitudinal unification or, 154; unity synonymous with, 155

T

Tabla rasa (blank tablet) (wax), experimentation and, 105; the individual as a, 121; on which to write life's foundational experiences, 143; Dewey, Locke, writing as a passive experience, 143
Teach(ing) (teacher), Dewey as, 8; Dewey, non-traditional ideas to, 8; Dewey's influence on the practice of, 9; Dewey, education theory of, 9; stubble of schools to, 10; valuable lesson, 22; Dewey and administration of, 31; experience as, 37; dogma, theory and, 38; Dewey's influence on, 38; facts and, 46; schools and the authority to, 51, 124, 130; Dewey, practical experience as, 52; facts and the necessary humanity, 56; has sold when no one has bought, 60; limitation of the, 60; of ends, 65; and history, 67; obstacles to, 74; and judgment, 74; and Dewey's standards of practice, 75; wisdom: student knowing and doing, 81; biased imagination of the, 90; and administrator, student-individual, 90; frustration, 90; and administrative correction of students, 91; nature as, 98; source of , 103, 156; community, the world and its objects as, 105; and hope for true community, 126, 127; and student-individual freedom, 129; and administrators and the reality of experience in the school, 130; and the certainty of maintaining a proper environment, 131; rote and, 134; educational community and moral, 135; facilitators and, 135; and student and multidirectional learning, 136; Dewey and dry, 137; school failures and progressive education, 146; Dewey, group and individual for the modern, 162; Dewey pedagogical fallacy, 166
Technology, Bacon and technology, 25; Dewey's optimism for, 46; Dewey's understanding of, 137; hyper-, 137; classroom, 137; Dewey, abstractions and, 137; Dewey, pragmatism and, 138
Teleology,common sense and external, 14; and experience, Locke, 26; Hume, no requirement for, 58; Kant, and prediction of consequences, 80

Index

difference" in paradox of, 154
Theory of mind, and Hume and Locke, not truly empirical, 34; Hume and Locke and empiricism and experience-directed, 35
Theory of truth, pragmatic, 49, 66; convergent, 63, 64, 74; convergent, 63, 64, 74; constructivist, 66, 74; consensus, 103; coherence, 34, 62, 63, 74, 76; correspondence 66, 74, 76; common sense, 74, 75, 76
Thoreau, Henry David, premier American transcendentalist, 22; teacher, 22
Tolerant (tolerance) (tolerate), in issues of epistemology and morality, 5; truth labeled, 5; unanalyzed, fragmented and radically, 28; expression of language, 44; doubt of knowledge shows, 65; truth and extending group, 74; certainty not seen as, 95, 96; freedom of thought and, 100; of individual and bending to other's needs, 108; pragmatism and, 154
Tradition(al), modern values and, 5; replacement of, 5; values to modern, 7; public education, 7; education, non-, 8; public education's standard praxis, 8; Dewey and philosophical, 13; Dewey and "Scotch realism" as, 14, 19; Emerson and, 22; intellectual habits, 23; change to unquestionable, 23; of common sense, 27; Dewey, alternative to, 30; Dewey, empirical process and historical-philosophical, 36; Dewey, and metaphysics, 36; learning, 48; time, agency and educational, 59; dogmatic, 59; fixity and, 72, 81; as a comfortable knowing, 72; immorality and a challenge to, 89; mores and reason, 96; Dewey, justification for independence from, 96; replaced by uncertainty of immediacy, 110; Dewey, custom and restraint coerce the young, 114; knowledge, 115; few of animal and human instincts, 116; impulses arise to replace habits of, 119; repairing and renovating custom and, 120; view of human nature and individuation, 127; educational practice, 129; and formal education, 133; experience to replace, 134; teacher and facilitator, 135; of "textbook" education, 140; view of human nature, 141; Dewey, tradition and progressive education movement, 145; problems were pseudo problems, 150; Dewey, two attitudes, radical and, 150; Dewey's interest " in the grand tradition," 151; and educating beyond material ends, 162
Traditionalism, dogmatic, 59
Training, teacher certification, 7; and the young's "original modifiability," 115; instruction and manual, 137; job, 138; hands-on, 138; limiting educational possibilities with specialized, 138; vocational

education, 139; as a habit, job, 139; Dewey, all student should experience manual, 140; occupational 146

Transcendent(al) (alism) (alist) (transcendence), "Scotch realism," an inner faith in God, an, 14; and solutions to daily problems, 15; Emerson, the inwardness of, 16, 109; Dewey, as a Vermont, 16; James Marsh and, 16; premier, 22; romanticism, idealism and American, 22; Dewey, "fixity" and the 30, 168; practical tools and attachments not like the, 36; Plato, rationalism and, 42; all experience as non-, 44; Dewey, projected collectivism: universalism or, 48; absolutism or, 48, 49, 73; schooling and knowing, in the fashion of, 41; activity and objects, 57; "fixed principles," not experience that is 64; to world meaning, 69; personal analogy which questions reality and, 76; and individualism in universal terms, 97; of Dewey, Plato and future group unity, 98; Emile, wise savage and seer as, 99, 100; Descartes, the empirical world and , 109; Descartes individual authority and , 109; object-based experiential empiricism, 109; and Dewey, eruptions of impulses to inform, 129; "professional philosophers" and, 146; Dewey as, 154, 155, 161, 162, 165; convergence of group members and, 154; Dewey, common purpose and, 154;

Trust(ed) (entrusted) (trustworthy) (trustworthiness), Bacon, to solve the problems of the physical world, 46; in immediate knowing, 59; Dewey, science not, 67; science not derived from certainty and values of the physical world, 67; Dewey, truth and, 75; of primary experience, 90; in experience with change, 95; Dewey, nature not beneficiary of blind, 101; Dewey, in hypothesis, mis-, 105; in truth, 150

Truth, is intolerant, 5, 95, 96; government and, 6; education and theoretical, 6; Dewey and shadowy, 8; "Scotch realism" and, 14; as a tool, 15; Hegel, knowledge and, 20; Dewey, Hegel and meaning of, 37; historically from deity, 37; as learned, 37; prescribed for oneself, 37; supplanting the lessons of, 37; in "social medium," 37; Bacon, discovery of new, 48; possessed by the mind, 48; knowing, 49, 56; for new needs, 49; theory of, 49; a go-between, new, 49; as an "approximation," 49; close to, 49; as a proposition, 49; action and, 49; a doing of, 50; experience of, 50; "metaphysical" judgment of, 50; defined by meaning, 50; from usefulness action takes its, 50; individual action and, 53; James as a property of certain ideas, 55; James, and the credit system, 55; Dewey, has collective meaning, 55, 59; conflicts and veracity for all, 55; individualistic authority for meaning and, 56; pragmatic understanding of knowing and, 56; and meaning and the event horizon, 57; lost in the past, 57; Dewey and James and, 57; Dewey's view of, 57; the real and a matter of, 57; Hume, is disputable, 58; Hume, subjective, 58; Dewey, relations and, 58; only the name, 58; dogma of, 58, 85; Dewey, pragmatic line of, 58, 59; Dewey would loosen the reins on, 59; Dewey's view and theory of, 60; correspondence theory of, 60, 61, 62, 63, 74; Dewey, as needs require, 61; shared, 61; as a tool, 61; narrative and, 62; incompleteness of, 62; another's, 62; coherence theory of, 62, 63, 74; acceptable, 63; commonality of, 63; authority over, 63; Dewey and coherence theory of, 63; science and philosophical, 63; convergence theory of, 63, 64, 74; convergent and inclusive, 63; Dewey as an unfolding, 63; individually held, 64; doubt, knowledge and, 65; pragmatism and, 65; Dewey, reluctance to define, 65; constructivist theory, 66; Dewey, eschewed constructivist theory of, 66; as constructivist and "pure reasoning," 66; Bacon, without preconceptions, 66; Dewey, loss of, 66; Dewey, education and, 66, 75; as "temporarily satisfactory," 68; as replaceable, 70; as a comfortable knowing, 72; as tenuous, 73, no fixed, 73; absolute, 74; Dewey, instrumental, 74; Dewey, purpose of, 74; as what works, 74; as optimistic skepticism, 75; as a personal analogy, 76; situational, 82; claim of, 91; usefulness of, 95; natural world of objects and, 98; minds filled with, 98; consensus of, 103; scientific, 110; fixed, 113; "indisputable," 117; accredited, 149; little agreement on, 149; trustworthiness of, 150; thoughts, objects and, 152; Dewey's epistemology avoids, 162

U

Uncertainty, inspired by Dewey 10; contemporary American, 13; Dewey, persistent, 14; Dewey's pragmatism and, 22, 41, 46; Dewey, Hegel and, 37; of pedagogical practice, 38; generalized philosophy of, 39; school vacillates in, 43; Dewey, science and, 44; education and procedural, 52; unity and, 74; and bottom-line morality, 80; role models and, 80; thought and observation fraught with, 85; doubt and, 91, 93; Dewey and standards of inquiry, 94; Dewey's epistemology of, 95; 131; every idea diminished by, 96; of immediacy, 110; and habit replacement, 130; Dewey, the future and, 138; of knowing, 142; Dewey, existentialism and postmodern, 161; from Kant and Hegel, 162

Unification, Dewey's philosophy of, 16, 23, 149; of One and the Many, 17; Dewey, requires action, 23; of action is a sign of appropriate conduct, 120; methodology for 150; of antithetical issues, 150; does not permit dualism, 151; and the inseparability of agents and actions, 152; on in the present, 154; or "synthesis," 154; of the self ands religion, 155; Dewey, a bind involving individuals and the community, 166; and group assimilation, 166; of conflicting elements of experimental life, 169

Unity, and America's melting pot, 6, and dubious authoritative behavioralism, 8; the myth of, 73; of method, 16; and opposites, 16; nature only has, 16; Dewey, philosophical, 19, 29, 107, 149, 151; Dewey, and real life, 20; of inwardness and outwardness, 23; proof of, 23; problems of collective, 24; assuming a functional, 25; individualism and, 31, 94; thread of, 43; Descartes, of mind and matter, 62; eventuality of communal, 84; Plato, spiritual, 85; in all of life, 92; and group purpose, 101; democratic, 104; of One and the Many, 110; as a mind-body holism, 110; of life and pragmatism, 110; theoretical, 111; not possible with mind but without action, 116, 117; of nature and mind, 120; of individualism and society, 127; Dewey, did little to show individualism and group, 142; Hegel, Dewey, and dualism, 149; through reasonable action through experience, 151; of method and subject matter, 152; separation and cooperative, 152; of eating, Dewey's analogy, 152; remote directive, theory and, 152, 153; something sought, 153; of theories of knowledge and behavior, 153, 154; of understanding, 153; of the human being, 153, 157; deteriorates out of time, 154; of conduct, 154, 155; of responses, 154; "and difference," duality, 154; pragmatic, 155; of all ideal ends, 155; of society and religion, 155; in human interaction, Dewey, 155; synonymous with "synthesis," 155; "striving to," 155; and non-earthly, metaphysical, 155; the whole world in, 156; of communal present, in time, 156; and a perpetual alternation of life, 156; as universality, 156; education and, 156; of learning, 156; of larger society, as educative, 157; Dewey, Plato, of collectivism, 158; direct methodology of, 159; paradox of, 160; of morality and knowledge, 160; of action and culture as a laboratory, 160; of ideas and philosophy, 161; of mind and body, 162; suffering, 165

Universal(ity), Dewey's, 25; Dewey, experience and, 26; as "prejudice" and "dogmas," 33; and special cases, Dewey, 39; Dewey, values, 42; Dewey, experiment and, 45; for others, 45; transcendence and, Dewey, 48; as a dream, 49; have no specific referent action, 49; authority and coercion, 50, 92; and "guiding and ruling influence," 67; principles filled in by experience, 73; Kant, imperative as duty, 83; Dewey, egoism and, 83; Kant, non-binding, 92; terms of individualism, 97; set of behaviors and a flexible nature, 113; limitations and conditions, 120; and individual situations and actions, 123; often valued above impulses, 123, 124; morality, 124; authority, individual not, 131; Kant, unity by, 151; and "intrinsic goods," 156

Universalism, Hegel's idealistic, 16; Dewey, logical positivists and, 25; transcendence and, 48

Unreason (ed) (able), understanding as true, 5; serious pursuit of knowledge, 52; classroom communication as, 89; of student-individual will among the group, 128

Unwillingness, to define truth, 65

Utilitarian(ism), and hedonism, 22; and materialism of ownership, Dewey, 22; ownership and the good society, 22; and the fixity of goals, 22; "utility" and Jeremy Bentham, 61; and one's own good, 86; Mill and the group, 88; and the student-individual as prime authority, 93; Bentham, and self-interest, 93; skewed, 168

Useful(ness), and modernity, 9; action and pragmatism, 14; instruments and Dewey's methodology, 15; as instrumental, 16, 50; permanent, 27; replaceable, 27, 36, 39, 120; Dewey, philosophy of, 27, 28, 39; practice as educative, 28; Dewey's boarder import to, 28, philosophy's inclusive, 28; Dewey, acts, experimentally, 36; temporal, 41; James, of science, 44; James, religion and metaphysical, 44; thought-action, 45; holism, 45; pragmatism, empiricism made, 45, 50, 130; truth as, 49, 56; and purpose, 49; action's value in, 50; expectations of value and, 51; of certain knowledge, 51; value of experience in, 52; Locke, knowing, 52; and the individual, 55; meaning and 57; preconceptions and, 58; retentive, 59; and "imagination," 67; Dewey, of science, 68; Dewey, of truth, 74; Dewey, truth, morality and, 95; uniting individual meaning and action that is, 109; habit change and, 115, 116; thought and, 121; character like immediate, 123; everyday, 144, Dewey's ideas as, 162

Utopia(n), Bacon and knowledge, 25; Bacon and the New Atlantis, 46; Bacon, nature, collective man and, 47; Bacon, human differences and, 47; Dewey optimism and, 49; outlook, optimism and the individual, 83; Dewey, and meliorism, 87; Dewey, idealism as melioristic, 94

Utopianism, Dewey and community positivity, 46; and melioristic improvement in the collective, 87, 99

V

Value(s) (valuable), modern and traditional, 5; and roots of change, 7; equivocal valuation of Dewey's ideas, 9; Dewey's optimism, 13; "instrumental," 15, 44, 45, 86; "hierarchy of," 15; of the group, 19; a teacher, a student, and a lesson of,22; "program of," 28; universals, 42; Plato, universals, 42; James, understanding and, 43; James, of science, 44; Dewey and the in-, 44; "intrinsic,: 44, 45, 86; as meaningful, as instrumental, 44; "degrees of," 45; of arithmetic, 45; Dewey, science, instrumental, 48; "cash," 49; of experiential knowing, 50; action has, 50; thought's, 51; usefulness has, 52; Dewey, an itch and whimsy, 56; found by others, 57; practical, 57, 80; inclusiveness and, 58; and revaluing knowledge, 59; trustworthy, 67; of educational tools, 68; of knowing, 71; of history, 71; of literature 71; and remoteness, 72; learning meaning and, 76; fixed, 81; determinative, 84, 88; formal procedure of, 84; Dewey, of "thinking," 84; not individualistic, 86; in-, 86; measureless, 86; loss of, 86; agency of, 86; preferential order of, 86; instrumental and situational, 86; morality, a group, 87; student action and consequences of behavior, 88; individual experience, morally, 89; arguments of, 90; experience of dubious, 95; core of group, 98; democratic, 101; of motive and action, 106; of habit, intelligent deliberations, 115; of action in habit, 117; above impulse, the universals, 124; punitive, 127; "deeper standards of judgments of, 136; of past in exacting benefit for the present, 146; of truth, 150; Dewey, of order, methodology of education, 161; immediate primary agency, time and, 167

Verify, judgment about the past, 67

W

Will (ed) (ful) (fully), Kant, good in action, 16, 17; individual and collective, 17; group, 17, 88, 128, 161; coalescing of "voluntary," 17; actionable, 17; and "intent," 17; Kant, duty against one's, 18; Nietzsche, "to power," 24, 105; to "creation of the world," 24; to cause prima, 24; Ones being given freedom to act as they, 43; Dewey, Kant and prescribing civil action by, 45; universally, 45; standard of individual, 56; personal, 67; for others, 75; to commit to trust, 75; attitudinal averaging of general, 77; of the naturally evolving group, 77; purpose of imposing, 77; Kant, morality as action to be, 80; Kant, by individual, reasonable judgments, 80; the One for the Many, 80; Kant, individual, 80; appropriate of action 81; moral, good agents of community, 82, 83; Kant, optimism of action as good, 83; disciplinary policy and student, 90; philosophically, 91; -ful law breaking, 91; Kant, a non-binding universal for all, 92; self-determined and self-serving purpose, 93; disciplined individual with deliberative, 99; social improvement and good, 102; Mankind, intellect and, 105; habits become the, 121; action, "mind and," 121; thought at, 121, 122; character, and transformation over time, 122; of the prisoner, 126; of society, 128; Dewey, authority of the individual, 141; categorically, 152; allegiance and the human, 155; of community, 166

Will to power, the most spiritual, 24; and the individual, 105

Wisdom, of the past, 73; of the "good creator," 99; to the authority of the individual, 109; children and conventional, 114; Emerson, "infused into every form," 133

World(s), philosophy of the outside, 8; Dewey, a prominence in the, 8; Dewey, and man's wont to see the, 11; Dewey's philosophy, a simple way to see the, 11; Dewey, theology in youth, no Biblical understanding in the, 14, 15; Hegel, duality and attraction to the real, 16; Dewey, Hegel, interdependencies within the, 16; Dewey, knowledge as individualized and dependent on the, 19; meliorism, better, actionable, 23; group will provide a better, 23; Emerson, oneness of the, 23; Dewey, holism of inner thought, objects, morality and the physical, 23; Dewey, physical understanding of the, 23; philosophy "always creates the," 24; methods for investigating the physical, 25; Bacon's *The New Atlantis* as a future, 25; Bacon, God and the problems of the, 26, 46; thought creates an objective, 26; theism and a foundational understanding of the, 27; "Ego" as creator of the, 27; individual and re-creating

Index

the, 27; Dewey's fame spread around the, 30; philosophical understanding of the, 33; Plato, experience and practical meaning in the, 33; Cartesian understanding of a possibly illusory, 33; Dewey, of immediate physicality, 33; Locke and Hume, explained by experience through the senses, 33; Bishop Berkeley, objects in the, 34; Dewey, no immaterialism, objects beyond sensational empiricism in a real, 34; Hume, a chaotic, 34, 35; Dewey, life not lived as isolated events, 35; Dewey, no imperative for how to see the, 35; Dewey, order in the 35; Dewey, habituation and the, 36; Hegel's idealistic, 36; Hegel, unique experience for the real, 36; Hegel, already ideal, not responsive to "specific problems," 36; Dewey, metaphysics and a fixed, 36; Dewey and empiricism in the real, 37; Dewey, Hegel, inconsistency in imaging an ideal, 36; Dewey, Hook, unified by Hegel, 36; Dewey's philosophical ideas and the modern Western, 39; James, enlarge man's perception of the, 42; Dewey, pragmatism and ideas help in viewing the, 42; pragmatism through immediate action, 42; Dewey, no divided, 42; dualism of Plato and Kant, 42; Plato, universals external to the physical, 42; Dewey, united physical and mental, 42; Dewey, rationalism and the objects changing in the, 45; rationalism rendering the physical, 46; Dewey's campaign of knowing the, 47; Dewey, Middle Ages and fixity of the concrete, 49; certainty and a changing, 50; knowing in a changing, 50; Dewey, causality and understanding the, 51, 55; pragmatism and the Western, 51 Locke and uncertainty of the, 52; Tennyson, experience and the untravelled, 57; individual through experience forms the, 58; pupils thought to live in two, 59, 60 Dewey, objects in action express the physical, 62; truth, between subject and object in the, 62; narrative and events in the natural, 62; truth, knowing with the objects in the world, 63; defining, fixed knowing and the way we view our, 66; Dewey, methodology, science and the constructivist, 67; trustworthy values and the structure of the physical, 67; Dewey, physical laws given from outside the real, 67; pure science, applied science and the, 68; facts could be transcendent to the, 69; Dewey, merged Kant's physical and metaphysical, 69; Dewey, anchoring theory to action in the, 72; Aristotelean ends and "regulated" "moral theory" in the, 78; purpose, dedication and success in the work, 82; Dewey, intellect and morality bring man into a better, 87; education and a better community and, 87; Dewey, no perfection in the real, 94; Dewey gave America a new way to see the, 96; objects in the natural, 98; relationships, in real time and in the real, 100; Locke, isolated mind from the objective, 100; Locke, left impression upon the mind, 100; Locke, as reflections of one's mental state, 101; Dewey, melioristic nature of the, 101; Dewey, individual changing with the material, 102; Dewey, man elevated above nature in the real, 103; duality of mind and matter in the, 103; outer and inner physical world, 103; experience and identity in the, 103; community, objects and the, 105; pragmatic experience and objects in the, 105; remote knowing and the experiential, 105; changes and everything in it, 105; education is more than interaction in the physical, 109; Descartes, the mind and the empirical, 109; individual authority to know objects in the, 109; becoming and the progressive, 115; education and a changing, 118; impulse, habit and a new understanding of the, 121; Dewey, children not to struggle in the, 126; dualism, individualism and the, 149; methodology for unification in the real, 150; all problems and questions arise in the, 150; Dewey, duality would compromise the real, 150; unification of mind and body meaningful to the 151; rationalism could not justify action in the physical, 151; inner and outer, 151, 152, 168; active learning and thought not separate in the physical, 151; changes in the empirical, 151; change in the objective and moral, 151; Dewey, man and nature working for a better, 152, 153; an indeterminate, 152; as one in unity, 156; man, "continuous with nature in a physical, 158; man not remote in the physical, 158; overlapping lessons in the, 158; education and understanding the, 162

World of objects, holism of thought and the, 23; Berkeley and the immateriality of the, 34; Dewey, rationalism and the, 45; truth and knowing within a, 63; knower, the known and the, 63; harmonious truth in the natural, 98

Worshipful, Dewey's consideration of nature, 111